D1571957

Awaken, Children!

Dialogues With
Sri Sri Mata Amritanandamayi

Volume I

Adaptation & Translation

Swami Amritaswarupananda

MATA AMRITANANDAMAYI MISSION TRUST
Vallickavu, Kerala
India

PUBLISHED BY:
MATA AMRITANANDAMAYI MISSION TRUST
Vallickavu (Parayakadavu)
(Via) Athinad, Quilon Dt., Kerala
INDIA 690542

ADAPTED AND TRANSLATED FROM THE MALAYALAM
Mata Amritanandamayi Sambhashanangal
by Prof. M. Ramakrishnan Nair

FIRST EDITION, January 1989, 3000 copies
SECOND EDITION, March 1990, 3000 copies

ALSO AVAILABLE FROM:
Mata Amritanandamayi Centers
P.O. Box 613
San Ramon, CA 94583-0613
U.S.A
Tel. (415) 537-9417

COMPUTER LASER TYPESET AT:
Mata Amritanandamayi Mission Trust
Desktop Publishing Unit
Vallickavu, Quilon Dt., 690542, INDIA

PRINTED IN INDIA
by offset at:
Jeyakar Offset Printers, Sivakasi - 626 123

This book is humbly offered at the

Lotus Feet of Her Holiness
Sri Sri Mata Amritanandamayi,

*the Resplendent Luminary immanent in the
hearts of all beings.*

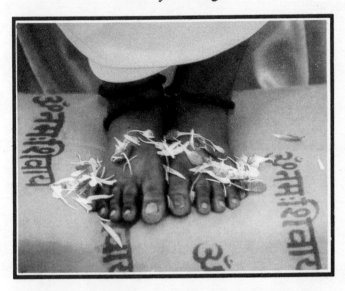

*Shôshanam pâpapankasya dîpanam jñânatejasâm
Guru pâdôdakam samyak, samsârârnava târakam*

The holy water that has washed the Guru's Feet,
dries the mine of sins, lights the Lamp of
Knowledge and helps one cross the Ocean of
Transmigration.

*Ajñâna mûlaharanam janmakarma nivâranam
Jñâna vairâgya siddhyartham gurupâdôdakam
pibet*

It uproots ignorance of the Self, puts an end to
rebirth and its cause, actions. One should sip the
holy water of the Guru's Feet for Enlightenment
and Dispassion.

ACKNOWLEDGEMENTS

My heartfelt gratitude is due to Professor M. Ramakrishnan Nair, the compiler of *Mata Amritanandamayi Sambhashanangal*, the Holy Mother's conversations in Malayalam. The present book, *Awaken, Children!* is a faithful translation of the same, interspersed with some additional materials which were recorded by me. I would like to thank my spiritual sisters Kusuma, Ambal and Durga who typed the text. Also, my thanks are due to brahmachari Nealu who did the editing and typesetting.

INTRODUCTION

Only in a Great Master who is established in the Supreme Reality can one see the perfect balance of Divine Fatherhood and Divine Motherhood, the beautiful blending of masculine and feminine qualities. Only such a person can transform another and mould the character of others. Integration of one's own inner personality, being higher than anything else, is possible only through discipline motivated by selflessness and unconditional love.

The Holy Mother Amritanandamayi's teachings, sayings and conversations are equally inspiring and throw light on the mystical expressions expounded in the scriptural texts. The Mother's teachings are surcharged with spiritual power and are a tremendous source of inspiration for people from all walks of life, especially for spiritual seekers. The Holy Mother has her own simple and lucid way of expressing spiritual Truths with examples which make the points clear and intellectually satisfying.

From a worldly standpoint, she has not attended school beyond the fourth grade, yet her knowledge, wisdom and philosophical insight is immeasurable. In the early days, due to the visitors' lack of spiritual interest, only a few paid attention to the Mother's words. At that time, most peoples' interest was to fulfill their material desires. Thus, they gave less importance to the Mother's precious gospel regarding the Supreme Goal of human birth. Needless to say, her parents, relatives and villagers who were deadly against her 'strange' behaviour considered her as one gone mad and took these words of the Mother to be crazy utterances.

However, at the age of 21, the Holy Mother began initiating some educated young men who had renounced their hearth and home to dedicate their lives to God-Realisation, and they noticed the depth and simplicity of her explanations and began writing down her teachings. By the end of 1983, Prof. M. Ramakrishnan Nair, an ardent devotee of the Mother, started taperecording the Mother's talks whenever he stayed in the Ashram. Later, he compiled the "Conversations with Mata Amritanandamayi." in Malayalam from the said materials. This English translation of that book is interspersed with other interesting incidents which took place over the course of the last ten or twelve years in the presence of the Holy Mother. From 1979 onwards, at which time I came and settled near the Holy Mother, I recorded many of her conversations and it is from that material that the additional incidents have been woven into the narrative.

With the blessings of the Holy Mother, I hope to be able to present the readers with the remaining volumes of the present book in the near future.

Swami Amritaswarupananda

PREFACE

Dear brothers and sisters, herein is contained a direct translation of Holy Mother's *divya upadesha* (Divine advices) into the English language. The tremendous blessing that is bestowed by presenting the Mother's teaching to the English speaking world is not yet fully realized. Now it is left to the reader to sanctify his or her life by a careful reading of the material and a whole-hearted practice of it in daily life.

Several points should be remembered in order that this translation is approached with right understanding. First of all, these conversations have occurred between the Mother and Indian householders and renunciates in the cultural context of India. Also the Mother's advices are given according to the level of understanding of each person to whom she is speaking. Often a word for word English translation falls short of conveying the totality of what the Mother has expressed through her mother tongue, Malayalam. One must consider these factors when contemplating her words to achieve deeper insight.

Secondly, the Mother's use of language is direct and earthy. Her words convey an immediacy and intensity of purpose to transmit the Essential, particularly when speaking to *sâdhaks* (spiritual aspirants). For instance, when it comes time to bring a point across to a renunciate, the Mother does not mince words. Thus we can understand her expres-

sion, "Worldly pleasure is equal to dog excreta" to
be sound advice to one whose sole aim is God-Re-
alization.

In a separate conversation with a householder, the
Mother's advice takes on an entirely different tone.
"Mother does not say that you must give up all desires.
You can enjoy them, but do not think that this life is for
that only." Keep in mind that in the Mother's language, the word 'world' literally means, 'That which is
seen' as opposed to the invisible Reality or God.
Knowing this will be of great help in interpreting her
use of the word 'worldly.' When the Mother contrasts
that which is spiritual to that which is worldly, she re-
fers to the attitude with which actions are done. Spiritual actions are those actions which lead one to God
through selflessness and purity. Worldly actions are
those actions which lead one away from God, performed as they are in a spirit of selfishness.

Finally, the Mother speaks to us from the exalted
state of *sahaja samādhi,* the natural abidance of a
Self-Realised Master in the Absolute Reality. The
challenge in translating is to render the Mother's
transcendental vision into English for the layman.
The vital ingredient in this process is the contemplative mind of the reader. Abandoning all superfi-
ciality, may our mind and intellect become subtle
and assimilate the eternal Wisdom of the Mother's
words. Firmly established in their practice, may
we all revel in the direct experience of the Supreme
Absolute without delay.

1 August 1976

The sun with it's golden rays blessed the earth on this beautiful day soon after the rainy season. Though a sunny day, it was not very hot. The trees and plants with their green leaves danced in the gentle breeze blowing from the sea. The melodious sound of the sacred chakora bird (Greek partridge) gladdened the ears. The Arabian Sea to the west with its blue waves reverberated with the sound 'AUM' which served as the drone (sruti) underlying the song chanted by the fishermen as they pulled in their nets. The large canoes made of wooden planks stitched together with coconut fibers glided slowly up and down the backwaters to the east presenting a charming sight.

At 10 o'clock in the morning the ashram atmosphere was extraordinarily calm and quiet. Peace permeated everywhere. The Holy Mother dressed in pure white clothes was sitting on the verandah of the old temple. A group of college students interested in spiritual life came to see the her. They prostrated before the Holy Mother and sat near her. Mother smilingly asked them, "Children, have you eaten anything?" One student replied, "We had breakfast." After a few moments the conversation turned to spiritual topics.

GOD

Student: *It is said that there is a God but I am unable to believe that it is so.*

Mother: Children, to say that there is no God is like saying "I have no tongue" with your own tongue. Is it possible for a person who has no tongue to say "I have no tongue?" Likewise, when we say, "There is no God," at that moment itself we agree that there is God. In order to say that a particular object is 'not,' we must have had a general knowledge of that object previously. How can we prove the non-existence of something which is not known to us? Truth is only one. That is God. God-Realisation is our life's aim.

Student: *What is meant by God?*

Mother: Son, if you can answer the questions which Mother is going to ask, Mother will tell you what God is.

Student: *All right, I will answer.*

Mother: Son, what did you eat this morning?

Student: *I ate* dosa *(pancakes).*

Mother: What other dish was there with it?

Student: *Chutney.*

Mother: What was it made of?

Student: *Coconut.*

Mother: Where did you get the coconut from?

Student: *From a coconut tree.*

Mother: Where did the coconut tree come from?

Student: *From a coconut.*

Mother: Which was first, the coconut or the coconut tree? That is what Mother wants to know.

The student sat tongue-tied.

Mother: Son, why are you sitting silent? (Pause) Therefore, you should agree that there is a Power beyond the coconut and the coconut tree which is the substratum of everything. That is God. A unique Power which is inexpressible and beyond words. That is God.

The First Cause for everything. That is what is known as God.

Student: *It can be believed if it is said that this building and that coconut tree exist but how does one believe in something which is not seen?*

Mother: Son, would you feel angry if Mother asks you one thing?

Student: *No.*

Mother: Is your father still alive?

Student: *Yes.*

Mother: What about your father's father?

Student: *He died long before my birth.*

Mother: Do any grandchildren call their father a bastard because they have not seen their grandfather? Son, do you remember who gave birth to you? When you grew a little older everyone told you, "This is your mother." You believed it, not that you had seen the person when she gave birth to you. Do you believe if it is said that there is cooking gas in cow dung? Cooking gas is not visible but gas is extracted when it is used in the proper manner. It often is blind faith that leads us to the goal. Son, you left your house to come here and you got into the bus which comes here. Is it not because of your faith that you will reach the destination? You got into the bus even though there are many vehicle accidents. Was your expectation that you would reach here itself not blind faith? Children, is it not because of your blind faith that Mother will talk to you that makes you talk to her? Children, all beliefs or faiths are blind.

Student: *It is said that God is everywhere. If so, what is the necessity of going to particular places of worship?*

Mother: There is wind everywhere but the person

who comes to rest under a tree out of the scorching heat gets a special kind of rejuvenating coolness which filters through the leaves of the tree. Likewise, we can experience a unique peace when we go to *Mahâtmas* (Great Souls). The significance of going to other places of worship is also the same. The atmosphere in a temple and a liquor shop are different, are they not?

Student: *Mother, how can we see God?*

Mother: Children, when there is good sunlight we can see numerous dust particles in the ray of sunlight which enters the room through a small hole in the roof of the house. Due to the lack of concentrated light, this is not seen in other places. Our mind is very dim. It has no subtlety. Just like charging a battery, through subtlety we illuminate our mind; we can see God. Having searched with our external eyes, do not say, "I am not seeing God; therefore, I don't believe in God." We should not make a big fuss saying, "I will only believe in the things that I see." Search, certainly you can see.

Without God's Grace, we cannot see Him. If we want to get His Grace, the ego in us should go. The well would say, "Everyone is drinking water from me. If I am not here, how will they cook food?" But the well does not know that it was dug by someone and that the bricks which make it beautiful were made by somebody else. Our situation is also the same. We become egotistical thinking "I am greater than everything else." But even to move a finger we need God's power. (Pointing her finger at a distance) However powerful a cyclone is, it cannot do anything to that blade of grass. Whereas the huge trees standing with their heads high will be uprooted. All grace will flow to us if a servant-like attitude (*dâsa bhâvana* or attitude of humility) comes to us. After that, nothing can move us. But God will not abide where there is ego. We will be uprooted by the cyclone of ego.

Another student: *Mother, what about people who do not have time to go to ashrams?*

Mother: Do not say that there is no time. Children, for many years we will sit at the courthouse to litigate for a foot of land. We won't care about rain, heat, or any other impediments. Because of our desire to acquire some land we will find time to try the case and toil for it. Nobody would say that there is no time for that. Similarly, we will wait any number of hours to see a doctor. Children, when you go to the theatre you will buy a ticket, not caring how large the crowd may be or even how many kicks and shoves you may get. That much desire you have to see the movie. These are not difficulties at all if one is intent on the goal (*lakshya bôdha*). Those who sincerely desire to see God will not feel that there is a lack of time.

By this time a householder devotee and his family had come from Quilon, a town 35 kilometers south of the Mother's ashram. They prostrated before the Holy Mother and took a seat near her. After some light conversation with them, the Mother again turned to the students.

GOD IS COMPASSIONATE

Student: *Mother, there are many people who are suf-*

fering in this world. Some are rich and enjoy life, but others die from starvation. What is the meaning in saying that God is compassionate? Is God not cruel?

Mother: Children, God is compassionate only but we must be deserving of His Grace which is constantly showering forth. The river is always flowing. Having constructed a dam, we complain that we do not get water. It is we who make the dam. We will get the constantly flowing Grace of God if the dam of ignorance and ego built by us is removed. Our mother gave birth to us and taught us the ways to progress. No progress will be made if we do not obey her. Imposing cruelty on God is like blaming our mother for our disobedience. Our case also is similar. God the Creator has given human beings the power to discriminate between the eternal and non-eternal. We commit errors indiscriminately and as a result we suffer. Seeing her son going to the forest, a mother tells her son, "Son, do not go into the forest. A forest fire is there, ferocious animals are there." Why should the mother be blamed for the troubles which may happen if he goes into the forest without listening to her warning?

Student: *What is the cause of the sorrows which happen in life?*

Mother: Desire is the cause of sorrow. The happiness that we get from worldly objects is only an infinitesimal fraction of the bliss that we get from within. The result will always be sorrow when we think that we are this body. This is only a rented body. We will be asked to leave at a certain time. Then we must depart. Before that, that which is eternal should be gained while we reside in this body. If we have a house of our own, we can happily move out when we are asked to vacate this rented one. Then we can live in the eternal house of God.

Student: *Mother, there are many people who still experience sorrow even after crying to God.*

Mother: We call God with many desires in our mind. The mind is filled with desires, not with God's Form. That means that we see God as a labourer which should not be so. Even though God is the servant of His devotees, it is not proper for us to treat Him as a servant. Dedicate everything at His Feet. We must have the attitude of surrender, then He will definitely protect us. After getting into the boat or bus, you won't still carry the luggage, will you? You will set it down. Likewise, surrender everything to God. He will protect us. Have the thought that God is near you. If there is a resting place nearby, the mere thought that the luggage which you are carrying on your head can soon be unloaded lightens the burden. The thought that the resting place is still far away increases the weight. In the same way, when we think that God is near, all our burdens will diminish.

Many of the householder devotees tell Mother, "However much we householders meditate or do *mantra japa*, not much benefit is gained." Devotedly we go to the temple to pray to the Lord. Finishing the circumambulation and standing before the inner sanctum, our mood will change if somebody comes and stands in front of us. We will get angry at him. Even if God Himself comes in disguise assuming a form, we will get angry. This is our character. How then are you children going to get the benefit of meditation?

Student: *If God is omnipresent, then why am I not realising the God-consciousness in me?*

Mother: Son, He is very close to you, that is why you cannot see Him. Is it possible to see our own face without the aid of a mirror? And will it be possible to see our image in a mirror if the mirror is completely covered with dust? Look after wiping away the dust particles and cleaning the mirror; then certainly you can see.

Student: *How is it possible to remove this ignorance?*

Mother: Through devotion, through worship, with pure divine love and knowledge.

Student: *Mother, I have seen a disturbing sight while leaving the house. Two crows were pecking and injuring an owl's fledgling. It was fluttering and crying from pain. What injustice is this? You say that God is compassionate. Then why does He allow such cruelties in Nature? Innocent deer become prey to lions. Human beings slaughter cows and eat their flesh. Is there no end to this?*

Mother: Children, nothing is in excess in this world. Everything is accurately weighed and measured and noted down. It is according to the *rāsanas* (latent tendencies) that beings take birth as a bird, cow or lion. Is God going to be responsible for that? Higher births are gained by exhausting each *rāsana*. If this human birth, which we have finally attained, is again spent living like an animal without using it for God-

Realisation, then we might take birth in this world as birds or animals. Therefore, God is not cruel. Each creature is only experiencing the fruit of its actions.

Question: *Mother, why is it necessary to worship God through a form when He is, in truth, formless?*

Mother: Children, it is our present habit to share our sorrows with our friends in order to get peace. Instead, the sharing of sorrows should be with the Universal Being. This is the aim of worshipping God with a form.

Once Shiva and Parvati were sitting together. Suddenly Shiva got up and started running but returned immediately. Parvati asked Him, "Why did You return so quickly?" Shiva replied, "One of My devotees used to tell his sorrows, big and small, to Me only; he never used to tell others. Today while returning to his house, he was mistaken for a thief and beaten up. Seeing this, I went to rescue him, but on My way I saw him telling his sorrow to some other man 'They beat me up for no reason! You should help me take revenge.' Since My help was not needed, I came back."

Do not increase your sorrows by sharing them with others. Tell them to God and try to solve them. If we share our sorrows with the Universal Being, we will get Eternal Peace.

An ordinary man may not develop love as easily for the formless aspect of God as he would if he worshipped God with form. Following the Path of Knowledge without devotion is like eating stones. The formless and omnipotent God can easily assume form for the sake of His devotees. If one has

full faith and confidence in the form of one's Beloved
Deity, he can reach the goal. We should think that God
is our own Self and worship Him seeing all-forms as different aspects of the same God.

Question: *If God is one and non-dual, why should we
worship Shiva, Vishnu and other such gods?*

Mother: An actor takes many roles, but he remains
the same. God is like this. Truth is one; different
are the names, and forms. Men have different natures and characters. The different forms of God
were described by the ancient sages to enable us to
realise Him by selecting names and forms according to our mental constitution. It is not that these
are different gods. The sages have portrayed the
non-dual God in different ways at different times
according to the taste and temperament of the
people.

Question: *If God is one, what then is the need for separate places of worship for each religion?*

Mother: Will an object change just because it is
known by different names? For example, water
may be called 'vellom' in Malayalam and 'pani' in
Hindi, but does the colour and taste change? No. Is
there any difference between the electric current
which passes through the refrigerator, the lamp
and the fan? No, only the object differs. Christians
say Christ is God and Muslims call Him Allah. Each
person understands God according to his culture and
worships as such.

Question: *Mother, a lot of money is offered to God in
temples in the name of ritualistic worship kand other
offerings. What for does God require money?*

Mother: God does not require anything from us. An electric lamp does not require the help of a kerosene lamp. God is like the sun. He sheds light equally on all things in the world. It is to this all-illuminating God that we offer a lamp and oil. This is due to our ignorance. It is like holding a burning candle in the daytime and saying, "O Sun God, here is light for You so that You can see the path clearly and walk." The offerings in temples are made for our benefit. God is the Giver of everything. He does not need or want anything from us.

TEMPLES

Question: *What are the temples for? Is not the sculptor who chiselled the beautiful idol the one who deserves to be adored?*

Mother: Just as we remember our father when we see his portrait, we are reminded of God, the Creator of the world, when we see the idol. When a devotee of Krishna sees the idol of Sri Krishna, he remembers the real Lord Krishna and not the stone image. Temples and idols are needed for those of us who are drowned in ignorance.

Question: *Are temples necessary for remembering God?*

Mother: Small children study things by looking at pictures of animals in books. These pictures will help them in their studies. They get an idea of what a camel, lizard or tiger are. At a later stage they understand that it is only a picture, but at a young age these pictures facilitate development of intellect.

Question: *It is said that if the daily worship is stopped in temples adverse reactions will occur. Is this true?*

Mother: As a result of man's resolve, the power of the temple gods will increase. If the worship is stopped, that power will diminish. The power of the god depends on the attitude of the person who installs it. Don't stop the daily worship performed in temples or to the family deity. If these rites are stopped, great misfortunes may happen.

Suppose we feed a crow for ten days. On the eleventh day, if we don't feed it, it will follow us cawing. We will be unable to work attentively. In the same way, if we stop the daily worship of the gods, they will always trouble us in their subtle forms. This will affect weak-minded people a great deal although a spiritual aspirant will not be affected much.

It is not enough that we build a boat but we should also learn how to row it. If we get into a boat without knowing how to row, it will move hither and thither. Is it proper to blame the boat if we have not learned how to row? Similarly, it is not enough that we construct temples. They must be properly looked after as well. Daily worship should be performed. If not, misfortune may result. It is meaningless to blame the temples at that time.

Question: *Are gods and God different?*

Mother: The gods are created and installed by man's resolve. Man's resolve has limitations, and therefore, his creations will reflect this fact. God, on the other hand, is all-powerful; His power neither decreases nor increases but remains eternally the same. The difference between the gods and God is like the difference between animals and man. Even though everything is one Reality, a dog does not have the discrimination that man has. A dog loves only those who love it; it may bite others.

Question: *If so, then won't temples become harmful to human beings?*

Mother: Never. This applies only to the temples where gods are worshipped. As regards such temples, we should be a bit careful. The installation of gods is done by priests who are incapable of controlling their own life force (*prâna shakti*). Never stop the daily worship in such temples. If worship is performed every day and in a proper way, material prosperity will result. Have you seen fish living in aquariums? The water must be changed frequently or it will become harmful to the fish. Similarly, temple worship must be done regularly.

The greatness of temples where *Mahâtmas* have installed the idols is unique. By their mere will, they give divine power to the idols which they install. They make the resolve that the idols should be identified with the Undivided Existence, Awareness, Bliss. Such temples and their idols will be full of divine power. They are not like fish living in aquariums, but like fish that live in the river. In such temples the daily *pooja* will never stop. Even if the *pooja* is stopped for some reason, there will be no loss of power. These temples will be centres of great attraction and will have eternally auspicious attributes. The temples at Tirupathi, Guruvayur and Chottanikara are examples of this.

Question: *Why were human sacrifices conducted in temples?*

Mother: The ignorance of people of olden times prompted them to do this. They believed that such sacrifices would please God. Misunderstanding the words of the scriptures, they performed these sacrifices. Look at our present day world. In the name of politics there is so much bloodshed. Atrocities like killing a man who changes his political party, killing the members of a different political party, shootings and stabbings have become commonplace. Does any party's by-laws or ideology sanction murder or such atrocities? The manifestos and preachings are very good, but what is carried out is entirely different. Similarly, there were such fools in those days. Blind devotion and erroneous belief prompted them make improper so-called sacrifices.

Question: *Do such people incur sin?*

Mother: If an act is for a universal cause, there is no sin but if it is for a selfish end, it is a sin. Once there were two brahmins in a village. Both became afflicted with the same disease. When they consulted a doctor, he told them that if they ate fish they would be cured. As both were strict vegetarians, they were at their wits' end. The first man, yielding to the demand of his wife and children, ate fish and was cured. The second man, being afraid of sin, refused to eat fish, and as a result, died. His family was orphaned and subjected to many troubles.

Here the first man, by eating the comparatively insignificant fish, protected his whole family. This is not cruelty. The second man refused to eat fish and died leaving his whole family to suffer. A family is of far greater importance than one or two fish.

Don't we cut down trees to build a house? Such things are not selfish. When we act with vengeance or out of hatred or passion, it becomes a sin.

Question: *Mother, what is the reason for the loss of sanctity in the temples?*

Mother: In the name of festivals people collect money and conduct worldly programmes in temples. This makes the surroundings of temples impure. Instead of cultivating devotion and good thoughts in people, such programmes create vulgar thoughts and passions. What nonsense is done in the name of festivals; people get drunk and fight. In the temple compounds they conduct drama, dance and programmes which arouse worldliness in the minds of the audience. Young children are also affected by this. At the tender age when good thoughts should be developed, these programmes make them stray from the right path. These kinds of thought waves make the temple atmosphere unholy.

Children, we alone destroy ourselves. First we should become good. We should see that the temples are kept pure. Only the arts of a divine nature which will increase devotion and faith should be held in temples. The daily *pooja* should be done properly. Having made the temple surroundings impure, there is no use in accusing the deities. In the olden days meditation, reading of the ancient scriptures, yogic postures and other spiritual activities were practiced in temples. Only stories connected with God would be presented as dramas during festivals.

The money collected from the public for festivals should be utilized for humanitarian purposes. There are so many people who are struggling without a house in our villages. We can build houses for them. Clothes and food can be given in charity to the poor. Help can be given to those who are unable to conduct a marriage ceremony for lack of money. Religious books can be printed and distributed free of charge and used for teaching children. Orphanages can be built and the children therein can be raised with culture and good character. If so, there will not be any orphans in the future. All this will help create unity among people.

Children, look at the Christians and Muslims and all the good things that they do. They build orphanages and schools and teach orphans religion and look after their requirements. Have you seen any churches in a dilapidated condition? No. But look at the plight of Hindu temples. So many temples remain uncared for and unattended. The Devaswom Board (government agency for the maintenance of temples) will take over the management of big temples because they can make money, while they ignore the smaller temples.

We should take special care to renovate temples and conduct divine arts during festival seasons. Unitedly we ourselves should take care of temples in the proper way. Their holiness should be preserved, otherwise our culture will degenerate.

Question: *Is it possible to attain Liberation through temple worship?*

Mother: It is possible, but one must worship with the understanding of the inner significance of the temples. God resides in temples, but don't think that He is limited by the four walls of the temple. Have firm belief that God is omnipresent. A bus will take us to the bus stop nearest to our house; from there we can easily walk the remaining distance. Similarly, the correct way of temple worship will take us to the threshold of *Satchidânanda* (Pure Being-Knowledge-Bliss); from there only a short distance remains before attaining Perfection. You can take birth in a temple, but don't die there. That is to say that, in the beginning, a seeker can do temple worship as stepping stone, but the final and real goal is beyond all these things.

MANTRA

Question: *Do words have the power to change the character of a person?*

Mother: Definitely. Once in a temple a brahmin was teaching spiritual matters to his students. At that time the king of the country arrived. The brahmin, engrossed in his teaching, was unaware of the king's arrival. The king became angry and berated the brahmin for not noticing him. The brahmin explained that as he was deeply involved with teaching, he was unaware of the king's arrival. The king then asked what the brahmin was teaching so earnestly that he was not aware of the king's presence. The brahmin replied, "I was teaching the children things which will purify their characters. There is no use if this is not taught with full attention and sincerity." The king mockingly asked, "Can mere words change the character?" The brahmin replied, "Certainly! Change will happen." The king retorted, "It will not change just like that." At that moment one of the brahmin's students, a small boy, told the king to get out. As soon as the king heard this, he was enraged and roared, "How dare you say that! I will kill you, your Guru and destroy this ashram as well!" Thus said, the king caught hold of the brahmin by the neck. Then the brahmin told the king, "Please forgive me. You just now said that mere words cannot change the character of a person. Yet, when a small boy said a few words to you, you changed so much from your normal character. You were even ready to kill me and destroy everything."

Children, through words character can be changed. If ordinary words can change the character, then what can we say of the power of a mantra which emanated from the *rishis* (ancient sages) and contains *bijāksharas* (seed letters, e.g., 'om,' 'hrim,' 'klim').

Question: *Mother, if a mantra is chanted will one get the benefit?*

Mother: Definitely. But one thing, mantras should be chanted with concentration. Depending on one's attitude one will get power. Mental attitude is the criteria. A doctor will prescribe medicine and tell the patient to take rest and avoid certain foods. If the patient follows the instructions, the disease will be cured. Thus, the *rishis* have taught that if a mantra is chanted in a prescribed way, then certain results will accrue. If we follow their instructions meticulously, we will definitely get the fruit of it.

RITUALS

Question: *Mother do the rituals peformed during* pitrukarma *(ancestral ceremonies) have any effect?*

Mother: Children, pure *sankalpa* (resolve) has great power, but only when *sankalpa* is pure will rituals bear fruit. When *pitrukarma* is performed, the name, birthstar, form and attitude of the dead person is remembered and the proper mantras are chanted. Each ritual has its respective *devata* (deity). Just as a properly addressed letter sent by a son to his parents in a distant place will be received correctly, the effect of rituals will also reach the intended person. If *the sankalpa* is pure, the *devata* pertaining to that ritual will make its result reach that particular soul.

RISHIS-SAGES

Question: *What is the guarantee that the* rishis *predictions will come true?*

Mother: The ancient *rishis* were *mantradrishtas* (visionaries); whatever they have expressed has come true. Everything written in the *Srimad Bhâgavatam*[1] about the *Kaliyuga*[2] has been accurate. "The father will eat the son; the son will eat the father. All the forests will become houses; all the houses will become shops." Are these things not happening? We cut down the trees and build houses and shops in their place. Truth and *dharma* have no place at all. Are there mutual trust, love, sincerity, patience, and sacrifice for higher

---

[1] An ancient scripture describing the deeds of Lord Vishnu's Incarnations.
[2] The present dark age of materialism.

ideals? Weather in the rainy season and in the sunny season is extreme one way or the other. During the growing season, due to lack of rain, crops dry up. All these things were predicted by the sages.

The ancient *rishis*, eating only leaves and fruits, did *tapas* (severe austerities) and realised the secret of the universe. The whole creation was like a mustard seed in the palm of their hand. Even inanimate objects would obey their command. The *rishis* made many discoveries in ancient times. Even present day inventions, which we consider to be very great, were brought forth effortlessly by them. For example, scientists have produced test tube babies. Yet the sage Vyasa brought forth the hundred and one Kauravas from clay pots; he imparted life to mere hunks of flesh. When compared with this, the test tube baby is nothing. In the *Ramayana*[3] reference is made to *"pushpaka vimâna"* (airplane made of flowers), yet the modern airplane was invented only recently. There are many examples like this.

Mother does not consider present day scientists and their inventions to be insignificant. Rather, this is to show that there is nothing that cannot be gained by *tapas*. For the *rishis* all these things were quite simple; they were able to create anything through their *sankalpa*.

18 September 1976

The Mother was conversing with a few devotees sitting in front of the temple. Unnikrishnan, one of the first Ashram resi-

[3]A scripture describing the birth and life of Sri Rama, an Incarnation of Lord Vishnu.

dents, was also present. He keenly listened to the conversation that Mother was having with the other devotees.

PATH TO LIBERATION

Devotee: *Mother, what is the path to Liberation?*
Mother: Children, what does Mother know? Mother is crazy. She would simply say some crazy things. Shiva! Shiva! Children, accept what you think is correct.

Permanent happiness will not be gained from the world which is changing every moment. If we depend on the Eternal Reality, Eternal Bliss will be gained. So much the better if the effort begins from a young age.
Devotee: *Why does man commit errors?*
Mother: We are caught in the illusion that we will get happiness from the world. Then we madly run here and there craving to acquire it. Having unfulfilled desires, we experience frustration and anger. Without discriminating between the necessary and the unnecessary, we do things as we like. Can we say that this is life? Whose fault is it?
Devotee: *It is said that without God even a blade of grass won't move. Can human beings be blamed for the errors if God is making them do everything?*
Mother: For a person who has the conviction, "The real doer is not me, but God," it is then impossible to commit any mistakes. He sees everything permeated by God. It is impossible for that devotee even to think about making mistakes. To say it in another way, one who has transcended all errors alone will have the faith, "God alone is the doer, even a blade

of grass will not move without Him." There is no error or sin for one who has the conviction that God is the doer; whereas, the fruits of the mistakes committed by a person who thinks, "I am the doer," must be accepted by him. He alone is responsible for his own good and bad actions if he thinks, "I am doing everything," without having the awareness that God is the doer. Having committed a murder, it is not right to then say that God is the doer. One whose thought is, "God is the doer" would not commit murder, would he?

Devotee: *We would not commit murder or mistakes if God didn't give us ignorance.*

Mother: In Creation there is ignorance and knowledge, discrimination and indiscrimination, everything exists. God's Will is that we should go forward and perform actions which will result only in goodness by using the discriminative power given by Him. A student may make mistakes while studying in school, but why should he be adamant in thinking that he should only make mistakes? He can progress towards goodness by using the circumstances in the proper way, can't he? There is right and wrong in the Creation just as there is night and day. God has also given discrimination to human beings to refrain from committing any errors. We have to make use of it. The field is there and the seed is also there. Cultivate carefully and reap the fruit. Having acted as you like, do not say that God is the mischief maker. If you say, "It is God who made me murder," console yourself that, "It is God who is hanging me." Do not make any complaints. How many times has God, dwelling within, prevented us, saying,

"Don't, don't," when we were about to commit a murder or some other evil deed? Why do we not consider that? Afterwards, are you putting the burden of the responsibility of your errors on God's head? If it is spiritual progress that you children want, then what is needed is to take refuge in God with a pure heart without blaming God or indulging in unnecessary disputes.

The effect should merge in the cause some day. The effects are the sense organs, mind, intellect, and vital forces. The world itself is an effect. Real life is a dispassionate, constant effort to merge the effects into the Supreme Self (*Paramâtma*) which is the Cause. There is nothing that cannot be gained through a human birth. If the feeling that something should be gained is there, that life is not full. That state should come where nothing needs to be gained. We must become eternally satisfied. That is Perfection. There will be no sorrow if and when the sense organs are withdrawn from sense objects.

Devotee: *In which shape does God's radiant Power assume a form?*

Mother: That cannot be told. Everything is God's Will. He will assume forms according to the need. None of them are fruitless.

Devotee: *Can there be more than one* Avatâr *(Incarnation) at a time?*

Mother: It can happen. Why doubt? Did not Parasurama, Sri Rama and Sita all exist at one time? What about Balarama, Krishna and Rukmini? There should be no doubt about more than one Incarnation of God being able to exist at the same time when it is the same God who has become all these worlds of diversity simultaneously.

Devotee: *Mother, can* sankalpa *(resolve) come true?*

Mother: When the world is true, *sankalpa* is also true. If the world is illusory, *sankalpa* is also illusory. *Sankalpa*, if it is strong and sincere, will come true.

ELIMINATION OF MIND

Devotee: *Mother, I have been worshipping God for a long time, but there is no peace of mind. What to do?*

Mother: Is it not the mind which has no peace? Eliminate the mind. Thus the problem is solved, is it not?

Devotee: *Is it possible to eradicate the mind?*

Mother: Why not? Are not all paths for that only? Do not let the mind go towards sense objects. This is possible through *sâdhana* (spiritual practice). Now and then the mind will go outward. Immediately make it turn inward saying, "No, I won't let you go."

Devotee: *How do human beings become good or bad?*

Mother: Due to *vâsanas,* actions arise, and from actions, *vâsanas* arise. From God alone we received the first *vâsana*. From that, action followed. According to the actions, good and bad come.

THE LAW OF KARMA

Devotee: *Each one experiences the fruit of his actions. Then why should the suffering one be helped?*

Mother: If what he is experiencing is the fruit of his actions, then can't it be the fruit of your actions to save him? If his *vâsana* becomes a cause for experiencing sorrow, your *vâsana* becomes a cause to help. Both are the continuation of past actions. Remember that if you do not help the ailing, you will have to enjoy the fruit of that evil action.

Devotee: *No faith comes because God cannot be seen. The* Mahâtmas *can be seen. Therefore, is it not better to worship them?*

Mother: That is all right, but you should also understand the relationship between the *Mahâtmas* and God. It is the Essence of God which manifests through the *Mahâtmas*, just as electricity manifests through a light bulb. *Mahâtmas* should be approached with *iswara bhâvana* (the attitude that they are equal to God). Only then is there benefit. The Guru should be considered as God.

SARIRA TYAGA
Committing Suicide

Another devotee: *Mother, I have no interest in sustaining the body, but there is the desire for God-Realisation. What shall I do?*

Mother: The body will exist as long as there is desire. When one body is given up, another will be gained. The body is the representation of desire. Desire is of different kinds. There is no harm in the desire to know God. Not only that, that desire must be there. To attain God, spiritual practices should be done. The body is needed for that; therefore, the thought to give up the body is wrong.

Your mind is always in the body; that is why you feel that the body is a burden, that it should be given up. There is no meaning if one who always thinks of the body says that he is thinking of God. There will be no body-consciousness if the mind merges in God. Let the body exist or fall off; after realizing the Truth, it is not a problem. Therefore, son, think of God at all times. That is what is needed now.

Mother knows that this suicidal tendency in you is not based purely on your longing to realise God. Is not the basic cause the calamities which recently occurred in your family? Son, you feel frightened thinking that those calamities which have subsided for the time being are still waiting to burst out at any moment, don't you? You are fearful about the future, aren't you? Son, don't worry. Nothing will happen. Cast off this fear; Mother is with you.

The devotee was wonderstruck when he heard Mother clearly and precisely reveal her knowledge of even his subtlest thoughts. It was perfectly true that a calamity had happened in his family instilling intense fear into him. Upon the death of his father a few weeks earlier, there occurred a verbal duel between the relatives who each wanted to seize the ancestral wealth. This culminated in a terrible fight. This unfortunate incident sowed the seeds of dread and terror in this young man's heart, the youngest of the family and a lover of peace.

Now he wondered how the Mother came to know all of this. He tried to fathom the mystery but failed. The young man looked with wide-open eyes at Mother's face and then with eyes cast down, he shed silent tears.

While Mother lovingly stroked his back and comforted him, another devotee asked,

HOW TO KNOW THE TRUTH

Devotee: *Mother, how can one know the Truth while living in this world of plurality?*

Mother: It is difficult to know God as we live in this world. Both God and the world can be known if the world is seen as God. Suppose a white crane is sitting in the midst of many crows. When viewed from a distance, everything will seem black and dark. As we move closer, the crows can be distinguished. Coming a little closer still, we will see the crane. Then our attention will be on that. Likewise, Pure Consciousness will not come into sight if we stand at a distance. Truth cannot be gained by searching outside. Truth is One. Search for It within. Truth is ever-existent, all else lasts for a short period of time. In reality the essence of the world is only God, but you must have the eye to see it.

Devotee: *It is said that God and the world are one. Then why are they seen as two?*

Mother: Just as the sun during the sunrise and sunset is the same, God and the world are one. If all our energy is wasted on trivial things, that which is the Essence cannot be known. Discrimination must be used. *Satsang* (companionship with the Great Ones) is necessary.

Devotee: *I would like to know certain things from Mother.*

Mother: That which is made known will not become knowledge. Then what can Mother make you know?

Devotee: *With what attitude should we visualize God?*

Mother: It can be imagined that "I am God's child." God's existence will also become more convincing when one's resolve becomes stronger and stronger.

Devotee: *Whatever is seen is not Truth. The scriptures say that God alone is Truth. So how should one live in this world?*

Mother: Live a detached life. Don't attach yourself to the work or to its fruit. Perform it as a sacrifice. Then your actions will become beautiful and beneficial to others.

Devotee: *I am worshipping God in an image. While travelling, I am not able to continue doing it. Is there any harm because of this?*

Mother: Harm may occur if you feel worried and think that the worship has been discontinued, whereas the worship will not be broken if the Beloved Deity is carried in your heart and worshipped mentally even when you go out. Not only that, *mânasa pooja* (mental worship) is the greatest. Those who are unable to do that should worship with flowers.

Devotee: *When will I be liberated from this cycle of birth and death?*

Mother: To get liberated, 'I' should go. This present body is the result of *sanchita karma* (accumulated actions) performed in the previous births. The human body is something higher than other bodies. God-Realisation can be attained by doing *sâdhana* with this body. It is due to the acquired merits in the previous birth that one feels interested to search for God in this birth. Your desire will be fulfilled in this birth itself if your resolve and effort is continued in the same way.

The tendency to enjoy sensual pleasures should completely leave the mind.

DO NOT BECOME A SLAVE
TO THE CIRCUMSTANCES

As the conversation continued, another devotee came to see the Holy Mother. He was a newcomer. Having prostrated before the Mother, he also sat among the other devotees. When the opportunity came to clear some of his doubts, he asked,

Devotee: *Mother, for a long time I have been thinking to come and see you. I could finally come today. There is a time and circumstance for all these things, is there not?*

Mother: Son, time is always favourable, but we are not favouring time, that is all. Both favour and adversity is within us only. Not knowing this, human beings become slaves to their circumstances. Many good things will pass through your hands if you sit saying, "Let a good time come." Do not wait looking for an opportunity to do a good thing. Do it immediately if it is good.

Devotee: *It is said that God dwells within yet why is it that nobody knows Him?*

Mother: Ordinary people think that they are the body only. They are attached to their wives, children and other relatives. Unknowingly they persist in wrong actions. While drowned in ignorance, how can we know God who is dwelling in the heart? God not only dwells in the heart, but He is all-pervasive as well. The only thing is, we should try to know Him. Instead of making the mind extroverted, make it turn Godward.

Devotee: *Among fears, such as fear of enemies, of poverty, of starvation and other calamities, the most terrifying is the fear of death. How can it be conquered?*
Mother: Fear of death will be removed when we become convinced that "I am deathless," will it not? We should understand the truth that "I am the Self, I am Brahman, I am deathless."

THE GLORY OF THE GURU

Devotee: *How can that be understood?*
Mother: A Guru who is established in that knowledge should be approached. It is impossible without a Guru. Suppose we are going to travel to a strange place. Somebody must be there who knows the path to protect us. Satsang is the easiest path. A scholar who has scriptural knowledge is not sufficient. A Guru who is a knower of the Self must be there. Only one who has known the path can show the way.

19 September 1976

As usual, the sun god, the illuminer of the universe, emerged on the eastern horizon slowly sending forth brilliant rays to caress the earth and its creatures. Gazing at the beautiful rising sun, the Holy Mother was lying in the front yard of the old temple. While looking at the sun, her mind soared to the heights of supreme bliss, and getting up in a semi-conscious mood, she walked into the shrine with faltering steps like one intoxicated. Having

entered the temple, Mother started singing loudly calling out
now and then, "Amma...Amma." After a few minutes, the
Mother abruptly stopped singing, and placing her head on the
peetham (the seat she sits on for the *Devi Bhâva*), she started
chanting 'Aum,' the sacred syllable. She became totally lost to
this world. Eventually, she began rolling on the ground from
this side to that side.

One hour passed like this when she suddenly got up and began dancing blissfully, having placed on her head the idol of
Lord Krishna which was kept in the temple. Replacing the idol in
the same spot, the Holy Mother emerged from the temple still in
the same blissful mood. It was then that she noticed that the milk
brought for her by a devotee had been tipped over by the crows
and had spilled on the floor. The Mother sat on the floor and
drank some of the milk by scooping it from the floor with her
cupped hands. Thus the Mother still fulfilled the wish of the
devotee who had brought the milk especially for her even
though it was no longer in the cup. The next moment, the
Mother joined the children who were playing games in the front
yard of the temple. Now she looked exactly like a small mischievous child making merry with her playmates.

Although seemingly contradictory, these crazy actions of
the Mother were full of significance in the eyes of spiritually-
elevated people. Such childlike plays of the Holy Mother gave
delight to the eyes of the devotees.

While the Holy Mother was playing with the children,
some devotees came to see her. Having stopped her play,
the Mother approached the devotees benignly smiling at
them. Now her mood again changed from that of a child
to a compassionate mother. Followed by the devotees,
the Mother went to the temple verandah and sat there
with them. She lovingly asked, *"Children, did you eat
anything?"* They replied, "Yes, we ate our lunch,
Mother." The Mother enquired, *"From where?"* "From
the shop," they answered. Mother smiled as the devotees
sat looking at her, wondering at her compassion and
love. They had many things to ask. It was often the expe-

rience of the devotees and aspirants who came to see the Mother that the Masterhood in her would be invoked by one's thirst for knowledge. During such occasions one could see the unending flow of the Mother's profound wisdom streaming forth in all its beauty.

TRUE KNOWLEDGE

Devotee: *Isn't it disappointing to see* bheda buddhi *(differentiating mind) even in famous* sannyâsins?
Mother: Children, true knowledge cannot be gained by merely studying the scriptures. *Bheda buddhi* will be there as long as there is no Self-Knowledge. Scriptural knowledge is external, whereas knowledge of the Self is internal experience. *Bheda buddhi* will not be seen in one whose mind has merged in God. Book scholars will speak about renunciation but cannot withdraw their minds from the sensual objects. A real Master is a knower of the Self. Such beings should work among people giving guidance to them.

MONKS AND RENUNCIATION

Devotee: *Shouldn't a monk keep away from the world? Isn't he someone who has renounced the world? Can he engage in material affairs again?*
Mother: *Sannyâsa* (formal renunciation, becoming a monk) is not renouncing the world and action. *Tyâga* (renunciation) is renunciation of the fruits (of action). It is the *dharma* of the *sannyâsins* to lead the world. *Sannyâsins* are the ones who give peace to the world. Whoever may protest, there will

always be a group of Knowers of the Self in this world.
Even today there are people who can sanctify the world
by mere *sankalpa* (resolve). Not everyone will know
about them. There are also many institutions which
sincerely work for world peace.

Devotee: *Can awareness of the Truth be gained
through institutions?*

Mother: What is meant by an institution is not an institution like a factory or a bank. It is a charitable
institution. Many people would be working for
each charitable institution. Several such institutions should be formed, that is what Mother
wants to say. Let at least ten people take the righteous path through each institution. Among them,
at least in one person, awareness of the Truth might
awaken. They, in turn, will protect many others.

Devotee: *In this way, after how many years would the
entire human race be turned into knowers of the Self?
Would such a thing be possible?*

Mother: God's resolve is not there for this to happen. Everything must be there in the Creation.
Otherwise, how could the *leela* (God's play) take
place?

See, it is not Mother's intention to keep the children who are here inside the four walls of the
ashram. Tomorrow they have to do good things in
the world. Even though the world may not know
the value of this now, in the future it will be known.
Until then, the protests and abuses should be accepted happily.

Listening and getting absorbed in the ambrosial
words and presence of the Holy Mother, the devotees were quite

unaware of the passing of time. It was now one in the afternoon yet no one wanted to get up and eat lunch. Hunger and thirst will disappear in the presence of a great Master. Presently some more devotees arrived. The Holy Mother was cheerful and compassionate as ever.

Question: *Mother, I always want to come and see you, but I should get time, shouldn't I?*
Mother: (Smiling) All those who come here say that there is no time. Then for whom is all this time? Each day some time should be kept apart for Godly matters.
Devotee: *We are doing spiritual practices as instructed by Mother. Our children are also doing* japa[4] *and* dhyâna.[5]
Mother: Good, they will not swerve from the path in the future because they have begun doing this at such a young age.
Another devotee: *(Pointing to his son) It is a school holiday. He came and told me that he wants to stay here for two or three days. I agreed.*
Mother: Then let both the children stay. (Smilingly) Here I will play with the children. In the middle of the game I will play tricks on them. Afraid of me, the children will go along with all this.
Devotee: *Mother, during meditation I feel headaches. Why is this happening?*
Mother: It can happen if meditation is not done at the correct time. A regular discipline is needed. Headaches may also occur if one meditates between the eye-

[4]Repetition of a mantra.
[5]Meditation

brows. At that time stop meditation for two days and switch to japa and *kirtana*.[6] If headaches return when you resume meditation, then meditation should be done in the heart. Then there will be no problem.

Question: *Mother, how can we think of God with our limited intellect?*

Mother: It is possible if the intellect, limited in the individual, is expanded. The intellect should be fixed on the *átma bháva*[7] giving up the *deha bháva*.[8]

Devotee: *Is this possible for ordinary people?*

Mother: Anyone can do so if they really have the desire. The only thing is that they have to do *sádhana*. They must understand that which stands as the Cause behind the perceptible non-eternal objects. The goal of human effort is to know that Divine Power which illumines even the sun, moon and stars.

BRAHMAN AND JAGAT
Absolute Consciousness and the World

Question: *Mother, it is said that* Brahman *and* jagat *are one. How can that be?*

Mother: Just as every object that exists has a name, the world exists in Brahman. Name and form are inseparable. When there is the awareness of the world, there is no awareness of the Self. When there is awareness of the Self, awareness of the world is not there either. There is butter in milk, but it is not seen.

---

[6]Singing of God's Names and songs in praise of Him or Her.
[7]The attitude that "I am the Self."
[8]The attitude that "I am the body.

When butter is obtained through churning, it forms a ball. If heated, it melts, and the shape changes. In the same manner, Brahman is not seen in diversity. It can be found when *sâdhana* is performed. When butter is heated, there is no form; when frozen it solidifies. God's form and formlessness is like this. No dross in either, no waste.

Question: *The scriptures say that we are not the body but the Self. If one believes this, is it necessary to trouble oneself with* sâdhana?

Mother: Is it not a belief which is obtained through telling, hearing and reading? It will not last long. Whereas, the faith gained from experience will last forever. Suppose a person was travelling with his son. They felt very hungry and thirsty. Then, pointing out the rice paddy plants on the roadside, the father started saying, "Look, this is a paddy plant. After some time the grain will grow there. If the paddy is husked, rice will be obtained. Delicious food made by mixing rice flour, coconut and molasses which, when eaten, will stop hunger." But hunger will not be removed simply with this knowledge. You must eat the food if hunger is to be removed. Scriptures will tell about the *Atman*, but what is the use if it is not experienced by oneself? What guarantee is there that we will get the time later when we think, "I will try for that." Therefore, without wasting time, start the effort immediately.

JIVATMA AND PARAMATMA
Individual Self and Supreme Self

Question: *Mother, are* jîvâtma *and* Paramâtma *two?*
Mother: In *vyavahâra*[9] they are two. When *samsâra*[10] is given up, there is only one. There is a dam in the middle of a lake. The lake is two when the dam is there; if the dam is not there, then it is one. The dam is ignorance or maya. If that is removed, it becomes Non-dual Knowledge. Duality is only seemingly real. In truth everything is strung together on one strand, the thread of Atman. The perception of duality happens when we are established in the pride of body-consciousness. Like air and movement, or fire and the power of burning, *Paramâtma* and *jîvâtma* are one and the same. This perception of Unity is *Jñâna*.[11] Perception of plurality is *ajñâna*.[12] Those possessing a one-pointed mind understand that it is the same witness-consciousness within everything. Ordinary people do not know this. A powerful person is one who has known the unity of *jîvâtma* and *Paramâtma*. He has no fear, no afflictions. *Jagat* (the world) is apparent; God is beyond the world. The goal is to reach the Non-dual State, abandoning all imaginings born of plurality.

EVOLUTION OF THE INDIVIDUAL SELF

Devotee: *To where is the evolution of the* jîva *leading?*
Mother: This journey is to attain something great.

---

[9]The phenomenal world.
[10]The Ocean of Transmigration or the cycle of birth, death and rebirth.
[11]Spiritual knowledge or wisdom.
[12]Spiritual ignorance.

Searching and roaming about the whole world, one becomes dissatisfied. One then thinks of a way to gain satisfaction. From the mind arises all thoughts and doubts. Next one looks to see whether peace can be gained if searched for in the mind. From then onwards the mind begins to turn inward. The enquiry continues. In between, the path gets obstructed. Then we approach a *Sadguru*. Again we move forward. At last, the goal of Self-Realisation is reached. Such souls will later come forward to protect the world.

Devotee: *Mother, will there be body-consciousness even after attaining Knowledge?*

Mother: In *Jñānis*[13] it is the awareness of the Self which is always there. A *Jñāni* knows that the body is not real. Descending a little from the plane of the Real, the *Jñāni* acts for the protection of the world. They can give up the body whenever it is necessary. After going to your village and spreading the news about the ashram to many people, you can return at any time. Like this, a *Jñāni* will do many things while being in the world, but he will stand in the awareness of the Truth at all times. A *Jñāni* has no body-consciousness. He has only awareness of the Self. But others will feel that he has a body.

All of a sudden the Holy Mother closed her eyes and sat motionless, her face lit up with a blissful smile. All the devotees who were gathered around her began meditating. A few of minutes passed and when the Mother slowly opened her eyes, she began rapturously singing,

---

13A Realised Soul.

By which Power this world had been created,
By which Power it is sustained,
By which Power it returns to the unmanifest state,
Let us offer our salutations to that Great Power...

Everyone joined her and went into an ecstatic mood. The Holy Mother shed tears of bliss, now and then calling out *"Amma, Amma"* while continuing the singing. Her poignant song and elevated spiritual mood filled the devotees' hearts with tremendous peace and tranquillity. Forgetting the world around them, they sang with great devotion.

THE SIGNS OF SELF-REALISATION

One of the resident *brahmachárins* had a doubt whether the Mother was a Realised Soul or not, but he was a bit hesitant to open his heart to her. One day while talking to some of the residents, Mother turned to the *brahmachárin* who had the doubt and said,

Mother: A Self-Realised Soul is one who sees the Fundamental Principle in everything without even an iota of doubt. In him there is no place for the argument, "There is or there is not." He has the constant Vision of the Truth alone, everywhere, in the front, back, above and below. There is not even an iota of *prapancha bhávana*[14] in him. In the plane of Real Awareness there is no place for the world. The world merges in *Satta*[15]. Both within and without is the same Consciousness. It is beyond even the intellect. Only such a person can work for the protection of the world. Renunciation,

---

[14]Feeling of the existence of the apparent world.
[15]The Essence.

feeling of equality, humility and simplicity are his characteristics.

The resident who was listening to the Mother's words with great wonder shed tears, thinking of the compassion that she had just shown him.

THE WAY A SADGURU DISCIPLINES

One of the residents was talking about the things which made him sad to the Mother.

Devotee: *In the beginning stages Mother would show great affection to me, telling me stories and feeding me with her own hand. But now there is nothing. The only thing she says is to study the scriptures and do* sâdhana *(spiritual practices).*
Mother: (Affectionately) In those days that was necessary. Now this is what is needed. Fathers build playhouses with leaves and boughs of a palm tree for their young children. In those days you could not understand spiritual principles. Therefore, more external love was shown. Now Mother keeps that love within. What you need now is serious spiritual training. It is not that Mother has any less love for her children.

Mother looked most lovingly at the him and his face lost the sadness from which he had been suffering. Later a group of youths arrived. From their appearance it was clear that they were college students. They stood at a little distance from where Mother was seated. She smiled benignly at them and asked where they had come from. Perhaps it was the Mother's natural way of enquiring that made the students come closer to her. As they approached, she asked them to sit down, which they did.

Moments passed in silence while the Holy Mother sat in front of them with the same smiling face radiating compassion and love. One of the students broke the silence, asking a question which made it clear that they were interested in spiritual life.

Question: *Is there a God?*
Mother: Why doubt? What is, is only God.
Question: *Why then is He not seen?*
Mother: What then is all this that is seen? What we see in different forms is God alone.
Question: *Then why don't I feel like that? What should be done to develop that feeling? Can it be said that everything of this diverse Nature is God?*
Mother: Why not? Could there be diversity in God because you see Him as diverse? Diversity is felt because of the difference of each one's vision. Otherwise there is no difference in God. God's real nature will be understood when the attitude of difference in us is removed. What is the difficulty in perceiving unity in diversity? We have hands, legs, eyes, nose, etc., but are these different organs not part of our own body? The limbs are not different from the body, are they? Like this, see everything that is seen as His limbs. The sun gets concealed by the clouds. In a like manner, God is concealed by our *vāsanas*. He becomes visible when the dirt of latent tendencies is removed.
Question: *How shall I do that, Mother?*
Mother: The *vāsanas* should be gotten rid of through *sādhana*. We are not the body. There is Truth within. That is what should be known. If we enquire outside, we won't get That. But there is another thing. Just as He is within, He is there without also. But searching for God outside is like trying to catch fish by emptying

the ocean. Therefore, become introspective. When God is seen within, then He can be seen everywhere. The mind should be purified by getting rid of bad thoughts. God will shine in a pure mind.

MERITS AND DEMERITS, PRARABDHAM[16]

Question: *Mother, what is* punya *and* pâpa?[17]
Mother: The result of auspicious action is *punya*; the fruit of inauspicious action is *pâpa*. Action which brings *dosha*[18] to oneself and others is inauspicious, and that which brings prosperity and goodness is auspicious. The origin of *punya* and *pâpa* can be transcended if *vâsanas* are exhausted. For that, the mind should be cleansed through *sâdhana*.

The *Atman* is not affected by merits and demerits, happiness and sorrow and other opposites. They affect the mind only. The *Atman* is only a witness to everything.

Question: *Mother, what is this* prârabdha karma?
Mother: Children, *prârabdha karmas* are those *vâsanas* alone which exist in the *chitta*[19] in the subtle form. The *prârabdha* will exist until knowledge of the Self is gained. *Prârabdha* will persist as long as body-consciousness is present. The body does not have to perish. If awareness of the body is overcome, *prârabdha* will cease. *Prârabdha* is related to the body. It will fall off when the knowledge that "I am not the body; I am the Self" is gained.

---

[16] The results of actions done in previous births and now bearing fruit.
[17] Merit and demerit (virtue and sin).
[18] Evil.
[19] The mind.

There is no birth and death for a *Jñâni*. Everything has only an apparent existence as far as he is concerned. For him, there is nothing different from *Brahman*. The body will exist for some time even after one becomes a Knower of the Self. The feeling that he has a body is in the eyes of others only. As far as a *Jñâni* is concerned, what is called a body is also *Brahman*. There are people who live peacefully even in the midst of all this confusion. Nobody is bound by this *samsâra* once an iota of the principle of Stillness is experienced.

Question: *Mother, what is tyâga?*

Mother: Tyâga is abandoning the desire for the fruit of one's actions. One who is desireless is liberated. The desire rising up from the feeling "I" and "mine" is the cause of bondage.

Question: *There is only one God. Then isn't one path enough? For what are all these different methods of* sâdhana?

Mother: Different means can be chosen for travelling. Travel can be done by water, air and land, but the destination will be the same.

Question: *Where is the best place to concentrate when doing* rûpa dhyâna?[20]

Mother: Meditation in the heart is the best.

Question: *Mother, when does the thought of God arise in a person?*

Mother: The thought of God can arise all of a sudden due to the accumulated merits of past births. Then if it is properly nourished, we can make progress. Otherwise, we will again fall into inauspiciousness. If *sâdhana* can be started from a very young age, that is the best.

[20]Meditation on a form of God.

Question: *Why are most people not interested in Godly matters?*

Mother: Due to the lack of accumulated merits from previous births, the desire for sense objects will be more predominant.

TIME NEEDED FOR GOD-REALISATION

Some householders, who were serious spiritual practitioners, came to see the Holy Mother. They sat among the other devotees and listened keenly to the topic which she was discussing. One of them asked,

Devotee: *Mother, I am a householder. All my time has been wasted. The* brahmachârins[21] *who stay here with Mother have started doing* sâdhana *at a very young age. Is it possible for me to reach the goal even now if I try?*

Mother: Why not? The mind should be firm. Not much time is needed for God-Realisation. When one feels the interest, then and there one should start the effort. Quicker will be the effect if there is sincerity in the effort.

Question: *For those of us who are ordinary people, is it possible to know God?*

Mother: Children, God is also ordinary at all times and therefore, He is not difficult to know. But there is one thing; the ignorant ones who are drowning themselves in worldliness cannot know the Truth. Whoever it may be, he who has sincere interest can know and see God.

---

[21]Celibate resident students of the ashram.

THAT WHICH IS NEEDED FIRST

Question: *What should a person who has become interested in spirituality do first?*
Mother: Approach a real Master. *Sâdhana* should be performed as instructed by the Master. Faith and devotion in the Guru is necessary. A *Sadguru* (a Self-Realised Master) alone is the refuge.
Question: *How does one search for and find such a person?*
Mother: The Guru will come before one who has intense desire to know. That omniscient Guru will gradually take the disciple to the goal. *Sadguru* is one who is capable of taking the disciple to the goal.
Question: *Mother, I have saved a lot of money, but there is no happiness anywhere. What is the way?*
Mother: Not everyone will have this thought. As this is a good time for you children, these thoughts arise because of the merit of the good actions done in the previous birth. Happiness will not be gained if you go after sense objects. No one will wait for anyone in this world. Each one runs after his own happiness. God is of the nature of bliss. Therefore, we can live happily if we can live in God. Faith is needed. The thought that "I am the doer" should go. God is the doer. The mind should be always fixed in God. *Satsang*[22] is necessary. *Sâdhana* should be performed as instructed by the Guru. Meditation should be practiced. In the beginning stages, try to meditate for a short time. Later, it will be possible to meditate for a longer time. The Lord's Name should

[22]Satsang means to associate with the Sat or Reality as embodied in sages, scriptures, spiritual discourses and other spiritual activities.

always be remembered without wasting time associating with friends and cutting jokes.

Devotee: *Mother, you should guide us.*

Mother: Shiva! Shiva! This crazy one?! God will do all that.

The Holy Mother was talking with some of the residents sitting in the front yard of the temple. It was 11 o'clock in the morning.

Brahmachârin: *Mother, how does one gain bliss?*

Mother: Children, everything depends on the mind. All is well when the mind improves. Chanting, *japa*, meditation, etc., are to make the mind pure and one-pointed.

Another brahmachârin: *Mother, what is fate?*

Mother: There are people who take God's Will to be fate and who think that it is unchangeable. This is not correct. We perform actions according to our *vâsanas*, the result of which will eventually come to us. The fruits of the actions which we have done in our previous births is known as our fate. Fate can be changed and transformed through self-effort, i.e., through sincere prayer and meditation.

Question: *Mother, there are many religions. Of these, which one is the best?*

Mother: All religions are good. All religions which help one realise God are good. The path which is not helpful for Gold-Realisation should not be accepted as a religion. Religion is that which helps for Self-Realisation. (Turning to the *brahmachârins*) You children are all lucky. You have a mind to relinquish *samsâra* at such a young age, have you not? This is not possible within one lifetime's merit. This is the fruit of many lifetimes' merits. We might also have met together before. Otherwise, we would not be bonded together like this. Some of those who come here seem very familiar (to Mother). It is impossible to get separated, having been together before. The *brahmachârins* do not think about the opposition and difficulties from their families. That is why some do not even feel like going home.

At 6 o'clock in the evening, the sun set in all its glory on the western horizon into the Arabian Sea. The waves gleefully danced, singing the ever vibrant sound OM. The Holy Mother, accompanied by the residents and devotees, began singing devotional songs as they sat on the front verandah of the temple. Mother slowly became more and more absorbed in the singing.

> *O Thou Who art meditated upon in thousands of*
> *hearts,*
> *Thou blazest forth forever in the minds of those who*
> *have realised God...*

As the Mother sang these lines, she became overwhelmed with bliss and merged in a state of divine inebriation. She began crying like a small child, now and then calling out, *"Amma, Amma!"* followed by ecstatic laughter which continued for a long time. The residents and devotees also were filled with bliss as they continued singing, drinking in the nectar of the Divine Name. By this time the Holy Mother had arisen from her seat and had come to the front yard of the temple. She began a rapturous dance punctuated with blissful laughter. Some of the *brahmachârins* who were watching the scene became oblivious to the surroundings and shed tears of joy. Some others sat and merged into meditation.

Eventually, Mother's father came to the spot and caught hold of her and made her lie down on a mat, thinking that something very serious had happened to his daughter. But the Holy Mother was still in another world, her hand showing a mudra[23] and her face radiating like the rising sun. When she finally came down to the normal plane of consciousness, one among the devotees said,

Devotee: *We were concerned that Mother would have gone on and on dancing if Sugunanandan had not caught hold of her.*
Mother: He should not have done that. It was not good. It is unbearable if someone even touches the body during such occasions. Now the whole body is burning. It is due to being touched. In the future, be attentive without letting anyone touch.

Without saying anything more about it, the Mother walked away. It was almost 11 o'clock at night. Some of the *brahmachárins* went to meditate at the seashore, some went inside the temple and others went to their rooms.

PRAPANCHA AND VEDANTA

1 September 1977

A devotee from Quilon had come to see the Holy Mother. Prompted by what he had heard and read about spirituality, he began asking her questions. When the Mother began answering his questions, many devotees and a few residents came and keenly listened to the conversation. The time was 10 o'clock in the morning. In the silent and peaceful atmosphere the dialogue commenced.

Devotee: Vedanta[24] *says that the world is an illusion,*

---

[23]A symbolic gesture done with the fingers.
[24]The system of philosophy expounded in the Upanishads.

doesn't it? If this is so, then there is no relevance to worldly life, is there?
Mother: Son, *Vedanta* does not deny the material plane. *Vedanta* views the world in a slightly different way which diverges from the ordinary outlook. That is all. *Vedanta* says that all this that is seen is not as we think, but it is *Brahman* (the Absolute) alone. Was it not because Sankara, the *Vedantin*, recognized the existence of the world that he worked hard during his whole life for the uplifting of the world? Look at the life of Vivekananda who was a *Vedantin*. *Vedanta* is only saying to imbibe the correct awareness and to remove wrong understanding about ourselves and the world. If do not, it would be difficult to reach the shore surmounting all sorrows.

In the beginning the Guru will tell the disciple, who is a practitioner, "The world is an illusion. Reject it and become established in the Self." This is to speed up the *sâdhana*. But at last he will understand that this whole world is part of God when he reaches Realisation. Then there will not be anything to reject, only to love and serve all. This state is not hypothetical, but is derived from experience.

VEDANTA AND IMAGE WORSHIP

Question: *Mother, isn't* Vedânta *against image worship?*
Mother: No, *Vedânta* denies nothing. Son, each and every one has a befitting path to make the mind concentrated on the Self. Hasn't Sankaracharya renovated temples, installed idols and composed poetry about

gods and goddesses? But do not get entangled in image worship forever. At a certain stage of *sâdhana*, all forms will merge and disappear, and one will reach the Formless State. Even if one or two may understand that the world is an illusion, for others the material world is real.

Scriptures and paths are to uplift those who are rambling in ignorance, not for knowers of Truth who have already attained the Goal.

Question: *Can a devotee become a* Vedântin?

Mother: *Parâbhakti* (Supreme devotion) is pure *Vedânta*. A true devotee sees everything as pervaded by God. He does not see anything except God everywhere. When a devotee says, "Everything is pervaded by God," the *Vedântin* says, "Everything is pervaded by *Brahman*." Both are one and the same.

Question: *Who is the real "I?" When will I become aware that everything which is seen is "I?"*

Mother: That "I" which fills the whole universe is the real "I." When the awareness that "I am not the body, I am the Self" awakens, we will understand that nothing is different from *Brahman*. At that time, we will know through experience that everything is "I" alone.

Question: *Mother, everything is happening according to God's Will. Therefore, there is not much scope for our effort. It is not possible to prevent God's Will.*

Mother: If you have that much conviction, can't you request Him to alter your fate? One who judges can also take back the judgement. Can you not just try and see?

If you accept what is not wanted and do not accept what is needed, there is no sense in blaming fate. Pride will not allow some people to search for God; sensual pleasures will not let go of others, and still others do not have time. What is the result? Sorrow.

Everyone sat silently gazing at the Holy Mother's radiant face with wonder and amazement.

PRANAYAMA[25]

After a few moments had passed, another devotee continued to ask questions.

Devotee: *Mother, will* prânayâma *be helpful to attain* Âtma Jñâna. *(Knowledge of the Self)?*
Mother: The mind will gain concentration through *prânayâma*. It is easily possible to fix the one-pointed mind on the *Atman*, is it not? The mind fixed on the Self becomes liberated from *samsâra (samsâra vimuktam)*.
Question: *Mother, many come here for worldly purposes. Why?*
Mother: Everyone will not come to spirituality at the same time. If they did, then one Sankaracharya or one Sri Ramakrishna would have been enough. Different people will reach the road to Liberation at different times, according to the standard of their *samskâra*.[26]

WHAT IS BONDAGE?

Devotee: *Mother has entrapped me in the family, therefore I cannot come often.*

---

[25]Control of the mind through control of the vital force, particularly the breath.
[26]Mental tendencies inherited from past births.

Mother: This is what all the children are saying. Having glued themselves to the sense objects, they then complain that God has bound them. God hears everything, but keeps quiet.

Devotee: *Then I am not going away from here anymore. Let all the necessities be looked after by Him alone.*

Mother: That is good! Once the lentil curry and buttermilk which we serve here is eaten, then he will not be seen anymore! (All burst into laughter) It seems that until now you alone have been looking after all the household matters. Now you say, "I am not going from here. Let God look after the necessities." It is God alone who is looking after you at all times. Son, bondage is nothing but the feeling "I am doing."

Another devotee mockingly said to him, "Here, only watery lentil curry is available. If you are at your home, thick lentils and polished rice are available." (All laugh)

Mother: None of you have to mock him. This son proceeds only with caution.

That devotee, who was thoroughly convinced that Mother understood he was living as a *sādhak* in his daily life even though he was asking such *Vedāntic* questions, turned to the others and said, "Mother is seeing each movement of mine. That is why she said that I am moving cautiously."

Question: *Mother, I am having no peace of mind nowadays.*

Mother: Son, can't you decrease a few of your outside affairs? Practice meditation for a few days in solitude. Otherwise, the strain on the mind will worsen.

13 September 1977

WHAT IS FREEDOM?

Some people arrived to see the Holy Mother in the afternoon. With them came a scholar. Mother was sitting in the southern part of the old temple. Two elderly women devotees from the neighbourhood were trying to make Mother eat something, but like an innocent and stubborn child, she refused to eat, regardless of their affectionate pleading. Every time they requested her to eat something, Mother would begin her playful antics and divert their attention from the food to herself. The devotees watched the charming sight from a distance when eventually the Holy Mother saw them. With childlike innocence she said, *"Look, these mothers are trying to feed me but I am not hungry!"* One of the women said, "Dear sir, Amma has not eaten anything for the last three days except some coconut water. Please tell her to eat something."

Finally, due to continuous persistence and prayers, Mother ate just one ball of rice and then ran away like a child from its mother. She sat in front of the temple while the elderly ladies helplessly stood there holding the plate of rice in their hands. The devotees followed Mother and sat near her after offering their prostrations. A few moments passed and her *bála bháva* (childlike mood) slowly disappeared. She closed her eyes sitting motionless as the devotees gazed at her face in wonder and reverence. A few minutes passed in silence before the Mother opened her eyes. Now she looked like a great Master, withdrawing all her other aspects within. Nobody would say that this was the same person who was making merry like a child-a few moments ago. The scholar began the conversation, "Mother, we would like to know certain things."

Mother: Shiva! Shiva! From this crazy girl? She knows only one thing and that is that she does not know anything.

The devotees, however, put forth their questions one by one.

Devotee: *Mother, what is meant by freedom?*
Mother: Freedom from worldly existence. Freedom from the cycle of birth and death. Total surrender to God alone is the easiest way. Either cultivate the attitude "I am Brahman, I am everything," or think "I am nothing, I am God's child, His servant."

Devotee: *What shall I do to get purity of mind?*
Mother: Mental purity will come through constant chanting of the Divine Name. This is the simplest way. Everyone will not have the faith to chant. Belief and disbelief are there at all times. Even this world is the result of disbelief. Then how can disbelief be completely eliminated? Disbelief will go if belief becomes firm. Once faith comes, inquiry is no longer needed. Inquiry ends in faith. The faith that you children have now is not full. Therefore, try for perfect faith. Full faith means Realisation.

THE GRACE OF LOVE

Scholar: *It seems as if Mother has practiced yoga and other disciplines very well.*
Mother: Shiva, Shiva! I have not practiced anything. But there is one thing which is natural to me, the nature to love. Love constantly flows from me to the Creation.

Scholar: *How many people can love everyone equally like this?*
Mother: Do not care about the number of people who

can love. Those who imbibe love are not lowly. Blessed
are their lives.

MOTHER'S KNOWLEDGE AND
THE PURPOSE OF HER BIRTH

Scholar: *What are Mother's future programmes?*
Mother: *Bhagavân* (the Lord) will look after all
those things.
Scholar: *Mother must have come down with that same
knowledge, isn't that so?*
Mother: After coming here I have returned that
knowledge to Him also. Otherwise, who could
keep all this knowledge? It will sit safely there in
the hands of God, will it not? He will hand it over,
little by little, to us when necessary.
Scholar: *I have wandered a lot. I did not get peace anywhere. Mother, please bless me.*

Mother smiled and then all of a sudden entered into
deep *samâdhi*. Her body became stiff like a log of wood.
Everyone silently watched her. Regaining partial consciousness, she requested the scholar to sing a song.

> *O Lord, if the blue mountain be ink, the ocean
> the inkstand, the branch of the Heavenly Tree
> be the pen, the earth the writing leaf,
> And by taking these, if the Goddess of Learning
> writes for eternity,
> Even then, the limit of Thy virtues will not be
> reached...*

He sang with great devotion and all the others sat in
deep meditation. When the song was over the Mother went on

uttering *"Shiva! Shiva!"* One of the devotees again asked, "Mother, what should be done to quiet the mind?"

Mother: *Japa, dhyâna* and other spiritual disciplines should be practiced.

Devotee: *How long would it take to attain the goal?*

Mother: That depends upon each one's inner disposition.

Devotee: *Mother's gracious look should always be there on this one.*

Mother: Certainly. Is it not children like you to whom Mother should especially pay attention? (Pointing to herself) Look here, this life itself is for that.

Usually, Mother would never speak so directly as this. Rarely would she give such hints, even indirectly, which would let people know that she had come down with that awareness.

14 September 1977

One devotee from Trivandrum came and prostrated before the Holy Mother. He was a doctor, a dermatologist, and an ardent devotee of Lord Krishna. Mother smilingly asked him, *"Son, where are you coming from?"*

Doctor: *Do you know me, Mother? Your question was so natural, as if you are seeing your son again after a long absence.*

Mother: Do you think you would come here if we had no prior acquaintance? Many people are familiar.

The time in between acquaintances remains forgotten; some people can refresh their memory.

Doctor: *When I was in Guruvayoor[27] one man told me about Mother and that she is an embodiment of love.*

Mother: Mother knows only love. (Looking at the book which the doctor was holding) What is that book, son?

Doctor: *The* **Bhagavad-Gita**. *In Mother I see everything that* Bhagavân *tells Arjuna about a* Jîvanmukta.[28]

Mother: (Like a small child) What does it say in there?

Doctor: *Did Mother ever read it?*

Mother: (Shaking her hands) No, it is not possible for me. Shouldn't I know reading? Even if I manage to read, after three or four lines, I lose control.

Doctor: *What a fool am I! What is a book for Mother? Is not Mother beyond all this? That is why so many people like me are coming here.*

Mother: Let that be. What does it say in the *Gita*?

Doctor:

> átmanyevátmaná tushtaha
> sthita prajñasta dóchyte

> Sthitaprajña is one who is content
> in the Atman, by the Atman.

(Gita, Chap.II, Verse 55)

---

[27]A famous Krishna temple in Kerala.
[28]A Liberated Soul.

Having heard these lines, the Mother became totally Self-absorbed. In a semi-conscious mood she chanted, *"Aum, Aum,"* lifting her hands up in the air and shaking her head sideways. This continued for a few minutes, and slowly coming down to the normal plane of consciousness, she said,

Mother: Always remember one thing. Studying the scriptures is good but a shortage of devotion should not occur. You can read the books. Mere reading is not enough. Practice is also necessary. Mother cannot read or hear such books without her mind suddenly going to another world.

Doctor: *And Mother again comes down for something.*

Mother: It is enough if you learn to fix the mind in God once. After that the mind will not leave at all.

MANTRA DIKSHA
The Necessity of Initiation

A few more devotees came and saluted the Mother.

A doctor: *Is initiation necessary? Can't Perfection be attained without that?*

Mother: Partial progress can be made. In Kashmir apples will grow abundantly. Apple trees will grow in our village as well, but will not bear that much fruit. There will not be any taste either. They need to be grown very carefully. The Guru's presence is the favourable circumstance. If there is no Guru, one should be very careful. There are possibilities of falling. God's Presence cannot be felt without purity of heart.

The purpose of initiation is mental purity. Milk will spoil in a dirty vessel. First the vessel should be cleaned. Only then can milk be poured into it. Besides that, initiation will also help awaken the inner divine power. The mantra which is of the nature of power enters the heart of the disciple from within the Guru, a knower of *Brahman*. Just as water is used for external cleanliness, internal purity is gained through initiation. When a spark of fire is blown upon and ignites, it becomes a great power.

There is a natural way of making yogurt by adding a little buttermilk to warm milk. If this is kept still for a day, it will turn into yogurt. In a similar manner, initiation, which the process of transmitting a portion of the Guru's power to the disciple, will enable the disciple to develop the power fully if he works on it sincerely applying self-effort. Great power can also be created if mantras are chanted repeatedly.

Devotee: *Is it ineffective if* mantra diksha *is given without the customary rites?*

Mother: Guru's initiation will never be fruitless. It is to get rid of the vacillation of the disciple's mind that the initiation is given with established customs and pomp. The disciple might doubt the mantra if it is not given according to the established customary ritual. If the disciple has doubts, his practice will not be correct. Not only that, if âchâra[29] is transgressed, the sanctity might be gradually lost.

Another devotee: *Mother, I am a devotee of Devi. Having seen my enthusiasm, one* sannyâsin *said, "Child, there is no doubt that you will soon gain a perfect teacher."*

---

[29] Customary observances and code of conduct.

Shortly after the swami said this, I happened to see Mother.

Mother: Everything is God's Will. His Grace is always there for His devotees. That Embodiment of Compassion is gazing at us. What do we have with us with which we can repay that mercy?

Devotee: *Is God's Grace and the Guru's Grace one?*

Mother: Yes. What is received through the Guru's Grace is God's Grace.

Devotee: *Mother, when will we be liberated?*

Mother: Children, unload the burden from your head. At that time you will become liberated. It is not enough if it is simply turned over. It should be surrendered to God. Then happily continue doing what He makes you do.

Devotee: *It is said that pure food should be taken, is it not? How should that be done?*

Mother: Before taking food, it should be offered to God. If poor people come, give them food, seeing them as God. Then the food we eat will become pure.

As she was talking, the Mother's attention turned to the pictures of gods and goddesses hanging on the wall. Looking at the portrait of Lord Shiva, Mother said, *"Oh...You?...Ancient One. Is it enough to sit like that? Who is going to look after the responsibility of all these people? I cannot be here for a long time."*

Devotee: *Don't say like that, Mother! Who is there for us if you go?*

Mother: Do not be sad, son. Mother was simply saying that. Is it possible to simply go away like that? Are there not certain things to be done?

BHAVA DARSHAN
The Divine Mood

Devotee: *Mother, are you always aware of your divine moods or are you aware of them only during* Devi *and* Krishna Bhâva?

Mother: These things cannot be said in that way. Different people's faith is seen in different ways. Mother's intention is that each person somehow gets closer to God. Some people like it only if they see the dress of Devi and of Krishna. Not only that, many do not know anything about spirituality. Some people can understand certain things about spirituality because these *Bhâvas* are perpetuated. It is a little difficult for some people to believe if Mother tells them something now. If told during *Devi Bhâva*, they will believe.

A devotee who was sitting at a little distance asked, "Mother, why aren't you informing the people about the real facts of your coming?"

Mother: Shiva! Shiva! What shall Mother make them understand? What does Mother know? Everything is *Devi's leela*. Humility and simplicity are the characteristics of greatness, the attitude that "I am nothing." Instead, we walk around trying to exhibit our abilities. The coconut feels, "Because of me, the dish was tasty." The cook will say, "It was because of my skill that it was good." The fire would say, "Because of me the dish was well cooked." But all ability is God's.

Question: *Is it good to meditate sitting on the seashore? I am interested in doing so.*

Mother: Certainly. The seashore is holy. You should sit there having prayed to the goddess of the ocean. After some time, the roaring sound of the waves will not be heard. Then, only a slight sound, *pranava*[30] will be there. If the mind is fixed on that, then you will not feel like getting up. Very loud sound and silence are equal. In both instances, the mind will become concentrated by itself. *Omkara* (OM) can be heard on the seashore.

THE IMPORTANCE OF
ACHARAS

15 September 1977

The Holy Mother was sitting in front of the temple. One person was distributing Mother's *prasáda*[31] to the other devotees. A little bit of *prasáda* fell on the floor from the hands of the person who was distributing. Another devotee took it and threw it outside. Seeing this, Mother said,

Mother: What is that, son? Contempt for *prasáda*? Lovers of God must not do like that. *Prasáda* has no impurity even if it falls down. You can give it to birds if it has become dirty and you cannot eat it.
The devotee: *Forgive me, Mother, for the mistake.*
Mother: It is all right. Do not worry. It is enough if you touch that place where it dropped and salute. All Godly actions should be done with devotion. After we apply the sandal paste which we get from the temple, the remaining portion also should not be put

---

[30]The sound OM.
[31]Consecrated offering.

on the ground. It should be wiped on a tree or something.

Devotee: *Isn't this all external etiquette? Who can observe all these things? If they aren't observed, will* Brahman *be displeased?*

Mother: *Achâras* should be observed as long as we live in the world. Even a person who has reached the Non-dual State and is beyond purity and impurity or do's and don't's, will not negate *achâra* even though nothing affects him. Ordinary people cannot ascend without *achâra*. Whether or not we observe *achâra*, *Brahman* has nothing to gain. But for us to grow, we need to observe *achâra*. Nothing affects those who have reached there. *Dharma* will decay if *achâra* is not honoured. *Achâras* will be useful for mental purity.

Another devotee: *It is because of our merits accumulated in our previous birth that we could see Mother. Bless us, Mother.*

Mother: All of you children have come here because you have all been blessed by those who can bless. Hereafter, again it will happen.

Devotee: *Mother, will I get God-Realisation in this birth itself?*

Mother: It is possible, if you try.

Another devotee: *Here is God in front of us, isn't it so? What more then is needed? What else is Mother except an Incarnation of God?*

Mother: Shiva! Shiva! What are you saying, son! Mother does not know all these things. Look, Mother is crying for God. Your birth will also be fulfilled if you call for God.

26 September 1977

Some people who were very interested in spiritual matters came to see the Mother. They began talking to her.

Question: *Can the truth behind this world be known with our limited knowledge?*

Mother: It is not possible to know the truth of the world if you sit thinking of your limitations. The world can be perceived as the gross form of God. It is His Divine Play alone which is happening here. There is not a single place which is not holy here. Purity and impurity are our superimpositions.

Question: *Oh, but what* anâchâras [32] *are there even in* Bharata *(India).*

Mother: Do not judge things without knowing all the different aspects. The volition of the Eternal God might be there behind things which we consider to be *anâchâra.*

Devotee: *I am convinced that Mother can save me. Hereafter I am not going anywhere else. Frequently I will come here.*

Mother: That is correct. If all the commodities on the list are available from one shop, then you do not have to wander all around the marketplace. But money is needed to buy the goods. Faith and dispassion are needed to gain spiritual knowledge. The means of Liberation can be bought with the money of dispassion in the vessel of *sraddha* (faith).

---

[32]Improper conduct and harmful customs.

TYAGA AND BHOGA
Renunciation and Enjoyment

It was 8 o'clock Sunday morning and already many devotees were sitting around the Mother. Some of them had a misconception that her highest spiritual moods were only during *Devi* and *Krishna Bhāva*. They considered Mother to be an ordinary girl at other times. All of a sudden, Mother said (not to anyone in particular),

Mother: Not everyone will understand when God's actions are in operation in individuals. Ordinary people will misunderstand it as something else. Otherwise, what a benefit they would have by seeing God's greatness! For ordinary people, their household affairs should go on smoothly. Towards that end, they might go to certain temples and do worship. Or they may go and see some *Mahātmas.* [33] Then they will ask, "My son appeared for the B.A. exam. Make him pass," or "I have planned to purchase some land but there are several obstacles. Please remove them." How trivial they are!

Those who have faith will not say such things to the *Mahātmas.* They will search for the path of Eternal Bliss. They will renounce anything for that. Some people relinquish everything for God. Some others accumulate everything for themselves. Those who accumulate will suffer. Those who relinquish will be joyful.

Question: *Is it possible to give up all wealth?*

Mother: It is not necessary. But the mental attitude that wealth is "mine" can be given up, can't it? Do not be attached.

[33] Great Souls.

Question: *Is it enough to think that wealth is God's, that it is God-given?*

Mother: More than enough. But not enough only in words, it should be there in action also. What if we eat plenty and the neighbouring families are starving? If the wealth which is in our hands is God's, then why can we not give some to the poor? If it is not given, that money will become the cause of troubles.

Having stopped the conversation at this point, the Holy Mother got up. While stepping from the temple verandah, she moved her right hand in a circular motion several times lifting it in the air and showing a divine gesture while chanting *"Shiva! Shiva!"* Some of the devotees who had been listening to the Mother's conversation talked softly among themselves. One said, "See, Mother has understood everything. The whole talk was surely intended for us. Wasn't it you who said that Mother does not know anything at any time other than *Devi* and *Krishna Bhâva?* Did you hear what Mother said just now? There is nothing that she does not know!"

Another man who was an engineer said, "Although I have been here several other times, I never understood this much of her greatness because I never had a chance to talk to her." Another devotee had arrived just then and asked, "Did you talk with Mother?" "Yes, we did," replied the engineer. The latecomer, who had no spiritual leanings at all, referred to the Mother's usual words that she is just a crazy girl making some crazy utterances which he believed to be correct except during the *Bhâvas.* He said, "Mother would just burst out with some crazy things." The other devotee said to him, "What the Mother told us is not crazy. To tell you the truth, we are the ones who are crazy."

20 September 1977

A *sannyâsin* had come to see the Holy Mother. She was in an abstracted mood and was walking around the temple. The *sannyâsin* closely observed her neither blinking his eyes nor noticing anything else. A few more minutes passed and while going around the temple, she stopped at a certain point in front of the temple, her body slowly swaying from this side to that. All the time the *sannyâsin* was gazing at her and when she stopped in front of the temple, he slowly approached her and saluted. The Holy Mother compassionately looked at him and enquired, *"Swami mon (monk son),* [34] *where are you coming from? Have you had any food?"*

Sannyâsin: *We heard about Mother when we came to the Oachira* [35] *temple and an urge arose to see you. Different people said different things about you. Finally, I decided to come and see personally, but now it is clear to me that you are not as I heard.*

Mother: There are two opinions for everything. One person is interested in one thing and another person in another thing. Not everyone will recognize everything. Some people will deny out of jealousy. All is His Will. Because of His Will, millions and millions of planets and stars exist in the sky.

Sannyâsin: *Is it not because of gravity?*

Mother: That gravity itself is God. What if gravity is not there? Total disaster, isn't it? Again, look at the order and harmony in Nature. Seeing and ob-

---

[34] Mother often calls some of her children by adding son or daughter to the name of their profession.

[35] A famous temple dedicated to the formless aspect of the Supreme, unique in Kerala and perhaps in all of India.

serving all these things, can't an intelligent person easily guess that there is a Controller who controls everything systematically? Look at the millions of living beings. God's greatness cannot be expressed. Think of all the animals which live on the land, in the water and in the sky; some live both on land and in water. There are also people who live in God while being in *samsâra,* but very few.

Sannyâsin: *We have now reached the stage that even the people with ochre clothes don't need God.*

Mother: That is not God's fault. Whoever calls, He will hear. Especially if it is a selfless call. Compassionately, *Bhagavân* will give everything to His devotee.

DUALITY AND NON-DUALITY

Sannyâsin: *All this will seem primitive to a non-dualist.*

Mother: Does it seem like that? If so, what is primitive is in the non-dualist. It is only by His Grace that one gets the Non-dual Knowledge also. Nobody can acquire Knowledge without the Guru's Grace and God's Grace. Therefore, a real non-dualist will not reproach all this. For him, everything will be felt as different aspects of the same Truth. Those who walk the path of duality also ultimately reach Non-duality. The non-dualist goes by himself and catches hold of God. *Bhagavân* catches hold of the dualist and takes him closer to Him. This is the only difference. Why scuffle with each other for this? Is it not enough to reach there some way or other? One person travelled by water. Another one by land. Both reached the same place.

Sannyâsin: *This is quite true. Various paths, one goal.*

Two new visitors arrived and sat near Mother after offering their salutations. Mother asked, *"What are you doing, children?"* One of them replied, "We have no job, Mother."

Mother: Devotion is needed. A job is also needed. The detached one does not need a job. Others will need one. Obstacles will crop up for *japa* and *dhyâna* if one is starving. Food is important when one is hungery.

Devotee: *I have no interest in anything. Everything is kind of humdrum...*

Mother: Disgusted with the world? Good, if it is caused by a detachment from sensual pleasures. But you do not have that much dispassion. For the time being, live doing some kind of worldly job with remembrance of God.

Devotee: *But won't* vâsanas *increase if we continue in the world?*

Mother: That is no problem if the work is performed while dedicating it to God. *Satsang* is also necessary now and then.

TO HOUSEHOLDERS

21 September 1977

Some householder devotees were sitting around the Holy Mother while she kept a baby on her lap. She asked the child's mother, *"Will you give him to me?"* The mother of the child replied, "Even now he is Mother's." Mother laughed and said, *"It is enough if you give him when he grows up."*

At this time more devotees arrived to see the Holy Mother. Having offered the fruits which they brought to Mother, they joined the other devotees. Looking at one of the women devotees who had just come, Mother said, *"Daughter, my son has just been employed with the bus again, hasn't he?"* Hearing the words of the Holy Mother, the woman fell at her feet crying, "O my Mother, O my Mother!" Her husband, who was a bus driver, had been without employment for many days. That morning he had been appointed as a driver in another bus. The devotee was astounded that Mother already knew about it without having been informed. Overwhelmed with joy, she went on crying. Fondly patting her back, Mother said, *"Do not be sad, children. God will look after everything."* She turned to the householder devotees and said, *"See, you householder children should always have Godly thoughts while living in this world."*

An elderly man: *Where is the time for householders?*
Mother: Sorrow alone is yours if you run here and there always thinking "my" house, "my" wealth and "my" children. Live surrendering everything to God. Protect your family and those in your care thinking, "God has entrusted them to me." After all, when did this wealth and these children come to you? Where were your kids when you came to this world? Now you say that they are all yours. When you die, whose are they? These landed properties had belonged to somebody else before. In the future they will be in somebody else's hands. There is nothing here that can be considered as ours. Changing hands, it came to us for some time, that is all. Understanding all this, we should live in the house taking refuge in God. Whatever work we may be doing, God can be remembered if you have the mind to do it.

It was now lunchtime. Calling everyone, Mother went to the dining hall. When all were seated, the Holy Mother herself served food to them. While they were eating, she went to her hut after having said, *"Mother will be back soon, have your food children."* After lunch some devotees sat in solitude reading books while others discussed spiritual matters. Some simply sat alone in contemplation enjoying the solitude.

At 3 o'clock, Mother came to sit with the devotees again. She remarked, *"Today is an auspicious day."* "Why is that?" a devotee asked. Mother replied,

Mother: All the children who came today are interested in spirituality. Mother is happy to see people like you. Mother will tell you some crazy things. People say that they like all that.

Devotee: *Again and again we come here because Mother says what is necessary for us. Mother knows everything. Mother is just playing tricks when she says "Mother does not know anything. Mother is crazy." It is not possible to tell us this anymore. We have begun to understand Mother's tricks. (All laugh)*

Another Devotee: *People like Mother come to show the path to us, don't they? Mother, is it possible for us to get Liberation in this birth?*

Mother: Do not say "for us." There is no group Liberation. Liberation is attained in different births according to each one's course of karma.

Devotee: *All right, Mother. Do I have a chance to attain Liberation in this birth?*

Mother: Very many chances. Only you have to try.

Question: *Everything is in God's hands. Nothing can be done through mere virility.*

Mother: Not so. Virility and effort endowed with enthusiasm are necessary. The result is according to karma. Nothing can be gained by those lacking in strong determination. The ego must be destroyed. Otherwise, nothing can be achieved spiritually. The ego can be removed through *bhakti* (devotion). The attitude "I am God's servant" will come thereby. If not through devotion, the ego can also be removed through knowledge. Oh! How much devotion I had previously! Now that much is not there. (All laugh) Once I asked the Divine Mother to show Her true devotees to me. Having asked this, when I came from the temple, two real seekers were standing outside waiting for me. From then onwards true devotees of the Mother started coming. The number of worldly people who came only to fulfill worldly desires began decreasing.

One devotee told, "It was the same in Sri Ramakrishna's life." All of a sudden, the Holy Mother again became oblivious of the external surroundings, being transported to another world. Another devotee quietly said, "Whenever I come here I am reminded of Dakshineswara. But there are not many who can understand this." A second man said, " People who come here are those who are allowed to know about the Mother as a result of their karma. How could anyone come here without having acquired merits in previous births!"

Mother got up from her seat. She went to the backwaters and lay down under a coconut tree. Now 5 o'clock in the evening, two more devotees arrived to see the Holy Mother. After a few minutes, she got up from where she had been lying and came to greet them. When she began speaking, the others also joined them. At this moment, a woman devotee brought a glass of tea and offered it to Mother. Mother said, *"You should give it to Mother only after giving to all the children."* So saying, Mother made the devotee put the glass down. Mother asked the new-comers, *"Children, where are you coming from?"* One man replied, "I am coming from Chenganoor and he is from Tiruvalla." Mother exclaimed like a small child, *"I know where Chenganoor is, I have been there! Where is Tiruvalla? Is it in Quilon?"* Everyone laughed and one devotee replied, "No, Mother, Quilon is south of Chenganoor. Tiruvalla is to the north."

Mother: What does it matter, wherever it is? Everybody comes here, then why should Mother ask, "Where do you come from? How many cows, jackfruit trees and so on and so forth? (All laugh.) Even then, Mother will forget all this. One day I asked a *brahmachârin* son, "Are you returning from your house?" The *brahmachârin* asked, "Which house?" "My son's house." Then the *brahmachârin* replied, "I don't know where that is. If Mother can tell where that is, I will go there. Once gone, I will not return." When he said that I understood what he meant but even then I did not give up foolish talking. (Everyone burst into laughter.)

Tea was brought for everyone. Someone cracked a joke. Mother told, *"Children, do not laugh and crack jokes while eating."*

LIFE AFTER DEATH

Question: *Mother, is life after death true?*
Mother: Yes. If this life is true, then life after death is also true. Because we are alive now, we were also alive before. Hereafter we will also live. When one dies, the *vâsanas* will be there with the subtle body.

It is not possible to act according to the *vâsanas* without a gross body; therefore, the *jîva* enters a gross body suitable for it. The case of a liberated soul is different. He does not have to live in the same manner. There is no birth or death from the point of view of a *Jñâni*. Therefore, he does not have a life after death.

JNANA, VIJNANA,
THE PLANE OF PURE CONSCIOUSNESS

Devotee: *Mother,* jñâna *is destruction of ignorance. Then what is* vijñâna *the destruction of?*

Mother: (After laughing) It seems that you are going to go beyond death immediately. (All laugh)

Devotee: *Not that, Mother, I was just expressing my doubt.*

Mother: If *jñâna* is the destruction of *ajñâna,* it can be understood that *vijñâna* is the destruction of *jñâna.* If *jñâna* is hearing and reading about Delhi, *vijñâna* is like visiting Delhi. *Jñâna* is intellectual knowledge while *vijñâna* is transcending the intellect negating even that as untrue and affirming pure experience alone as the Supreme Truth. Is that not so, children?

Devotee: *Only Mother knows all this.*

Mother: There was once a man who would go and sit in a big academy of scholars. When the scholars discussed matters, he would stick his nose in without knowing the subject matter, although he had his opinions. The people would tease him but he did not care about all this. Eventually, he also became a scholar due to his association with them. He would say, "No harm came to me from my *ajñāna*. Because there was some discrimination, *jñāna* dawned from *ajñāna*. Even then, I did not let go of discrimination, and therefore *vijñāna* ensued from *jñāna*." There was a young man who used to visit a potter. In due course, he also learnt to make pots. Even though he had no idea how to make pots, he also learnt it through close association and companionship with the potter. Children, suppose we visit an incense factory. Having spent some time there, when we return home we can smell the fragrance of the incense on our body also. In a like manner, even weak-minded people or dullards would gradually evolve along the spiritual path through the constant association and companionship with spiritual people.

Once I said, "God is all-pervading and He is within us," and so on and so forth. Whereas, now I see everything as God alone. God is both outside and inside the veil of "I"; the veil of "I" is also God. Veil is the body. The veil is not a problem anymore. That is *vijñāna*. Then there is another thing. Once you reach the plane of consciousness of *jñāna* and *vijñāna*, all will flee. There is not even *vijñāna* in the plane of Pure Consciousness. Pure Consciousness alone is. That cannot be expressed.

NAME AND LIBERATION

Devotee: *Is there any hope for me?*
Mother: You should pray with great yearning. Then it is possible. It is enough to call, He will come before you without delay. *Bhagavān* is al-

ways standing ready to come running when the devotees call. (Mother laughs.) Because of that, mistakes
also happen to *Bhagavân* sometimes. Sometimes He
will come running even if He was not called. Ajamila
called his son "Narayana" and *Bhagavân* started running hearing this. He was not even caring whether it
was He who was being called. If you call His Name,
then He will come running. (All laugh blissfully.)

Bharata, a great saint, thought about a deer at the
time of death. *Bhagavân* did not come running. The
reason is that "deer" is not *Bhagavân's* Name. Nobody
had called *Bhagavân* "O Deer." So *Bhagavân* did not go
because His Name was not called. Therefore, Bharata
had to take birth as a deer. However, because he had
been a sage, he was saved. The other side can be seen if
there is only a thin screen in one room. In Bharata's
mind there was only a thin screen of being a deer. Therefore, he could know who he was even when he was born
as a deer. Because Bharata, a Knower of the Self, did not
chant the Lord's Name, he took birth as a deer.
Ajamila, an ignorant man, became liberated through
the name "Narayana." That much is the greatness of
the Lord's Name.

In this birth, this moment itself, they who fix their
mind on the Lord are liberated. Nothing else is a problem.

ENDLESS BEGINNING

Mother: What Mother has prayed to the Divine
Mother for was to bring to her those who have some
real stuff in them. Others come for temporary

peace. Still others, whether or not their desires get fulfilled, do not feel it necessary to come again and neither do they come.

Devotee: *How can they know unless Mother makes them know?*

Mother: What is the benefit if it is made known to those who do not have any interest to know? There are very many yet to come and join. This is just the beginning, the endless beginning.

Another devotee: *Are we also included in your list, Mother?*

Mother: All are there in God's accounts. But our birth will be fulfilled only if our calculations and estimations are cut off.

MOVEMENT-STILLNESS

Mother: (Pointing to one person) In the beginning when this son started coming here, some people asked him, "Why should you go there? She is possessed, isn't she?" But without caring he came here. Then what? He understood that it was they who were possessed. (All laugh.) Some people call the *Bhâva Darshan* "possession." That is incorrect. It shows their lack of proper understanding. Both movement and stillness are two different aspects of the same Truth. They are one. To reach the state of stillness, it is necessary to hold onto something which, of course, is changing. The means, whatever it is, must be a name or form, which is bound to change. Nobody can conceive of *Brahman* which has no form or attributes. The majority of people need name and form. Mother has to consider them as well. Is it possible for Mother to discard the thousands who are in need of name, form and attributes in order to progress spiritually, for the sake of one or two *jñânis* who do not need it? Stillness and movement are one and the same. If one is omitted, the other cannot be known. Enquiry is motion, the place where enquiry ends is stillness. Creating motion, God abides in stillness.

Twilight fell and the residents were about to begin the devotional singing. The Holy Mother got up from her seat and walked towards the temple verandah calling, *"Come, children."* Everyone got up and followed Mother. One devotee commented to his friend, "How long we have been coming here but we never heard Mother talking like this. The fact is that we have never stayed to hear it. We would come late in the evening to see the *Bhâva Darshan* and after entering the temple we would leave the place immediately." The friend replied, "Did you hear what Mother said about the *Bhâva*? It is to uplift ordinary people to God also. To bring them closer to God and to develop faith in them, such things are needed. For those who come in search of pure spirituality, Mother will reveal her real greatness." The singing had begun and the heart-capturing songs of the Holy Mother filled the atmosphere with a divine fervour. She sang,

> *There is nothing to tell to the all-knowing Mother...*
>
> *Walking beside us, She is seeing and understanding everything...*
>
> *The Primordial Being who is greater than the greatest, sees all the thoughts of the innermost self...*

The Mother's *bhajan* was always a source of tremendous inspiration to the devotees. While singing, she would always soar to the highest planes of supreme devotion equally elevating the listeners as well. Some of the devotees took leave of the Holy Mother after the *bhajan* and *árati*.[36]

January 1978

PRABHAKARA SIDDHA YOGI

As it was Sunday afternoon, devotees had already started coming for the *Bháva Darshan*. Some of them were talking about Prabhakara Siddha Yogi, an *Avadhúta*[37] who had many followers. These devotees who were talking about him had met him in Oachira on their way to the Mother's ashram. Some of Mother's devotees cherished a desire to see him and expressed their wish to her. Mother replied, *"If you are very desirous, Mother will make him come here."* The conversation ended there. At ten o'clock at night *Devi Bháva* had already begun. To the wonderment of the devotees who had expressed their desire to see Prabhakara Siddha Yogi, he came to the ashram this night accompanied by three other people. It was very difficult to understand the strange behaviour of the yogi. His peculiar ways were incomprehensible to the devotees gathered there. Sometimes he spoke in a strange language and acted as if mad.

It was nearly dawn by the time the *Bháva* was over. The Holy Mother came out of the temple and sat near the Yogi. When he saw Mother he started saying, "Kali...Kali." He asked Mother, "Why did you call me here?" Mother replied, *"I did not call, did I?"* "No, you called," came his reply. "For the last few days I was being attracted here."

---

[36]The waving of burning camphor before the Deity signifying the offering of the ego to God.

[37]A Realised Soul who does not observe any norms in his external behaviour, sometimes acting like a sage but at other times acting like a child, madman or ghoul.

Mother: The children here felt like seeing you. That is the reason. (Pointing to a resident) That son was very inspired to see you. Give what is needed.
Yogi: *What am I to give? (Turning to the resident) The person to give what is to be given is here. I am not needed for that.*

The Yogi pretended to be angry and pointed to Mother saying, "Do you know this person who is sitting here? No, you don't know anything. This is a place where many things will arise. Many are yet to come. Many will come by air and water. Everything is here." The Yogi then turned to the Holy Mother's father, Sugunanandan. "You must be very careful. This is not your house, it is the devotees.' You have to become a little better. Do not make the devotees sad. All this is theirs."

After roaming around the ashram for some time, the Yogi left. Later, Mother told the devotees and *brahmacharins,*

Mother: The Yogi was brought because the children said that they wanted to see him. You will not understand his ways and will not approve either. Children, now you go and do your *sadhana*. Everything that you want will come. Children, learn yourself. There is not much use in trying to study people like the Yogi. The path is different for different people. Everyone cannot assimilate everything. What you need is Self-Realisation, not *siddhis*[38.] Nothing else is needed for those who get that (Realisation).

---

[38]Psychic powers.

TAKING DISEASE

15 January 1978

Today the Holy Mother was not well. She came from the hut where she resides, later than usual. The number of visitors was not less, however, and having saluted her, the devotees stood around her.

Mother: Mother is not well today.

Devotee: *Perhaps Mother has taken somebody's disease.*

Mother: Oh, does Mother have the power to do it?

Devotee: *Of course! That day how quickly Mother removed my sickness. A few moments later the same symptoms were seen in Mother. Yet in Mother it lasted only a few minutes.*

Mother: On certain occasions such things are necessary. Otherwise, to whom will the children call? When Mother's children have pain she will say, "Mother (Devi, the Divine Mother), give it to me." Whether it is in your body or this body (pointing to her own), it is enough to suffer, is it not so? All is 'Thy' grace. Only if we get that there be will some benefit. No benefit will come, whoever else may help us. One look, one word or a touch from God is enough to get rid of all the impurities in a person. Because you are believers, Mother speaks in this manner. Mother does not know rationalism and such things. At the time of death, all reason will run away and hide. The inadequacy of those who pretend to be courageous will be proven then.

Devotee: *Not only for a skeptic, but a devotee also has death, hasn't he?*

Mother: All those who have taken birth will die. But the death of Knowers of God, that is something different. They are not afraid of death. Instead, they will welcome death. They enter not the world of death but the world of God.

Another devotee: *I heard that Mother has not eaten for several days. Why is that?*

Mother: There is no particular reason, son. Look, Mother has no problem. Very many times Mother has done this. So what? Did this body become weak? Good vigour is there.

Devotee: *(Laughing) Mother should teach us that trick also.*

Mother: It is not a thing which is possible through any trickery. It cannot be explained either. Such a nature is there during certain times, that is all.

By this time a group of women devotees had come to see the Holy Mother. They were members of a women's cultural centre and began by asking about the *dharma* of women.

Mother: There is only one *dharma.* That is to know God. There is no separate *dharma* specially made for women, but they have their own way to attain God. Women like yourselves should observe the scriptural statements and follow in the footsteps of Sita, Savitri, and Satyavati, who were embodiments of *sthri dharma* (women's dharma). Living in it is greater than simply talking about it. Set an example for other women by living it. Take the case of

Sita. The whole *Ramayana* entirely depends on the purity and virtuous character of Sita. What would the situation have been if Sita had obstinately said, "It is not possible to go to the forest, the country is rightfully ours?" But Sita did not do that. That shows her detachment towards worldly possessions. Her love for Rama shows attachment to God. Sita symbolizes a courageous woman who has acquired enough mental strength to confront the challenges of life through one-pointed devotion to her husband Rama. This also shows the infinite power of chastity. During her stay in Lanka, which symbolizes material wealth, surrounded by demonesses (negative tendencies), Sita would constantly remember Rama and shed tears due to the excruciating pain of separation. It was because of that power that Rama could come to Lanka and kill Ravana. It is impossible for *Bhagavân* not to give an ear to the devotees' grief-stricken call. Where there is love, there *Bhagavân* is.

1 January 1980

A householder devotee with four young men came to see Mother. Several of the youths had heard about Mother but this was the first time they had come to see Her in person. All four of them were humble and devoted. One of them was studying for his Master's degree and the other three for B.A. degrees. It was their inquisitive nature to want to know more about spirituality which brought them to Mother.

Mother came out of her hut and sat in front of the temple. All five of them prostrated before the Mother and stood by the side of the temple verandah. She affectionately asked them to sit down. Mother closed Her eyes and absorbed herself in meditation. After sometime, she opened her eyes, and turning to the students, enquired smilingly, *"Children, do all of you like spirituality?"* One of the students replied, "Yes, we go to temples and holy places." Mother remarked, *"It is a wonder that children who study in college have interest in such things."* The student replied, "We are interested to know spiritual things. Mother should give us some advice."

Mother: Children, Mother is crazy. She would just burst out with some crazy things. All of you children call her "Mother" and because of that she calls you "children." Other than that, Mother does not know anything.

MEDITATION

Mother: You children should live with the remembrance of God. Do not waste time. Repeat your mantra while doing each action. Every day do meditation for some time.

Student: *Mother, how to do meditation?*

Mother: Place a small picture of a god or goddess that you like in front of you. Sit gazing at the picture for some time. Then try to fix the form within while closing your eyes. Again look at the external picture when the form within fades away. Again the eyes should be closed. Imagine that you are talking to the Beloved Deity, "Mother, do not go away abandoning me. Come into my heart. Let me always see Your beautiful form," and so on. Cry, embracing your Beloved Deity. That which we meditate on will appear in front of us if constantly repeated like this with faith.

Meditation is good even for small children. Their intelligence will become clear, memory will increase and they will learn well. Mother does not say that all children must become *sannyásins*. Children, find a blissful life. You can understand the secret of bliss when you think of the nature of the Self. The waves of the mind will subside. Everything is there in you alone. If there is faith, you can find it. The happiness that we get from the objects of the world is only an infinitesimal fraction of the bliss that we get from within.

Just as the filter fixed on the water tap absorbs the impurities in the water, so we should absorb the impurities in us with the filter of meditation. In the olden days the forests were outside. Now having cleared all those forests away, they have come within everyone. In olden times animals were outside. Now they are also within. It is the dirt within the mind that should be removed. Give up selfishness and thereby be rid of sorrow.

Student: *What should be done to remove the dirt from the mind?*

Mother: If the mind is to become pure, love for God should come. Virtues should come. The main obstacle to becoming closer to God is our selfishness. Selfishness automatically falls off when we feel compassion for others. Just as the saline taste disappears when fresh water is constantly added to salt water, the bad will leave us when we constantly think of the good. See how many poor people are suffering around us without shelter, clothes, food or proper medical care. We will lose our selfishness when we have compassion for them.

Suppose we smoke ten rupees of cigarettes a day. In one month that is three hundred rupees. How much money will it be if calculated like this? A small hut can be built for a poor man to sleep in with the amount spent for one year's smoking. Presently, we are not understanding that bliss is not in the cigarette but in us.

You children might ask, "Then what about the cigarette manufacturers?" They themselves are saying that cigarette smoking is bad for health and that it will destroy the body and mind. Those who have discrimination will withdraw from it.

Children, find satisfaction in others' happiness. For example, suppose we are comfortably seated in a bus. An elderly person gets in at the next stop and there is no vacant seat. Immediately getting up from your seat, you should make room for him to sit. We will become worthy of God's Grace when each one of our little selfish actions is given up. Negative qualities thus get destroyed.

We are all children of one Mother. The same eagerness which we have to apply medicine to our burnt hand we must show towards others who are suffering. If the left arm is burnt, does the right arm refuse to apply medicine saying, "It is not me who has the burn?" "I" permeates the whole body. That "I" feels the pain in any part of the body. Likewise, we are unknowingly experiencing the pain of even a small creature because the same Consciousness pervades everywhere. Children, always act with compassion understanding this. We should not expect the fruit of our actions. It is enough to dedicate it to God. He will give what we need.

Question: *Mother, how do we get rid of sorrow?*
Mother: We do not know what is eternal and non-eternal. Our desire is not for the eternal. Because of this, we become sorrowful. The mind burns and burns due to sorrow and we become sick. Thus, our life span also decreases. To counter-act this, we should improve our actions. Our mind becomes restless because wherever we go, we find the faults and defects of others. This is not the point of view that we want. Look carefully at what is of value in others and respect that. Forget what we have seen which is lacking. When we go to a new place or meet someone new, instead of trying to find faults and being critical, try to see the good and appreciate that. You should only look at those qualities in which you are lacking. In this way, we should always see the good. Thus we can get rid of sorrow.

Student: *Mother, parents have a lot of expectations in regards to their children, don't they? Is it right to stay in an ashram without serving them?*
Mother: Children, parents would say "my" son, "my" daughter. We are only their step-children. It is true that the parents have many expectations in regards to their children, but think for a while. Do they discharge their duty towards their children properly? Mother would say "No" because their real duty towards their children is to give them good culture which they are not doing at all. If any one of the sons or daughters of any of the parents take to spirituality, Mother will consider it as a great blessing not only for their family but also for the whole world. By doing so, he or she is rendering a great service to their family as well as for the en-

tire human race. Children, tell Mother which is better, to ruin one's life just for one or two people or to sacrifice for the good of the world?

Anyhow, it can be said without a doubt that only *sannyásins* have served the world selflessly. Even today it is so. They never expect anything from the world. Whereas, worldly people have only expectations or desires which will eventually steal away all of their human qualities and make them behave like animals.

If we are our parents' own children, they should be able to save us from death as well. We are God's children. What use are we if His power is not there? Everyone might seem to be our relative while we stand in a bus. Each will go away when alighting at their stop. This is life. We alone will remain. Father, mother and everyone else are like these relatives in the bus. The Lord alone is always with us.

At this time *brahmachári* Sreekumar came and sat near Mother and she continued,

Mother: Children, however much wealth we have, if its place and use in life is not understood, sorrow will result. Even if there is immeasurable wealth, momentary is the happiness that we get from it. It cannot give Eternal Bliss. Didn't Kamsa, Hiranyakasipu and others all possess vast wealth? Did they ever have mental peace and tranquillity? What peace did Ravana have although he possessed fabulous wealth? They all lived egotistically swerving from the path of Truth. They did many actions which should not have been done. Thus they lost peace and tranquillity.

Eternal bliss is not gained from wealth. Only non-eternal happiness can be gained from wealth. Then you might ask, "How to live without riches? Do we have to abandon the wealth that we have?" Mother does not say to abandon anything. Bliss and peace will become our wealth if we understand the proper placement of what we have. For those who have turned Godward, wealth is like rice in which sand has fallen. It is of little use.

Seeing that the students were listening with interest, the Holy Mother continued,

Mother: In the olden days everyone first stayed at the residence of the Guru throughout the period of their education. As a result of that, they came to know what life is, how to live and how to behave in the world. Because of that, they were blissful. They became strong-minded and could cross over any obstacle whatsoever. They were ready to dedicate their life to Truth without fearing death. They were like good lion cubs - perfectly healthy, endowed with a long life span, magnificent stature and full of vigour. They were not like today's people, shortlived and weak like lambs. They were not afraid of anything. In those days, having lit the oil lamp, people would sing the Names of God during twilight. After that, they used to think of the mistakes that they had committed that day and would repent. They also tried not to repeat such mistakes again. That gave them consolation. But what about today? Times have changed. At dusk people sit in front of the television playing video tapes to watch movies. People think how to seize other people's money by fraudulent means or by killing them. They would not hesitate to kill their own mother for money. This is today's world. Even then, is there peace? There is no peace anywhere.

Ganja (marijuana), sleeping pills, intoxicants, liquor - these are the present-day gods for people. If these are not there, they cannot live. Becoming a slave to all these things, their lives are ruined and they are destroying others as well. Nowadays, three year old children are shouting slogans, "Hail revolution!" If somebody does not belong to his own (political) party he will even say, "I will kill him." Going to school, he incites strikes. My children, do not be ruined like this.

Having said this, Mother closed her eyes and sat in an abstracted mood. After some time, the Mother got up from her seat uttering *"Shiva...Shiva!"* showing a divine gesture with her fingers. As she walked out, Mother told Sreekumar, *"Sit and talk about something to these children. Mother will come back after some time."*

Student: *As I was thinking to ask some questions, Mother went on telling the answers to them!*
Sreekumar: *Such experiences are not unusual for us.*
Student: *What inspired you people to come to the ashram?*
Sreekumar: *Mother's pure love and unconditional motherhood. It kindled love for God and ailing humanity in us. It must be known through direct expe-*

rience. One cannot even dream of such love from one's own parents.

Mother's love comes from having known the Eternal. There is no selfishness in it. It is untainted love. Mother clears and cleans the path in front of us. It is enough to walk along it. At present, we are just like a pond with stagnant water in it. Mother connects it with the river by making furrows. Unknowingly, we get closer to God because Mother cuts off our selfishness with love. Mother acts selflessly, that is why she can do this. It is not possible for those who have desires to do this. This is the true relationship. This is not available anywhere else.

All of a sudden Sreekumar became disconsolate. His eyes were fixed on a distant point and he sat motionless. His eyes became wet with tears.

Student: *What happened, Sreekumar?*
Sreekumar: *Oh . . . nothing . . . I just remembered something which happened on the first* Thiruonam[39] *day after seeing Mother.*
Student: *We would like to hear about it.*
Sreekumar: *It was the day before* Thiruonam. *I was talking with Mother after* darshan *and she said, "Thiruonam is tomorrow, is it not? Children, please come." I and some of her other children were sitting nearby when she said this. When I returned home, my family would not let me go without first having food as it was* Thiruonam. *In those days my family was not so close to Mother. Mother wanted us to eat lunch with*

---

[39]The most important annual festival in Kerala.

her on that day which is why she had called us, but how to escape from the house? It was nearly eleven-thirty when the cooking was over. Soon after eating lunch, I started for Vallickavu. All the buses were very crowded and none of them stopped. I waited for a long time at the bus stop. Although it was late, I was fortunate to get a direct bus to Vallickavu. It was three-thirty when I arrived. Crossing the river on the ferry, I walked quickly towards the ashram. I can never forget the sight which I saw there, such a heart-breaking sight it was. Mother was lying on the bare ground full of sand all over her body. A temporary oven was seen near her. Crows were pecking and eating cooked roots from the pot and some pieces were lying scattered in the sand. Later, when Mother awoke, she related what had happened:

"Mother had asked the children to come, didn't she? What to give the children, Mother thought. I don't like to tell anything to the family members. Mother herself made an oven in the yard. Going to the garden, Mother plucked some roots and kept them on the oven to cook. When it was fully cooked, the pot was kept closed without removing it from the oven. Having extinguished the fire, Mother waited for the children to come. Several times Mother went to the jetty and looked to see whether the children were coming. Mother also did not eat anything. When it became late, Mother laid down on the sand thinking, 'It was wrong to call the children. Being *Thiruonam,* will their families let them leave their house?' At that moment a crow flew by pecking one piece of cooked root. Mother got up hurriedly. Some pieces had been scattered on the ground from the pot. Some more crows came and tried to eat. What will I give my children? Mother felt sad and was about to drive away the crows, but the next moment Mother thought, 'They are also my children. Let them eat.' Mother again laid down on the sand."

After a few moments some of the children arrived. Everyone had brought something for Mother. She asked them all to sit around her as she unwrapped the packages and distributed the banana chips and other edibles to each one. She smiled with tears in her eyes. This innocent smile of a small child made everyone cry also. Since that incident, all of us would only eat with Mother during Onam festival.

By this time Mother returned and called everyone for lunch. Everybody followed Mother to the dining hall.

Saturday, 5 December 1981
11 a.m.

Mother was sitting on a cot in the hut. All four sides as well as the roof were thatched with coconut leaves. The entrance, being on the western side, was facing towards the backwaters and the Arabian Sea. The roaring sound of the breaking ocean waves could be clearly heard from this side of the ashram though a full view was not seen. Big fish, diving through the backwaters gleefully moving their tails and fins, could be seen while sitting in the hut itself. Different varieties of flowering plants were growing on the raised ridge of the backwaters. On the walls of the hut hung pictures of great saints and sages and different gods and goddesses. The cot was situated along the southern side of the hut adjoining the wall. Grass mats were spread on the floor.

Some young men had come to see the Holy Mother. They entered the hut and sat on the floor having offered their salutations to the Mother. She also sat down on a mat and smilingly asked, *"Children, when did you come?"* One man replied, "Some time before." Mother asked if they had eaten anything to which they replied in the affirmative. One of the young men said, "Mother, we have certain doubts."

Mother: Mother is crazy. Mother does not know anything. She babbles something or other.

Question: *Mother, how can one lead the world?*

Mother: Only one who has studied can teach. Only one who has acquired can give. Only one who is completely free from sorrow can free others from sorrow completely.

Question: *Mother, what is meant by death?*

Mother: Son, death is only a change like all other changes. Each being takes birth on earth according to the fruit of its actions. Coming here, they proudly live thinking "my" wealth, "my" wife, etc. Each one dies as they are trying to fulfill their desires. Eventually we are forced to go, leaving everything behind that we considered as our own. While travelling in a bus, we have to get off at the stop where we must alight. When we sat in the bus we proudly thought "my" seat and even claimed it so. But when leaving the bus, we do not take the seat with us. Only God knows how long we will be here. The existence of all of us is in God. The *jiva*[40] which makes the body act, departs leaving behind

---

[40]Jiva is used here in the sense of the live force

the corpse. This is what we call death. But death is not the complete destruction of the body. It is the beginning of the decomposition of the five elements of which the body is made, only to merge with its original principles. This change of the body has nothing to do with the soul which will remain unchanged as ever.

EASY PATH

Devotee: *What is the easy way to attain God's Vision?*
Mother: An easy path is sought due to lack of surrender. God's Vision cannot be gained simply by torturing the body. Whatever the path is, the mind should merge in God, that is important. Regularly performing *sâdhana,* we should wait with patience. Here, there is no shortcut. Having put rock sugar candy in one's mouth, nobody would quickly swallow it just because it is sweet. If so, the throat would get cut. Let it dissolve and then swallow. *Sâdhana* is also the same. The path of devotion is simple.
Devotee: *Mother, what should be done to develop devotion?*
Mother: *Satsang, kirtan, mantra japa, dhyâna,* all these are helpful.
Devotee: *Mother, how can those who are involved in worldly affairs sustain devotion?*
Mother: Children, remember God while doing actions. (Mother points to a man who is leading ducks through the backwaters.) There is hardly any room in the boat even to keep his legs properly. It is such a small boat. Standing in the boat, he will

row with a long oar and lead the ducks as well. Making
noise by slapping the oar on the water, the man will
guide the ducks if they stray. At intervals, he will smoke
a cigarette. He will scoop out any water entering the
boat with his feet. He will also converse with the
people standing on the bank. Even while doing all
these things, his mind will always be on the boat. If his
attention wavers even for a moment, losing his balance, the boat will capsize and he will fall in. Children,
like this we should live in this world. Whatever work
we are doing, our mind should be centered on God.
This is easily possible through practice.

It was now time for lunch and one *brahmachárin* came
to call the young men. Mother affectionately said, *"Yes, my children, go and eat your lunch. It is ashram food. There will not be many
spices to add flavour. It is good to have some training!"* All moved
towards the dining hall.

PURPOSE OF BIRTH

Mother was eating while a few *brahmachárins* sat
nearby. She also fed them with small balls of rice. One
brahmachárin asked, "Mother, what is the purpose of
your birth?"

Mother: Mother's birth is for the good of the
world. Some people dig wells only for their own
use. There are others who dig wells for the use of
the whole village. Their intention is that all should
quench their thirst by drinking water from the
well. Mother dug at a place and there was water there.
Gradually it flowed as a river. Some bathed in it and

others quenched their thirst. Each one does as he requires.

Was not Sri Krishna the Supreme Self? The Lord had no attachment to anything. Even then, the Lord incarnated on the earth and acted ideally for the good of the world. It was not for Himself. He is not in need of anything. It is not for the Knowers of the Self that God takes birth. God assumes a body to bring the ignorant to the path of goodness. What defamations Sri Krishna heard! Was He not killed by an arrow? Jesus Christ was crucified. If necessary, they could have reduced their enemies to ashes in an instant. Yet, only to show the world what renunciation is, they did destroy their enemies.

All of us should learn to live with equality and to love each other with a brotherly attitude. Different kinds of people come to see Mother during *Bhâva Darshan,* for devotion, for fulfilling worldly desires, for curing diseases and for many other things. Mother discards no one. Could Mother discard them? Are they different from me? Are we not all beads strung on the one thread of the vital force? Each one understands Mother according to his own way of thinking. Those who criticize me and those who love me are the same to me. A continuous stream of love flows from me towards all beings in the cosmos. That is Mother's inborn nature.

Lifting both hands in the air and looking upwards, the Holy Mother called loudly, *"Shivane . . . Shivane . . . (O Shiva, O Shiva)."*

KUNDALINI

Question: *Mother, yesterday I read certain things about* kundalini shakti *but it was so confusing that I finally put the book down. What is* kundalini shakti? *How does it work? What is meant by "awakening of* kundal-ini?" *Mother, please could you say something about it?*
Mother: Son, first of all, a serious seeker should not think about and go on asking each and everyone about the working of *kundalini,* whether it is awak-ened or "Is it going to awaken soon?" Mother does not say that you should stop reading and gathering knowledge about such things. It is good. But too much reading is also dangerous. Mere reading without practice is harmful. Do your *sâdhana* regularly and with utmost sincerity and faith, sup-ported by self-surrender. All other developments will happen automatically. You do not have to worry about it. It must take place provided that your effort is sincere.

Because you asked, Mother will say something about it. Mother does not want to disappoint you. Son, *kundalini,* or the serpent power, is the vital force which flows in and through all living beings. This power is situated below the spine in the form of a coiled, sleeping female snake. It is awakened through incessant contemplation and Guru's Grace. When it is awakened, it ascends through the *sushumna*[41] which lies in the spine, yearning to see the male serpent which is residing in the *sahasrâra.*[42]

_____
[41]A vital nerve.
[42]The mystic thousand-petalled lotus at the crown of the head.

Mot.... paused for a moment and the *brahmachârin* took this opportunity to clear his doubts about *kundalini* by asking, "Does all this exist on the gross level or on the subtle level?"

Mother: This is subtler than the subtlest. As you know, there are six *chakras*.[43] *Sahasrâra* is the last and the subtlest. Each one of them is a storehouse of spiritual power which can be experienced only through yogic intuition. As the serpent power reaches each *chakra*, it makes that particular region fully blossom and mature before passing to the next. As the *kundalini* reaches each plexus, the seeker will get different kinds of visions, both divine and tempting. The *sâdhak* who is not under the strict control of a *Sadguru* might misunderstand these lower states as something very great or equal to Self-Realisation and become prey to a fall. That is why it is strictly said that a *Sadguru* is absolutely necessary to guide the aspirant during the course of his *sâdhana*.

Several changes also occur in the body when this power moves from one plexus to another. One feels a burning sensation all over the body, as if hot chillies have been rubbed on the body. The body also experiences tremendous heat and horripilates now and then. Water may ooze from the pores like sweat. In certain stages blood may come out through the pores and the body becomes gaunt like a skeleton.

Brahmachârin: *Isn't this a frightening situation, Mother?*

Mother: Yes, it is. The *sâdhak* who undergoes these

---

[43]Mystic centres along the spine.

experiences for the first time may get frightened. Not
only that, sometimes he might also become mentally
abnormal or perverted due to fear and lack of inner
strength to withstand the situation. That is why it is
strictly prescribed that *kundalini dhyâna* should be
performed only in the presence of a Realised Soul.

Brahmachârin: *What things should an aspirant be
careful about during this period?*

Mother: During this state the aspirant should be
very careful and alert. He should be looked after
with as much care as a pregnant woman would be.
The body should not be moved unnecessarily. He
should not even lie down on a mattress because the
smallest folds will be unbearable to him. He should
use a straight, well-smoothened wooden plank to
lie on. The spine should not receive any knocks, as
the after-effects will be great. When the *kundalini*
wakes up, the aspirant becomes a tremendous
centre of attraction and being deluded by this,
women and others may flock around him. In such a
state, the absence of a *Sadguru* to impart proper instructions may tempt him to indulge in sensual
pleasures, thus draining away all his accumulated
spiritual energy.

Brahmachârin: *Mother, what happens when the* kundalini shakti *finally reaches the* sahasrâra?

Mother: Transcending all six *âdhâras,* [44] including
the *mûlâdhara,* [45] it finally reaches the head which
is its real abode. The body experiences a rejuvenating
coolness and there follows a showering of ambrosia

---

[44] The first six chakras counting from the bottom of the spine upwards.
[45] The lowest chakra at the base of the spine.

throughout the body. The old body gets transformed into a new vessel of tremendous spiritual power.

Roots absorb water and manure from the soil and carry this to the leaves. Thereupon the leaves do their part of the process by dividing and distributing the substance among all parts of the organism, including the roots. This refined energy sustains the tree. Similarly, the spiritual energy which reaches the *sahasradala padma*[46] from the *mûlâdhara* transforms itself into ambrosia and, flowing through the nerves, pervades the whole body and nourishes it, imparting a rich glow and splendour, marvelous energy and vitality.

Another brahmachârin: *Mother, the mind is not getting any concentration during meditation. Why is it so?*

Mother: Children, the mind is naturally one-pointed and pure, but until yesterday we have made room for many impure worldly emotions there. Thus it becomes difficult to make the mind concentrated while sitting for meditation. They (the worldly thoughts and emotions) are like tenants. We have given them a small space to build a hut on our land which was lying independent and expansive. Not only do they not care when we ask them to leave, they come to fight with us. We have to toil to kick them out. We have to argue in court also. Likewise, to kick out the tenants of the mind we have to file a case in God's court. It is a constant fight. We must continue fighting until we come out victorious.

---

[46]The thousand-petalled lotus.

It will be experienced that more *râsanas* come up as you do more *sâdhana*. While sweeping a room, we can remove only the superficial dirt. Whereas, if the room is wiped with a wet cloth, more dirt will come out. In a similar way, more dirt will rise up when we do more *sâdhana*. It is only for the purpose of being destroyed that they will rise up like that.

Brahmachârin: *Mother, is it not necessary to fight against the injustice in the world?*

Mother: That is the work for worldly people endowed with *râjasic*[47] qualities and not for a seeker of Truth. Do not see the faults and defects of the world. God-Realisation is our goal. After attaining that, we can make the world good in accordance with God's instructions. Is it practical to worship God only after wiping out all the injustice in the world?

SADGURU
Self-Realised Master

Question: *How to know whether one's spiritual experiences are valid or invalid or just a fascination, or imagination?*

Mother: Son, for that a *Sadguru* is needed. A *Sadguru* is one who has gained God-Realisation. He will guide the disciple along the correct path and take him to the goal. Those who are sincere will get a Guru. It is not necessary to wander here and there.

Question: *Mother, which is better, meditation on God with attributes or without attributes?*

---

[47]One of the three *gunas* or qualities of Nature, the quality of passion or activity.

Mother: That depends on the seeker. Usually, to begin with God with attributes and to end in the Attributeless is good.

Question: *It is a little difficult to clearly get the form of the Beloved Deity in meditation. Why is it so, Mother?*

Mother: It will be like that. There is no other way than to continue the *sâdhana* correctly. The mind which runs here and there in the beginning will later become fixed on the Beloved Deity. Then the form will become unclouded.

Question: *Why does the mind run like that?*

Mother: Because of the *vâsanas.*

Question: *Can a householder attain God?*

Mother: Why such a question, son? Is a householder's life enough just because your meditation is not becoming firm? (Everyone laughs) A *grahastâshrami* [48] will attain God but not a *grahasta.* [49] No problem for a *grahasta* who leads an ashram life understanding the eternal and non-eternal. One can reach the goal if selfless action is performed with an attitude of dedicating everything to God. A seeker should stay firmly fixed in the goal. Do not stop the *sâdhana* out of disappointment and frustration. Intentness on reaching the goal should be there.

Question: *Can't the Guru remove the shortcomings of the disciple?*

Mother: A passenger can be dropped off at the station but it is he who has to get into the bus and

---

[48] A married person who makes his house into an ashram, i.e. who leads a spiritual life.
[49] An ordinary worldly soul leading a married life.

travel. The Guru will show the path. All the rest depends on the mind and effort of the disciple.

Question: *What is the difference between worshipping God with form and the formless aspect of God?*

Mother: What is gained through meditation upon God with form is *savikalpa samâdhi,* the perception of Reality while retaining the state of duality. Owing to the vision of one's Beloved Deity, the attitude of "I" is still there. The feeling of duality is there.

In meditation upon the Formless, the ego sense is completely removed. There is only One. What is gained is *sahaja nirvikalpa samâdhi*, the natural state of abidance in the Absolute.

Question: *Mother, how will the disciples be who come to do good for the world?*

Mother: They are *nitya siddhas.*[50] They are detached from the time of their birth itself.

Question: *Why does the world slip into errors?*

Mother: Due to *kâma* (lust) and *krôdha* (anger) human beings commit errors and become unrighteous. What is necessary is to control desires.

Sunday, 6 December 1981

Since it was a *Darshan* day, there was a big crowd to see the Mother as Devi and Krishna and to receive her blessings. At four in the morning when the *Bhâva* was completed, a moving incident took place which made this an unforgettable day.

A black cow which was living at the Ashram had given birth to a calf one year ago. It was a beautiful sight to see the glee-

_____
[50]Ever-perfect.

ful calf running here and there around the ashram premises. That night the calf suddenly became afflicted with an acute illness. Unable to bear the pain it cried aloud, "Ma...Ma!" as if it were calling the Holy Mother. Although many people tried to relieve the calf of its pain, it was to no avail and its condition became worse and worse. The poor creature was struggling for life.

Coming out of the temple after the *Bhâva*, Mother went straight to the calf and with great love and affection placed its head in her lap. She carressed it and asked everyone to chant the Divine Name. After some time, the Mother asked everyone to chant the sacred mantra *"Om Nama Shivaya."* As the chanting was going on, the Mother asked for some *tulasi* (basil) leaves and sacred water to be brought in a *kindi*.[51] When the water was brought, she poured some into its mouth which it drank and then took some in her palm which she sprinkled on its body along with the sacred *tulasi* leaves. The calf was lying down, gazing at the Holy Mother's face. After a couple of minutes the Mother again carressed its face and body and said, *"All right, you go."* After a few seconds the calf breathed its last, still keeping its head on the Mother's lap.

Mother later relating about this incident said,

Mother: That calf was a *sannyâsin* in its previous birth. Due to its karma it took birth as a cow. Because of the accumulated merits from its previous birth, it happened to be born in this ashram. The *brahmachârins* raised it. It grew up hearing the Divine Names. This way it left its body.

Thursday, 10 December 1981

At 10 o'clock in the morning Mother came into the kitchen. One *brahmachârin* was cooking tamarind seed for the cow on the gas stove. Mother commented, *"Cooking gas is very expensive.*

---

[51]A metal water pot with a fluted rim.

This can be cooked using firewood. The stove will be ruined if you keep big vessels like this on it." The *brahmachârin* did not heed the Mother's words. She continued, *"If you cannot, Mother will cook it."* He replied, "Where is the time to do *sâdhana* if I must sit here doing this kind of work?" Hearing this, the Mother became a bit serious and told him, *"From now on you don't have to look after anything to do with the cows."* Having said this, she entrusted the work to another resident. Then the *brahmachârin* became sad, but Mother would not agree to his request to continue doing the work. What followed was a beautiful piece of spiritual instruction.

Mother: One should learn to do every action with utter dedication to God, shouldn't one? What kind of spirituality is this? Spirituality is not sitting in a corner with closed eyes. We should be ready to become everyone's servant and also to see all equally. Going out into the world tomorrow, all of you should serve everyone without selfishness. Serving the cow is an especially meritorious action. It is said in the *Bhâgavatam* that Sri Krishna used to graze the cows, is it not?

Once a sage who was sitting under water in meditation got caught in a fisherman's net. As instructed by the sage, the fisherman took him to the king's palace to be sold. However much was offered, the sage did not agree to be sold to the king. At last, as suggested by a clever minister, the king offered a cow. Only then did the sage consent to be purchased by the king. The cow is that sacred of an animal. Serving a cow should be considered as a good fortune, it is a *sâdhana*. Son, do not do this work half-heartedly.

One who simultaneously does *karma* (action) and remembers God is the noblest. Son, can you not repeat your mantra while cooking the tamarind seed? Otherwise, can you not read spiritual books?

Sage Narada thought that he was a great devotee. Once Lord Krishna said, "Narada, there is one farmer on earth who is a greater devotee than you." Narada doubted this and came down to earth to see the peasant in person. He found that the farmer would chant the Lord's Name only three times a day. "How could he be a greater devotee than I?" thought Narada. Upon returning, he mentioned his doubt to the Lord. The Lord gave him a small vessel filled to the brim with oil and asked Narada to keep it on his head and go round a particular hill without spilling even a drop of it. When Narada returned after finishing the round, the Lord asked, "How many times did you chant My Name in between?" Narada thought and was surprised to discover that he had not remembered the Lord's Name even once because his attention had been fully concentrated on keeping the vessel of oil steady so as not to spill it. *Bhagavân* smilingly said, "Now do you understand what a great devotee that farmer is? Even in the midst of his toilsome work, thrice he is remembering Me, is he not?"

The *brahmachârin* who had tried to say that cooking tamarind seed was an obstacle for his *sâdhana* understood his mistake and apologized for his indiscrimination. But Mother did not allow him to resume that work. She said, *"When you are able to do these works with faith and without selfishness, then Mother will ask you to do it. Until then, meditate."* Out of remorse, the *brahmachârin* fasted that day. Learning that he had not eaten, the Holy Mother, out of her affection, also did not eat anything. Greatly pained at heart to hear that she was not eating because of him, the *brahmachârin* had his supper. Thereupon the Mother also ate.

Saturday, 19 December 1981

At 8 o'clock in the morning the *brahmachârins* were getting ready to chant the *Lalitasahasranâma* (The Thousand Names of the Divine Mother) as instructed by the Holy Mother. It was the first day of the *Laksharchana* when they would chant it one lakh (one hundred thousand) times. Everyone came into the temple and sat around the sacred seat ready to begin the worship. All preparations were ready and *brahmachârin* Unnikrishnan commenced the formal worship which would be followed by the chanting. Each one had kept flower petals in front of themselves on a piece of banana leaf. All sat with closed eyes as the verse for meditation was chanted. Unnikrishnan led the worship in the presence of the Holy Mother. He chanted the Names one by one as the *brahmachârins* repeated them and offered each flower petal on the holy seat. Noticing one *brahmachârin* who offered the flowers carelessly, Mother said,

Mother: Do not perform the offering disgustedly and drearily. If you feel disinclination, take some rest, then continue. Children, do not force the body to do the worship. It is not a problem even if the *pooja* finishes a little late. Visualize Devi's form sitting on the *peetham* (seat) while taking each flower petal. Offer the flowers at Devi's Feet. Then you will get good attention. External attentiveness becomes the cause of internal attentiveness.

SAHAJA SAMADHI
The Natural State

The time was now 3 o'clock in the afternoon. *brahmachârin* Nealu was conversing with the Holy Mother in the hut. Sitting nearby, *brahmachârin* Balu was keenly listening to the Holy Mother's words.

Nealu: *Mother, what is meant by* sahaja samâdhi?
Mother: Son, imagine that there is a rubber ball and ring within us. The ball is always moving up and down. This ball is the mind. At times it gets caught in the ring and remains motionless. This can be called *samâdhi*. But the ball does not rest there permanently. It will again move up and down as before. Eventually, a state will come when the ball rests permanently in the ring without any further motion. This is called *sahaja samâdhi*.

Merging of the mind is experienced by the *sâdhak* in an advanced state of meditation but the mind starts functioning as before when one gets up from meditation. *Sahaja samâdhi* is the state wherein the mind completely merges in the Reality. After this, the mind does not have any power to function independently. The person who has entered *sahaja samâdhi* can be blissful seeing his Real Nature in whatever object he sees.

Tuesday, 22 December 1981

At nine in the morning Mother was sitting under a coconut tree in front of the temple. Some *brahmachârins* came and sat around her. She said,

Mother: There is a lot of benefit in doing group meditation. The atmosphere gets permeated with the concentrated air of everyone and it becomes more conducive for doing meditation. Since eve-

110   AWAKEN, CHILDREN!

ryone's thought vibrations are of a similar pattern at that time, good concentration can be attained.

One *brahmacharin* liked to spend most of his time only in the presence of Mother. He asked, "Is my feeling correct?"

Mother: In the beginning stages attachment to the Guru's external form is good but the disciple should not observe the Guru's actions and try to judge him or her. In most cases the disciple becomes too attached to the Guru's external form and forgets about his all-pervasive nature. Attachment to the Guru's form supported by the awareness of his omniscience and all-pervasiveness is the perfect attitude. In the former case, which is more common, the disciple gets deluded due to lack of knowledge about the Guru's infinite nature and becomes an easy victim to all kinds of negative tendencies. Devotion to the Guru backed with the understanding of his higher nature is real devotion.

Mother paused for a while and then, fixing her eyes on the blue sky told, *"Balumon, sing a song."* He sang,

> O Thou Who appears as this illusory Universe
> filling it throughout,
> O Radiant One, won't Thou dawn in my mind
> and stay forever shedding Thy brilliance?
> I will surfeit myself drinking Thy motherly affection...

As the song went on, Mother sat motionless with her eyes still fixed on the expansive sky. Tears rolled down her cheeks. When the song was coming to the end, she laughed blissfully and pointed her index finger towards the sky, all the while uttering unintelligible words as if asking something of an unseen being, again and again bursting into a rapturous laughter. In a semi-conscious mood she turned to the *brahmachárins* and said,

Mother: Look here (pointing to her own body), this one's will has no separate existence from that One's Will. They are one and the same. If you take Mother as the body, then you cannot grow spiritually. Mother is not this body. She is her children's Self. Mother is ready to give all that she has to her children, but you should become deserving of it. Mother is always serving what her children need but you children are not yet ready to accept it.

Children, always think of the goal. Only if you have strength of your own can you serve others selflessly. What will you say when others ask you something (about spirituality)? Therefore, the scriptures should also be studied. Do not torture the body unnecessarily. Control of food should be gradual. You should meditate during the nighttime. Yogis will not sleep in the night, they will meditate. All of Nature becomes still at night. The vibrations of worldly activities diminish. Therefore, good concentration can be gained.

TO THE HOUSEHOLDERS

It was a *darshan* day and the householder devotees started coming one by one and in groups. Having saluted the Holy Mother, they all sat down. *Brahmachárin* Venu

was sitting near Mother fanning her while she distributed some
sweets brought by a householder devotee. While distributing
the *prasāda*, she sang:

> Hey Shiva who takes everyone,
> Take me also, hey Shiva...

(All laugh hearing Mother's song)

One devotee asked Mother if he could question her.
She replied, "*Shiva . . . yes, yes, . . . ask, ask.*"

Question: *Mother, is it possible to lead both a spiritual
and worldly life side by side?*
Mother: Certainly it is possible, son. But one
should be able to act selflessly. Sorrow comes
when we think, "I am doing. I must have the fruit of
it." A certain amount of detachment is needed.
Never think "my" wife, "my" child. When you consider everything as God's, then it is not possible to
be attached. When you die, wife and children will not
come with you, will they? God alone is Truth. A householder should also go to temples and ashrams.
Devotee: *To say all these things is easy, whereas, the difficult side of it is the practice. How can we do that? Can
Mother please say something about that?*
Mother: Children, it is not impossible because
nothing is impossible in this world, especially for
human beings. Strong determination and unshakable faith are the two factors needed for the success
of anything and everything. Mother clearly knows
that as far as a *grahasta* is concerned, it is not so easy
because of the pull from all directions. His mind is

much too involved in worldly affairs. Do your duty but do not get entangled in it. That is the problem. Suppose you are living in this world for eighty or ninety years. Why should you waste your entire energy only for enjoying worldly pleasures and fulfilling your desires? After all, think about what you are doing your whole life? Just repeating the same thing that you were doing the day before or jumping from one type of enjoyment to the next. Therefore, my children, slowly try to change your life. Out of thirty days in a month, at least spend two days for your spiritual development. Try to change your bad habits by gradually replacing them with good thoughts and actions. Every day before going to bed recollect the days activities and try to discriminate between the good and bad. Repent on the bad thoughts and actions. Make a strong determination to abstain from them the following day. The next day also do the same. Before going to bed, make a comparative study of the actions which you did that day and the previous day and see the differences. Pray to the Lord to bestow enough mental strength to fight against the negative tendencies. Surrender everything at His Feet. Have compassion for ailing humanity. Do charity for righteous purposes. Real charity or renunciation is giving up your dearest things. Actually, it is said that the mind should be offered to the Supreme. But the mind is immersed in money and other such worldy possessions. So offering money for righteous things is equal to offering our mind. Such actions will make your mind more and more expansive. Expansiveness is God. Let not your wealth be used only for fulfilling your desires and those of your family members. Let at least a small portion of it be used for the benefit of the world which in turn will purify you.

Another devotee asked: *Mother, you told us that house-holders should go to temples and ashrams, but there are many people who scoff at image worship. Why is this so?*

Mother: It is because of their ignorance about temples and the science behind image worship that they criticize. To put it in one sentence, the temple represents the body and the idol symbolizes *Atman,* the soul, which is situated in the sanctum sanctorum (innermost chamber) of the heart. The complete temple is the seeker's body in full prostration with all the *ádháras* including *sahasrára.* Ordinary people with gross intellects cannot conceive of a formless or nameless God which is His real nature. They need something to hold onto and someone to share their heart with. Being limited individuals, human beings are not satisfied with another limited being. Knowingly or unknowingly one is always in search of an infinite, Universal Person to whom one can unburden one's sorrow and find peace. The *rishis* knew that the people belonging to the forthcoming ages would be unable to grasp these subtle truths unless it was put in a different way. Thus the idea of temples dawned in their hearts to make Truth available even to the grossest. But we misinterpret it and make a mess. Whose fault? Whom to blame? Neither God nor the great forefathers, but us, us only.

In any case, son, why do you care if somebody out of utter ignorance says something about God or image worship? Let them babble. That is their lack of understanding. Let us pray and work to uplift them as well. But let our faith be unshakable.

Devotee: *What Mother says is perfectly true. If we can correct ourselves, then everything will become all right.*

Another devotee: *Mother, it is believed and said that one will get mental peace if one goes to temples and prays sincerely. How does that happen?*

Mother: It is true, but as you have said, sincerity should be there. We call "God" having looked at the idol once and then we close our eyes. Even then, we are looking within ourselves only. The case of meditation on God with form is also the same. We are meditating on our own Self. This means all other thoughts will be restrained and our mind will become concentrated on the image of God. This again means that there are no other thoughts, which cause all our external and internal problems and conflicts, except that one thought of God. Less thoughts means more peace of mind. More thoughts means less peace of mind. Moreover, when we go to a temple, the atmosphere is also calm because everyone stands there with one thought only. All minds will become one-pointed while waiting for the sanctum sanctorum to be opened and to behold God's image. The atmosphere there also becomes peaceful because of that concentrated thought. That is why we get peace when we go to temples.

Mother stopped and got absorbed in meditation. Opening her eyes, she called aloud, *"Sreemon, come with the harmonium."* Looking smilingly at the devotees, Mother told, *"Mere talking alone is not sufficient. Let us sing His glories. A little bit of practice too."* By that time Sreekumar had come with the harmonium followed by

Pai. Mother said, *"Pai mon, sing some verses"* Having saluted the Mother, Pai sang,

> *O Mother, I know neither the divine mantras nor the yantras which embody Thy Power, nor do I know any verses which praise Thy glories.*

> *O Mother, please tell me, there may be sons who are sinners on this earth, but is there a cruel mother?*

Hearing the Sanskrit verses, Mother became totally drawn inwards. Her body remained motionless. With half-closed eyes she sat there like a statue. Tears born of supreme bliss rolled down her cheeks and her face became most brilliant. Pai went on singing until he also burst into tears. Sreekumar who was playing the harmonium also slowly slid into a meditative mood. Everything became silent for a few minutes except the sobbings of Pai.

At this time, one *brahmachárin* burst into tears while embracing the Mother's feet. Do you know for what reason? He was thinking how fortunate he was to have Mother, the embodiment of innocent love and selflessness, as his Guru. How many devotees have wet those feet with their teardrops? How many are taking refuge at those holy feet? How many ailing people's teardrops have been wiped by those hands? Everything for others, nothing for herself.

When the Holy Mother emerged from her ecstatic mood, Krishna Shenoy, an ardent devotee of the Mother, arrived. He saluted Mother and sat near her. Mother, with a mischievious smile on her face exclaimed, *"Hey, Krishna, little thief, you got your job back, didn't you?"*

Krishna Shenoy was left speechless for a moment with an air of amazement on his face. Gazing at the Mother, he shed tears. He then fell at Mother's feet and cried like a small child. The Holy Mother, with great affection and love, carressed him and consoled him. The devotees who were standing around could not understand the meaning of all this. When Shenoy became normal, one of the devotees who was sitting near him asked, "What happened?"

Full of emotion, Shenoy said,

Shenoy: *How can I tell you? Everything is Mother's grace. After the last darshan, when I reached the factory where I work, the first thing I learned was that a suspension order was charged against me. It was for taking more holidays than was alloted without having officially informed the management. Those holidays were actually taken to come and see Mother. I became so crazy for Her after meeting Her. But the most astounding thing was that everything was straightened up within three hours and the suspension was withdrawn. How it happened I don't know. It is still a mystery. As far as I know, nobody supported me or recommended for the withdrawal of the suspension order.*

One devotee: *Who told you that nobody made a recommendation for you?*

Shenoy: *What do you mean?*

Devotee: *See, really I meant it. Don't you know that Mother was there to recommend for you? (All laugh)*

The first devotee: *But how did Mother know all about this?*

Shenoy: *That is a good question. Is there anything which Mother doesn't know?*

Mother: Yes, children, Mother knows one thing, that she doesn't know anything.

Question: *Mother, can you please tell us what we householders need?*

Mother: In olden days *Grahastâshrama* (householder life) and spirituality were led simultaneously. From the time of giving birth onwards, parents would chant mantras into the ears of their baby. Thus, the child would grow up hearing Godly mantras. Later, the child would be sent to a Gurukula.[52] There he or she would learn all the *Vedas* and *Sastras* (scriptures), observing perfect celibacy and practicing what they learnt. Later, having married a girl who had been raised in the same way, a man would become a *Grahastâshrami* and would lead a righteous life. They would serve others selflessly and feed those who came in hunger. They had no hesitation even to worship their feet.

Only for sustaining their family line would they procreate a child. The child was considered to be a portion of the husband which came out through the wife. When the child was in the womb of the mother, she would observe different kinds of religious vows. Because of that, the child who was born would become noble hearted, wise and a benefactor of the world. Both the husband and wife had perfect control over their minds and would never allow them to be influenced by petty emotions. The quality of thoughts of the woman during the period of pregnancy will influence the character of the child. The child born to a woman who maintains the remembrance of God during pregnancy will become a devotee. There is no doubt about that. From the day the child is born, the husband would see his wife as Mother. Later, having raised the child and made him

---

[52]Residential school of a Guru.

self-reliant, both the husband and wife would go to the forest and do *tapas*.[53]

But today everything is out of order because human beings have given up their intrinsic nature (*swadharma*). Great sages have written that in this *Kaliyuga* (dark age of materialism) people will be blind, deformed and with many other weaknesses.

> *Forests will become houses...*
> *Houses will become shops...*
> *Selling the temple, betel nuts*
> *Will be eaten...*
> *The father will be eaten by the son*
> *And son by the father...*

There will be only rain. There will not be any agricultural yield. Then there will be only excessive sunshine. The cause for all this is the selfishness and lack of mental purity of human beings.

Some more devotees came and prostrated before Mother. Having made some light talk with them, Mother went near the huts where the *brahmachārins* were staying. It was time for their meditation. Mother went to observe them.

Wednesday, 23 December 1981

THE MOTHER HEN AND HER CHICKS

Brahmachārin Venu was loudly singing Sri Sankara's *Nirvana Shatkam* sitting in his room :

---

[53]Austere penance.

*I am neither the mind, intellect, ego nor
memory;
Neither ears nor tongue nor the senses of smell and
sight;
Nor am I ether, earth, fire, water, or air;
I am Pure Awareness-Bliss,
I am Shiva! I am Shiva!*

Venu's nature was that of a child in those days and this
created a lot of problems for him. Constantly repeating
the Divine Name, he would do all the work entrusted to
him. One could always see his lips moving. Because of
this, sometimes his mind would lose its contact with the
external world and he would knock over or break bottles
that would happen to be near him. One day, Mother
scolded him for not having any external attention. She
said,

Mother: Son, constant remembrance of God is
good but if you cannot concentrate your mind on
the work that you are doing, then don't do it. Go
and meditate sitting somewhere. If God is everything, then work also is Him. Do your work as worship. You should not be careless while offering the
worship.

Hearing these words of the Mother, Venu felt a little
sad and went to his hut. It was then he sang the above
mentioned song. Having heard this, Mother again came
to his hut and said,

Mother: Son, nothing can be gained if we walk
around saying *"Shivoham"* (I am Shiva) in the beginning itself. If the egg is to be hatched, it must sit
under the mother hen to be incubated. They hatch

because of patiently sitting there that many days. Likewise, a *sâdhak* should perform *sâdhana* according to the Guru's instruction. It is not possible to hatch if you sit chanting *"Shivoham."* Would you say "I am a hen" before being hatched? Pure devotion is the best. That is the easiest. One should say, *"Dâsoham, Dâsoham"* (I am your servant) in the beginning. *"Shivoham"* is not something to be said. It is something to be verified through direct knowledge. If somebody beats you, is it possible for you to sit patiently thinking that he is Lord Shiva? If so, chant *"Shivoham."* Otherwise chant "Dâsoham" alone.

As Mother went out of Venu's hut she sang the following refrain of one song:

> *If Thou givest me another birth, then bestow the boon of taking birth as the servant of Thy servants forever.*

Thursday, 24th December 1981

It was a *Bhâva Darshan* day and there were many people to receive blessings from the Holy Mother. All of them were sitting in front of Mother. As she called the devotees one by one, keenly listening to their woeful stories, Mother bestowed peace and tranquillity on each of them, giving instructions according to their mental nature and reassuring them that she would always be with them. It was 2 p.m. when the daytime *darshan* was over. Getting up, Mother went to the hut of a *brahmachârin*. Having seen several things scattered here and there in the room, she said,

Mother: There should be order and discipline. In the olden days when a bridegroom went to see the bride for the first meeting to make the marriage proposal, he would judge the girl's character by observing the surroundings of the house and their cleanliness. Likewise, it is by seeing the character and orderliness of the children who stay with Mother in the ashram to do *sâdhana* that others learn.

Another *brahmachârin* came to the room where Mother was standing as he had become angry about something which somebody had said.

Mother: Son, imagine tht we are the servants of everyone. Children, suppose you become angry if somebody who comes here gets angry with you. If that happens, the mind should be immediately controlled, understanding that the ego in you is the cause of it.

Children, when you see a person for the first time, salute him. He may not salute back if he is an uncultured person. Again salute the next time you see him. That day also he may not return it. The next day also you salute him without any hesitation or hatred. Then he would think, "This man has been saluting me for the last two days and I haven't saluted him back. Again today he is saluting me. It is not correct that I don't salute him." Automatically he would salute. In a like manner, if there is virtue in us, we can make everyone good.

The *brahmachârin* listened to everything silently and full of remorse he prostrated at the Mother's feet.

The Mother walked towards her hut followed by Gayatri. At five in the evening, the *bhajan* before *Bhāva Darshan* began. The Holy Mother sang,

The sound OM is ringing everywhere
As an echo in every atom.
With a peaceful mind,
Let us chant "Om Shakti."

O Noble One Who is adored by the Universe,
We come to know Thee well
When this Universe is understood to be
worthless
Which so far was felt as great...

Sreekumar played the harmonium and Venu the drums. Balu and the other brahmachârins and devotees sang along with the Holy Mother. The Mother's songs were poignant with God-love, filling the atmosphere with waves of supreme devotion which penetrated the hearts of the *brahmachârins* and devotees. All were led into a meditative mood. It could be seen that some were silently shedding tears of inner joy.

Friday, 25th December 1981

DIFFICULT IS THE PATH OF KNOWLEDGE

At ten in the morning, Mother was giving *darshan* to the many devotees who were present. Some Westerners from Kanvashram in Varkala had just arrived. Most of them were newcomers. One of them named James was highly intellectual and did not believe in God with form. His strong conviction was that there is no truth beyond intelligence. He said, "There is a Cosmic Intelligence. I believe in that, not in Rama or Krishna or Christ. What I want is peace of mind which I don't have at all."

Mother: Son, if this is your belief, let it be so, but it is not correct to say that other paths are wrong and your path alone is true. You believe in a Cosmic Intelligence, do you not? That same Cosmic Intelligence we call Rama or Krishna or Christ. Whatever the path is, *sâdhana* should be performed and should be known through experience.

When we worship Rama, Krishna or Christ, we adore the eternal ideals which manifest through Them. If They were mere individuals, nobody would have worshipped Them. When They are worshipped, a true seeker is not adoring a limited individual but the same all-pervading Cosmic Intelligence which you believe is the only Truth. To climb a tree, we need a ladder or something else as a means. Nobody can simply reach the top of the tree in one leap. If somebody tries to do that, it is certain that he will fall down and break his arm or leg. (All laugh) These names and forms will serve as ladders to attain the Supreme without struggling too much. Anyhow, self-effort is implied in all paths. Self-effort and Grace are interdependent. Without one, the other is impossible.

The path of knowledge is possible only for a few who have the necessary mental disposition accumulated from the previous birth. Whichever is the path, it is not a problem if there is a real Guru. In meditation with form also we meditate on our own Self. During the midday when the sun is directly overhead, no shadow will be seen at all. Same is the case with meditation on a form. We become That. When you reach Perfection there is no shadow. No two. No illusion. Son, once you understand that from your own experience, Mother will not object. Anyhow, your path is a difficult one. Anything can be gained, attained, accomplished if there is faith. When you say, "Mine alone is true," think that it is the same Intelligence which you believe in as the same Truth that makes others also set out to work on their own paths.

Son, you yourself have said that you don't have mental peace. What is the use in saying "Intelligence, Intelligence" if there is no mental calmness?

Balu translated the Mother's words to James, who seemed very satisfied with her advice.

All the while, Ganga was sitting near Mother. It was obvious from the expression on his face that he had something on his mind. Before meeting Mother, he had been practising *átma dhyána* or meditation on one's Real Self. After seeing Mother, he had changed his meditation to *rúpa dhyána* or meditation on a form. Yet, he could not persist in it with the same enthusiasm and inspiration which he had in the beginning and felt a bit confused. He wanted to have his doubt cleared by Mother and was therefore waiting for her to finish her conversation with James.

Before Ganga could say anything, the Mother turned towards him at the end of her conversation with James and said,

Mother: Son, do *átma vichára* (self-enquiry) if you find it difficult to meditate on a form. You have more attraction to that, but more attention is needed in that path. Do not waste even a moment but continue to ask yourself "Who am I?" or think that "I am none of this" even during the work which you may be doing. Ramana Maharshi (Ganga's previous ideal) was a supreme devotee who had the attitude that "I am nothing." Now no one is applying that teaching of his. He did not want fame, yet that and everything else came of its own.

Ganga was happy to hear Mother's advice and at the same time astonished to find that Mother had understand what was on his mind even though he had not said anything about it to her. He became convinced that she was closely observing both his internal and extenal activities.

In the evening Mother went to a householder devotee's house in Quilon, some 35 kilometers away from the ashram. Every month this family would invite Mother and the *brahmachárins* to their house. Many people would come there to see Mother and listen to her *bhajans* and words. The day of Mother's visit was like a festival for them. Today Mother also took the Westerners with her. There were two cars. Mother, Balu, Gayatri, the mother of the family and her daughter with her three year old son travelled in one car. Five or six rode in the other car and the rest took a bus. The Holy Mother first enquired about their family affairs. Then slowly the subject turned to spiritual matters.

Mother: Children, don't think that you can start spiritual life after satisfying all your desires. The desires will go on and on. It is a never-ending circle. When one is satisfied, another one will occupy its place. If somebody thinks to take up spiritual life after fulfilling all his desires, he is like a person on the seashore who waits for all the waves to subside before taking a bath.

The housewife's daughter: *Mother, what is the way to overcome desires so that people like us can get closer to God?*

Mother: Daughter, the only way is to understand that each and every object that you desire is riddled with pain. If the desires are not controlled now, later they will control you and eventually they will swallow you. Mother doesn't say that you must give up all desires. You can enjoy them, but don't think that this life is only for that. That is dangerous. Let us control them gradually before their grip becomes too tight. Strong determination is needed. Try to lead a happy life with what you have. If you have more, give it to the poor and needy. For example, if you have twenty sarees, why can't you give at least two of them to those who don't even have one good saree? Usually rich people will purchase a minimum of two or sarees a day and then nicely arrange them in their closet. Every morning they will look at them and feel happy about their great achievement. No giving up at all. Children, just think for a moment. Is this the right way to live? Thousands of people are thrown in the midst of poverty and starvation and we go on enjoying. If all are God's children, then the poor are also His children. If so, they are our brothers and sisters who came from the womb of the same Mother. Instead of adding more and more to our existing negativities by creating more and more desires and fulfilling them by any means, why can't you help them? You can't take any of these so-called achievements from this world except the virtuous deeds that you have done. That alone will be there in the list of God. The final judgement entirely depends on that. Helping others results in helping ourselves to expand and to be purified. It will also help us a lot to gradually lessen the burden of attachment thus increasing the amount of peace.

As the talk went on, the three year old boy started to whimper. He caught hold of his mother's saree and asked for something to eat. As there weren't any edibles in the car, his mother said, "No, later when we reach home." The child kept quiet for a few moments, then again caught hold of her saree and repeated the same request. Now the mother became a bit angry and said, "Keep quiet. Let me listen to the Mother's words." But the child was hungry and could not keep quiet. After a few seconds he began crying out, "I want something to eat. I want something, I want something to eat." The mother this time became really angry and hit the child, pulling his hand from her saree. Now the child fell on his mother's lap bursting into tears, calling, "Amma...Amma..." Now the mother's face bloomed with love and affection for her child. Embracing him tightly and kissing both his cheeks several times, she consoled him uttering soothing words, "Mother's darling son...little thief, don't cry..." She asked the driver to stop the car and get some bananas for him which was immediately done.

Now the Holy Mother turned towards Balu and said,

Mother: Did you seen that? This is the correct attitude that a true seeker or devotee should have towards God or Guru. He may scold you or kick you out but don't loosen the hold. Like this innocent child, go on calling Him with more and more intensity. Go on asking while catching hold of His Feet. The relationship of the child to his mother is so strong that he didn't feel any hatred or anger towards her. Instead, he tightened his hold and finally laid down on her lap when she hit him. This was enough for the hidden compassion of the mother to overflow all its bounds. Son, this is the kind of attachment that a *sâdhak* should have towards God. Whatever happens, hold on to His Feet without loosening the grip even slightly. Then He is bound to shower His grace. Love with attachment to God is good but not with attachment to the world.

By this time, the group had reached Quilon and everyone alighted from the car. The family members led the Holy Mother into their house having worshipped her feet and offered *purnakumbha*.[54] The devotional singing started at 7 p.m. and the Mother's ecstatic singing went on until 10. Sometimes she burst into a blissful laughter while at other times she shed tears of joy. Occasionally she became lost to this world and sat motionless. All the devotees gathered there were full of bliss and remained spellbound until the end. After the *bhajan*, Mother gave *darshan* to all present. It was 12 o'clock when everything was over.

The Mother returned to the ashram at 1:15 a.m. She sat on the front verandah for sometime. All the Westerners sat around her. *Brahmachârin* Madhu, who was a native of Reunion Island, was there. He didn't know Malayalam. He was sad about it because he could neither understand what Mother said nor could he talk with her. Looking at him, Mother said,

---

[54]A pot full of consecrated water offered to God or holy persons as a form of reception.

Mother: Children, (referring to the Westerners) Mother is deaf and dumb in front of you and you too are in the same situation. Mother has seen your happiness when she utters any English words. Mother doesn't know your language. Mother knows that you are very sad about it. But Mother can understand the language of the heart. (Like an innocent child) Have you ever heard Mother speaking English? Yes, Mother knows some. (Pointing to Balu) He taught me a few words like (Mother recites, pausing after each word) "Open the door, congratulations." (All laugh - Mother also laughs - pointing to Sreekumar) He also taught me one or two words.

After a short pause Mother continued,

Mother: Others should be loved without any desire or expectation. You need not love me or respect me. I won't be bothered about it. Nor do I ask any of you to serve me. If you were to get involved in that you would become angry. You know, Mother is crazy, isn't she? Visualizing each and every atom of this world as the Truth, serve all with an attitude of equanimity. Equanimity is God.

Madhu: *There is hope for us. It will be easy if Mother can learn English. She can do it. (Mother smiles)*

Having spent a couple more minutes with them, Mother went to her hut.

Sunday, 27 December 1981

The Holy Mother always observes both the external and internal actions of the *brahmachárins* and instructs each one according to their mental consitution. Sometimes the instructions are general, at other times personal. These instructions are spontaneous and soul-stirring and come out irrespective of time and place. Sometimes it may happen in the middle of some work or while travelling or in the middle of devotional singing.

Today, while sitting with the *brahmachárins*, Mother said,

Mother: Either you should dedicate everything to Mother whom you say is all in all, considering everything as Mother's Will, or you should have faith in yourselves. Enquire in yourself believing that "I am the Self pervading the whole universe." Intentness to reach the goal should always be there. Attentiveness should be there while doing anything and everything.

SUBTLE BEINGS

The Holy Mother next went to the ashram library. A devotee who was sitting there reading then told the Mother about an experience he had with subtle beings. He asked, "Mother, are such experiences valid? Do subtle beings really exist?"

Mother: Everything depends on the mind. If you believe in their existence, then it is there. If not, then no. There are many beliefs which are not scientifically proven but they still remain as facts because they can be experienced or seen, not with these external eyes but with the inner eyes. We cannot simply deny them because we haven't seen them. After

all, have we seen or experienced even a corner of this
vast universe? Certainly not. Then how can we say that
they (subtle beings) do not exist? There are many
things that we cannot perceive with the external eyes
but they still exist. For example, look at that ray of sunlight which is entering the room through that hole in
the roof. You can see numerous dust particles moving
in it. Then why don't we see them when that shaft of
light is not there? Are they not there even when the
light is not coming? Yes. Likewise, subtle beings are
also there but our mind is not subtle enough to see
them. When the mind becomes clear and subtle
enough through *sâdhana* then one can see them.
But a *sâdhaka* should not give much importance to
such experiences. He must simply ignore them and
transcend them. This is nothing compared to the
experience that you are going to have. These silly
experiences will create obstacles on your path and
will distract your attention from the Real.

REAL GURU AND DISCIPLE

Another devotee: *Mother, what is the nature of a real*
Guru-sishya *(master-disciple) relationship?*
Mother: In a real Guru-sishya relationship it will
be difficult to recognise who is the Guru and who is
the disciple. The Guru would be a person who has a
more servant-like attitude than the disciple. The
only aim of the Guru will be the advancement of the
disciple. The Guru's sole intention is to somehow
mend (improve) the disciple. The Guru will observe
each and every action of the disciple. But the disciple

will not know it. Do you know how a real disciple will be? He will be one who serves the Guru with the attitude that the Guru shouldn't even know about his service. *Seva* (service) means obedience. Spontaneously, the Guru will shower his grace on that disciple who he sees moving with *sraddha* (faith). When the field is low, water will naturally flow into it. However high a mountain is, no water will get collected on the top of it. On the other hand, it will flow down into the stream. Son, humility and simplicity are the characteristics of a great soul.

At this time *brahmachârin* Venu approached Mother to clear one of his doubts.

Venu: *Mother, I have a big problem. I feel aversion to some people. What should I do to remove it?*

Mother: Son, are you not meditating on *Bhagavan's* (Lord Krishna's) form? Son, you ask Him, "Kanna! are You not the one who shines in me? Do You have hatred towards anyone? Is it not Your mind bereft of attachment and aversion that I should have?" We will not reach that Supreme Self if there is even an iota of selfishness.

Venu: *Mother, is it possible to completely remove likes and dislikes through meditation?*

Mother: Certainly! When the mind becomes pure through meditation, each atom can be seen as the form of one's meditation. Then we feel love towards all creatures.

We do not know anything. Everything is controlled by that Supreme Self. We are a log of wood in the water. Wherever the current carries it, there the wood goes. The wood doesn't have any power of its own. This "I" should become a corpse. Then only knowledge will dawn. If a corpse is put in water, it will move according to the course of the current. The corpse doesn't have the feeling of "I." God can be seen only if we develop this attitude. Either proceed according to His Will convinced that "Everything is You" or enquire "Who am I," having the strong conviction "Everything is in me."

One devotee who had been sent to a distant town for scriptural studies was at the ashram to spend a few days with the Holy Mother. He came and sat near Mother after saluting her.

Mother: (To the devotee) When you come back after completing your scriptural studies, don't waste time saying *"Shivoham, Shivoham"* without any experience. Without becoming a caretaker of someone else's wealth, become the owner of it. What is said in the scriptures should be brought into experience through *sádhana*. You will not get sweetness if "molasses" is written on a piece of paper and you lick it. Scriptures are pointers.

It was four in the afternoon and many devotees had arrived for the *Bháva Darshan*. They were all sitting around the Holy Mother on the verandah of the old temple. One householder devotee's family who had come for the first time was also there. Their daughter could sing devotional songs beautifully. Mother asked her to sing a song. She sang 'Atmávin Dukham'(Sorrow of the soul). That innocent girl's poignant song, full of love and devotion, stole the Mother's heart and she became lost to this world. Though there were about two hundred people sitting around Mother, complete silence pre-vailed. All silently gazed at the Holy Mother's face as if seeing an extraordinary sight.

The *Bhâva Darshan* started at 7 p.m. preceded by the usual devotional singing by the Holy Mother and the *brahmachârins*. The *Darshan* was over at 3 a.m. Werner, who had been sent to Tiruvannamalai, had arrived that day to spend a few days with Mother, so she talked with him for some time. He always had only one complaint; this was about the delay in attaining Self-Realization. The clock rang five when Mother went to the hut that day. There wasn't much time for her to take rest. Some devotees were waiting with a car to take the Holy Mother to Quilon to attend a pre-arranged program.

In the early morning itself the Mother with some *brahmachârins* and Gayatri went to their house. During the daytime, the *brahmachârins* conducted the reading of *Srimad Bhâgavatam* and chanted the Thousand Names of the Divine Mother. In the evening, many people came to participate in the *bhajan* and to receive the blessings of the Mother. After bhajan Mother herself distributed *prasâda* to everyone. With great enthusi-asm, Mother went on talking with the devotees, cutting jokes and enquiring about their family affairs. Since *Bhâva Darshan* was the previous night, Mother had not slept. Some of the close devotees felt very sad about this. At their persistant request, Mother finally went to bed at one o'clock. But, in a few minutes she again came out and straight away approached a person who had just arrived. Upon arrival, he discovered that Mother had just gone to bed. He felt very de-jected as he was a poor man who came from a far away place only to see Mother. He was cursing his own misfortune thinking, "I am a sinner; that is why I am not able to see Mother," when he saw Mother walking towards him. He could not control his emo-tions. Bursting into tears, he called aloud, "My compassionate Mother, it is so kind of you to come and see this worthless son." Mother spent a few minutes with him, consoled him and then went to her room at 2:30 a.m.

The next day Mother and the *brahmachárins* returned to the ashram by 3:30 p.m. In the middle of the journey Mother said,

Mother: God takes a body not for the knowers of the Self (*Vijñáni*). He doesn't need anything. God's Incarnation is to bring the *ajñáni* (ignorant) to the correct path. It is not necessary to improve the noble.

If the *brahmachárins* go to any householder's house, they should stand in front of the house. Go inside only if they invite you. If you enter the house, go into the *pooja* room and sit there. During the period of *sádhana*, you should not go to other rooms. Reply in a few words to the questions asked. Even then, do not forget the goal. Be very careful. We cannot understand the mental attitude of worldly people. Their thoughts will affect us also. The presence of a lustful woman will create lust even in a person with no lust. Butter will melt if kept near the fire. Keep this in mind.

The car stopped at the Vallickavu boat jetty and everyone alighted. The sun slowly journeyed to the western horizon. Having crossed the river, everyone reached the ashram premises. Hearing the pitiful cry of a goat, Mother hurried to that spot. A goat which had been raised by Mother's family was crying with great pain and lying on the ground. This goat had great love for the Holy Mother. The family members and a few devotees were standing around it helplessly watching. For a week it was afflicted by a disease in its udders. None of the treatments proved fruitful. The disease had continued to increase. By the time Mother reached the goat it was nearing its end. The Holy Mother, unable to watch the poor creature's struggle, sat at a distance and got lost in prayer and meditation. As everyone looked on, the goat approached the Holy Mother, crawling on its knees. Having reached her side, the poor animal placed its head on her lap and breathed its last gazing at her face. Seeing this extraordinary sight, all present there started singing Divine Names and chanted the sacred mantra *"Om Namah Shivaya"* with great devotion. A blessed death it was. Who knows what the goat may become in its next birth.

Friday, 1 January 1982

DISEASE AND MEDICINE

The Holy Mother was sitting in front of the dining hall. Ganga, Venu and some other devotees were also sitting near her. The devotees were all spiritual aspirants.

For the past few days, Mother had been very sick. She had been afflicted with a terrible cough and pain all over the body. The devotees, to express their love and concern, had brought different kinds of medicines. The Holy Mother, to fulfill their wish, drank from each bottle everyday. Out of his love and devotion to the Mother, Ganga became a little bit angry about her irregular and unsystematic way of taking medicines.

Ganga: *Why does Mother take all the medicines they bring?*

Mother: Son, they will bring it even if Mother says that she doesn't want it. Then, what will Mother do? It is for their happiness and satisfaction that Mother takes all these. If it is not taken they will become sad. Mother's disease won't go simply because of taking these medicines. The diseases of others are affecting Mother. That should be exhausted through suffering alone. You need not get angry with them. Why should you fear if you have faith in Mother? There is only one doctor to cure my disease - that Supreme Self alone.

One devotee: *Mother, can't you remove these diseases which you take from the devotees without undergoing suffering?*

Mother: Yes, they can be removed by burning them up in the Fire of Knowledge (*jñānāgni*). Even then, a little must be experienced and in order to show that by its very nature the body must undergo suffering, whether it is the body of a saint or a sinner, Mother accepts it. *Mahātmas* suffer in order to teach us renunciation (*tyāga*).

Another devotee: *Mother, can yogis live without air?*

Mother: Those who have reached a particular state can live without air. They can live merely by breathing air from within, without taking it from outside. They can live even if they go beyond the atmosphere.

ATTITUDE OF A SERVANT
INTENSE DISPASSION

Devotee: *Mother, no noticable progess is seen even though* sādhana *has been performed for a long time.*

Mother: Children, even if we sit all the twenty four hours with closed eyes, nothing will be gained if God's Grace is not there. God's Grace and Guru's Grace are one and the same. Many people come to Mother and say that they haven't had any spiritual experience inspite of their best efforts for many years. Children, presently what we are doing is like filling a tank by drawing water from a well from morning till evening and then putting a hole in it in the evening. What happens? All the water will flow out and the tank will become empty. All our efforts will be in vain. Likewise, children, we will do some kind of spiritual practice. But, the significant amount of energy which we acquire will be drained out by indulging in worldly activities. This is like producing sugar on one side and creating ants on the other. The ants will eat all the sugar.

One who does meditation can be understood from his character. His attitude will be "I am nothing." Humility will be there. We should have the mentality to prostrate to anyone without shame. The ego can be removed only if we develop an attitude that "I am the servant of everyone." Only then is God's Vision possible. Even four years is not needed if *sādhana* can be performed intensely. The goal can be attained within two or three years. Detachment should be there. Do you know what kind of dispassion it should be? Intense. Lying in the midst of a blazing fire, would we not call aloud screaming, "Save me, save me!" Forgetting body, mind and intellect, is there a call, a complete surrender to God? When we come close to death, when death stands before us, is it not so? God should be called just like that. Not much time is needed to attain the goal if God is constantly called like this.

Sunday, 3 January 1982

Though various medicines were given by different devotees, Mother's cough went on increasing. It was heart-breaking to see the Holy Mother coughing. This morning she again said to Balu, Nealu and Gayatri who were sitting near her, *"Don't worry children. In reality this is not bothering me as much as you think. It will only last for a few days or sometimes a couple of minutes. Anyhow, there is suffering even if it is only for a short period of time.*

Nealu: *Mother, why can't you stop taking different kinds of medicines? That is also harmful.*

Mother: Mother wants to show that these medicines can do nothing unless "She" wills. (Mother coughs for a long time holding onto Gayatri's shoulder while Gayatri softly rubs her back).

Balu: *Mother, it is already a week since this started. I can't bear to see Mother suffering like this. (His eyes become filled with tears).*

Mother: All right, no more medicines. This cough will go by tomorrow evening.

It was ten o'clock. Although she was very weak, the Holy Mother came out of her hut to see the devotees, and spent three hours with them. Nealu, Balu and Gayatri were wonderstruck at the tremendous enthusiasm which manifested in Mother while talking with the devotees.

Sundays are the most crowded days and many devotees had come. The Holy Mother received one and all. The cough troubled her several times, and the devotees were greatly pained at heart. A young man who was very devoted said, "Mother, it is unbearable to see you suffering. Give some of it to me."

Mother: (Laughingly) This love is good, but son, you know, it would be impossible for others to bear even an infinitesimal fraction of this weight. Son, Mother is not suffering at all. The body is suffering a little. That is quite natural. But Mother's mind is constantly revelling in the *Paramâtma*. Pain and pleasure are like the waves of the ocean. They come and go, but are only on the surface, beneath is calm and peaceful.

The daytime *darshan* finished at two-thirty. At four-thirty, the Holy Mother returned to begin the devotional singing before the *Bhâva Darshan*. She sang,

> *O blue clouds, how did you get this blue colour, this beautiful blue colour which is the colour of Nanda Kumara (Krishna) Who sported in Brindavan?*
>
> *O my beloved Lord, is Thy Will to make me drown in this excruciating pang of separation? O Lord of my life, O Beloved, my All in all, I am unable to go away from˜ Thee. Please abandon me not.*

The Mother was transported to another world. Her songs created wave after wave of devotional bliss. The devotees also sang aloud, clapping their hands, forgetting all about the surroundings. She again sang,

> *O Divine Mother, O Great Goddess, O Thou Whose nature is Illusion, O Creatress of the Universe, O Mother, I bow to Thee again and again...*
>
> *O Empress of the Universe, Blue sacred One, O Great Illusion with beautiful limbs, O Supreme Goddess, Thou art the Friend of the devotees granting both Liberation and bondage...*

The Mother entered the shrine at six-thirty and *Bhâva Darshan* started at seven, continuing until four o'clock the next morning. At the end of the *Darshan*, the Holy Mother sucked blood and pus from the wounds, especially those on his forehead, of the leper Dattan.

After *Darshan* Mother again spent some time with the devotees. At the end of *Devi Bhâva,* while Mother was still behind the closed doors of the temple, people could hear her coughing. What was amazing was that she had not coughed even once during the entire *Bhâva Darshan.* Finally, when she came out of the temple, she seemed like a mischievous innocent child, so brilliant and full of cheer. She moved among the devotees, cracking jokes and sometimes sitting on the lap of an elderly woman and playfully hitting one devotee on the back. Then she played with her pet black and white dog for some time, riding on him and playfully fighting with him. Even while doing all this, Mother coughed several times, but still went on with her innocent play until five o'clock when she finally went to bed due to the insistence of some of the devotees and *brahmachârins.*

Monday, 4 January 1982

The previous day Mother had stopped taking medicines, but still the cough did not subside. Today, during lunch she said, *"Don't worry about this body. Mother is not at all attached to it.* (Pointing to her body) *This is here to do service to others. This can be thrown away at any moment. The increase and decrease of its existence depends on the need."*

Today Mother fed one ball of rice to all those present with her own hands. At two-thirty she went to her hut accompanied by Gayatri.

The evening *bhajan* started as usual at six-thirty. The singing reached its peak as the Holy Mother sang,

O *Beautiful One, please come,*
O *Consort of Purandara (Lord Shiva),*

please come,
O Auspicious One, please come...

O Giver of radiance,
Thou art the All in all of those
Who consider Thee as their dear relation...

O Mother, please remain as the spring
of my inspiration...

Becoming intoxicated with God-love and standing up, the Mother began dancing ecstatically. The *brahma-chárins* went on singing with overflowing devotion. From the temple verandah the Mother moved towards the coconut trees in the front yard. Having reached there, the Mother went round and round completely lost to this world. She was showing a divine pose (*mudra*) with her right hand which was slightly raised. A beaming smile lit her face which was clear even in the dim light. This ecstatic mood had gone on for more than half an hour and it seemed as though there would be no end to it. Some sat near by and others at a distance watching the Mother. Some of the *brahmachárins* made a chain by holding hands to protect Mother from hitting the coconut trees. Eventually Sugunanandan, on account of his usual fear that his daughter would leave her body soon if this state persisted for a long time, appeared on the scene and without asking anybody's permission, carried her into the hut and laid her on a cot. Mother was totally lost to this world and her body now seemed like a corpse. Sugunanandan later related, 'The little one's body was so light in weight that it felt like I was lifting a basketful of flowers, but her face was glowing like the rising sun.'

It was only after two hours that the Mother came out of this deep *samádhi*. She asked for something to eat and Gayatri served her some rice and curry. She hardly ate two balls of rice. Then like a small child, she asked for peanuts and mixture (a combination of various titbits). Finally,

without eating anything, she got up and went away. The most
amazing thing was that as the Mother had said the previous day,
the cough had mysteriously disappeared. No symptoms of it
were seen from that evening onwards.

Wednesday, 12 May 1982

After the evening *bhajan*, Mother was sitting in front
of the temple with *brahmachârin* Venu and *brahmachârin*
Werner.

Venu: *Mother, can incense be lit during meditation?*
Mother: Children, you shouldn't. That will create
a distraction in the mind. The attention will be diverted to the smell. As far as a *sâdhak* is concerned,
it is not necessary. That is simply a sensual pleasure. It is impossible to control the mind without
conquering the senses. Whether it is food, fragrance,
women, whatever it may be, do not think that you can
satiate the desires by enjoying them. Each time that
you enjoy the pleasures of the senses, the *vâsanas* only
increase. (Pointing to her own head) Here there are all
five sense organs. (Pointing to the place between the
eyebrows) Here there is ambrosia also. But human
beings do not want that, they only want sensual pleasure which is equal to excreta.
Venu: *Mother, how can desire be controlled?*
Mother: Desire for anything will not rise up once
love for God arises. Attachment to other things
will automatically decrease. If intense love for
God comes, then that love is like one who is suffering from fever. A feverish person will not feel any
appetite at all. He will not feel anything if he sees

food, however delicious it may be. At present, control in everything is necessary for you due to the lack of intense love for God within. Because of our addiction to worldly pleasures we should physically refrain from them in the beginning. Thereby the tendency of the mind to enjoy them will gradually decrease. Through physical abstinence the mind can be controlled in due course. A drunkard cannot help drinking while seated in the midst of a hundred bottles of liquor. Therefore, first control physically.

Venu: *Mother, how can the "I" sense be destroyed?*

Mother: Either surrender everything to God or Guru and become the flute in His hands or have faith in "I" itself. It is good for a *sâdhak* to sit gazing skywards. There is no movement there at all, attributeless, formless. There is only undivided bliss. When looking down at the earth, we find ups and downs and other irregularities. There is no diversity in the Real Thing. Always be convinced "I am of the nature of *Satchidânanda*" (Pure Being-Awareness-Bliss). We can learn lessons from everything if we have *sraddha* (alertness). Everything is our Guru. Having imbibed the essence from any object, throw away the rest.

Sunday, 4 July 1982

Nowadays Werner is doing severe penance. For the past four days he had been meditating day and night without drinking even a glass of water. One *brahmachârin* told Mother about this. She replied,

Mother: I will not ask him to eat. You should also get such *vairâgya* (detachment). How much change has occured even in his complexion. It is a sign of getting closer to Truth. Let him continue his practice.

However, Mother did insist that Werner drink some tender coconut wafer. Then she said,

Mother: Remember that to blossom, a tree sheds its leaves. The flower of love is blossoming within, that is why your desires are falling away. But it is not enough if we alone attain Liberation through renunciation. It should also benefit all people. For that, this body should be taken care of. Not only that, we may have to take birth again if the body perishes before attaining Liberation and then the work will again increase.

Realizing with all humility that what the Holy Mother said was true, Werner started taking food from that day onwards. Mother said,

Mother: Ten *sâdhaks* like him is enough. I will become your servant if you are ready to sit like that. I will bring food for you to the place where you are sitting. Mother does not ask the one who meditates all the twenty-four hours to work.

A group of young men had arrived to see the Holy Mother. Some were still studying in college and others had finished. Among them onewas studying for his Master's degree in philosophy. Generally, such students would come only to ask some intricate questions to the Mother hoping to make her speechless. Only a few were really interested to learn from her. The former always returned disappointed or humbled as the Mother was always quick to reply with remarkable answers. The philosophy student asked, "Mother, have you taken *sannyâsa?*"

Mother: Namah Shivaya! Mother is one gone crazy. Some children came here. Mother told them that such and such is Truth. Mother did not ask them to believe. Mother has only told them, "Look within yourselves." They called me "Mother" and because of that I call them "children." Otherwise, Mother does not know anything more than that.

Young man: *Has Mother attained perfection?*

Mother: If Mother says, "I am perfect," then there is "I." Whereas, in the state of Perfection there is no sense of "I" at all. Not only that, such statements always have a feeling of ego implied in them. *Mahâtmas* set an example for the world through their humility and servant-like attitude, hoping that others will follow them. Therefore, Mother doesn't want to say such things. Above all, everything depends upon the children's faith.

The young men, particularly the one who had questioned Mother, appeared to be deeply contemplating Mother's statement about perfection. Afterwards, the philosophy student stopped asking questions and kept silent. Later, when they were about to leave, they met Balu and the philosophy student remarked, "To be frank, we came to corner her but we failed in the face of her wisdom, humility and simplicity."

Sunday, 8 August 1982

VASANAS
Tendencies

At 8 o'clock in the morning the atmosphere was calm and quiet except for the reverberating sound of the ocean waves. The ringing of the bell indicated that the morning worship was beginning. The chanting of the Thousand Names of the Divine Mother was heard emanating from the temple. The Holy Mother was meditating under a coconut tree near the backwaters. One *brahmachârin* came with a glass of tea for her. After some time she opened her eyes and gazed into the water for a long time, aimlessly throwing stones into it, enjoying the dance of light and shadow created by the ripples. There was a beautiful smile on the Mother's face. Having offered the tea to Mother, the *brahmachârin* sat nearby and asked, "Mother, I am unable to cry and call to God."

Mother: Son, sorrow should come if you truly long to become one with God. The attitude "You alone are enough for me" should come, while abandoning all other desires. There is no yearning because renunciation is not firm. The Vision of God will not be gained if an iota of ego lies within. The mind should become expansive. Everything should be seen as One. Compassion should be felt for the sorrow of others. Their difficulties should be felt as if they were our own.

Brahmachârin: *Mother, do* vâsanas *come from this birth or from the previous births?*

Mother: Child, the impressions created by the actions performed in the previous births are manifested in this birth. These inherited tendencies decide the course of action during this lifetime. What we should do is to exhaust them while doing spiritual practices and avoid adding new ones. Take ten eggs and keep them under a hen to hatch. Suppose that one of them is that of a duck, but the rest of them are chicken eggs. After being hatched, the duckling takes to water immediately when it sees it. But what about the baby chicks? Not a single one will go down to the water. This is the nature of *vâsana*. It is derived from previous births. If it was from this birth, was it not a hen who sat on the eggs? But the duckling does not show any traits of a hen.

The mother's thoughts during her pregnancy play an important part in the child's character. That is why in olden times a mother would always chant the Divine Name during pregnancy. If this is done, the child also will be one who remembers God.

As soon as a baby is born, he starts asking, *"Enge, enge?"* He is asking "Who am I? Where have I reached?" But what do we do? Suddenly taking the child, we breast feed it. The baby relishes the milk. Later, if we give fresh water it will not drink. It wants only sweetened milk. Then it experiences the comfort of the mother's contact. After some time it feels sad if it does not get milk. When milk is stopped, we give biscuits, bread, rice, etc. Why expatiate much? Thus the mother binds the child.

The first *vâsana* in a *jîva* (individual soul) is God-given. From that arises *karma* (action). From those actions arise new *vâsanas*. All these *vâsanas* accumulate as latent tendencies inherited from the previous birth and bring forth a new birth. This cycle will go on spinning like this. Liberation from *samsâra* (the birth-death cycle) is possible only through attenuation of the *vâsanas*. All spiritual practices like *satsang* (companionship with great souls), chanting the Divine Name, meditation and *japa* are helpful for weakening the *vâsanas*.

At this time another *brahmachârin* came to the Mother and asked, "Mother, what should be said at this evening's speech?" At the request of some of the devotees, Mother had agreed to send one of the *brahmachârins* to give a spiritual talk at a temple. He wanted to know from Mother the way in which he should present the subject.

Mother: Before talking about spiritual matters with anyone, you should first understand what sort of people they are. Many cannot understand if you use complicated, subtle *Vedantic* words when you speak. Only bread and milk can be given to a small child. His stomach will be in trouble if you give him rice and sweet pudding. When you talk with present day youths who do not believe in God, ask, "Let there be no God, but do you believe in 'I'?" We can tell them, "Try to know that 'I'." As far as possible, try to instill *bhaya bhakti* (devotion with reverence) in them. The world is benefited only by that.

Tuesday, 10 August 1982

SADHANA AND SCRIPTURAL STUDY

A discussion was going on about the syllabus that should be introduced for the *Vedanta* course which would be starting soon at the ashram. Some scholars and philosophy professors were present. Each one was offering his opinion about which teaching method and text should be used. Having listened to all the suggestions which were made, the Holy Mother said,

Mother: Mother gives importance to *sâdhana*. Scriptural knowledge is also necessary. But more time should be spent for *sâdhana*. Meditation should be done at least six hours each day. There is no benefit at all in mere studying. Having drawn the picture of a coconut tree, even if you think that you can quench your thirst by plucking a tender coconut from it, it is not possible. *Sâdhana* should also be there simultaneously with scriptural study. Then that will become a constant meditation. In any case, there must be innocence and sincerity in the work we are doing.

In the beginning stages, due to the power of the *vâsanas,* it is difficult to fix the mind firmly in meditation. At that time companionship with Great Souls is more beneficial. Meditation is also a type of *satsang*. There, the companionship is with God. But it will take some time for that state to come. In the beginning, *satsang* is more beneficial than meditation. *Satsang* can be a close association or companionship with a Self-Realised soul. It can also be discussing or listening to spiritual truths expressed by them, i.e., studying the scriptures. But studies shouldn't make one egoistic. Remember that everything is done to uproot the ego. In the former case, it is a direct physical, mental and intellectual relationship with a Great Soul. In the latter, it is also the same type of relationship, but indirectly, by studying, reflecting, and practicing their teaching. In both cases, the aspirant or devotee must have utter dedication and devotion supported by knowledge. In any case, in the presence of a living *Sadguru*, spiritual practice becomes smooth and less complicated. They are the souls with whom we must establish an unshakable relationship.

As Mother was talking, her mood suddenly and completely changed. In a semi-conscious state she said, "Everything is nothing but that Supreme Self alone. There is no form there, nor name, neither Krishna nor Rama, nor Incarnations." Mother entered into an abstracted mood. Her body became still and her face shone with the light of perfect peace. Everyone gazed at Mother with great devotion and wonder. One of the scholars sweetly sang:

> *Salutations to that all-pervading, all-knowing, omniscient, pure, attributeless, unchangeable, formless Omkâra, the Absolute Sound, the Unmanifest, the non-dual Turiya (the Fourth State of Reality beyond the three states of waking, dream and dreamless sleep), the Supreme Self.*

It took some time before Mother came down to the physical plane of consciousness. A few more minutes passed and then the bell for lunch was heard. All saluted the Holy Mother and moved off to the dining hall. As they were walking, the scholar who had chanted the Sanskrit verses said to his friend, "After hearing Mother's talk and seeing her state of *samâdhi,* I really feel sad to think how fruitless our long years of study have been. Yes, my friend, it was a waste." As he finished his sentence he turned and noticing a *brahmachârin*, he remarked, "Lucky fellow." That evening during the devotional singing, the Mother became intoxicated with divine love as she sang:

> *Aren't Thou my Mother, O aren't Thou the dear*
> *Mother Who wipes away one's tears?*

> *Aren't Thou the Mother of the fourteen worlds?*
> *O Mother, aren't Thou the Creatress of this*
> *world?*

> *Since how many days am I calling Thee, O Supreme*
> *Energy? Won't Thou come? Won't Thou come?*

Tears rolled down her cheeks. She laughed blissfully calling, "*Amma...Amma...!*" Now her mood was that of a perfect devotee crying for God's Vision with an overflowing heart. There were many devotees present and all were spellbound hearing the Mother's *bhajan*. Like her presence, her singing also gave tremendous solace to the devotees. Some sat in contemplation and others clapped their hands, their bodies swaying to the ecstatic music. The *brahmachârins* were also totally absorbed. It seemed like a kingdom of bliss.

Monday, 16 August 1982

After the evening *bhajan*, Mother sat with the *brahmachârins*. She called Gayatri and asked her to cut the apple offered by a devotee into small pieces which Mother then distributed it to all. As she was serving it she said,

Mother: Human beings can learn many things from Nature. For example, take an apple tree. It gives all its fruits to others, taking nothing for itself. Its very existence is for other living beings. Likewise, a river. Everyone comes and bathes in it. It washes away everyone's dirt, expecting nothing. It willingly accepts all the impurities and returns purity, sacrificing everything for others. Children, each and every object in this world teaches us sacrifice. If you observe closely, you can find that all of life is a sacrifice. Each one's life is a story of sacrifice. The husband sacrifices his life for his wife and the wife sacrifices hers for her husband, a mother for her children and the children for their family. Each one of us is sacrificing our lives in one way or another. But all of us are limited to our own little world. Without sacrifice, there is no world. Sacrificing everything for the good of the world is the greatest sacrifice. This little world of ours should evolve until it becomes the whole universe. As it grows, we can see our problems also dissolving slowly.

Brahmachârin: *Mother, is it possible to reach the goal only by sitting in a place and meditating with the eyes closed?*

Mother: Children, patience is *tapas*. Mental impurities will be removed if one patiently meditates constantly, sitting in one spot. If there is a Guru, the disciple only has to do *sâdhana* and the Guru will take care of the rest.

Brahmachârin: *Mother, it is said that Sri Krishna was a perfect Incarnation. Is that true?*

Mother: Children, if Sri Krishna is the ocean itself, then Sri Buddha, Jesus Christ and Sri Ramakrishna are each waves in the ocean. Sri Krishna is the embodiment of that Supreme Self having assumed a form.

Brahmachârin: *Doesn't a* Jñâni *attain Perfection when he gives up his body? Do such people come back?*

Mother: Children, that depends on their will. Just as a rubber ball bounces back if it is aimed and thrown at a particular spot, a *Jñâni,* having gone, can return according to the *sankalpa* which he made at the time of leaving his body. He would never think, "If I come back, I will have to suffer." *Jñânis* are ready to take any number of births for the upliftment of the world.

Tuesday, 17 August 1982

The time was ten in the morning and Mother was sitting with the devotees. Venu, Balu and Unni were also present.

Mother: Always move with faith. One who has faith (sraddha) will never swerve from the path. Remember the form of meditation while doing any work. When you see somebody, chant *"Hari Om"* or *"Nama Shivaya"* first. This will help to create Godly thoughts both in the other person and in ourselves. When you talk with someone, imagine them to be your form of meditation. Imagine the form of your meditation in the atmosphere while you travel in a boat or bus. Time will not be wasted if this is done.

Never become weak-minded. Do not see Mother only as this body. Sorrow will be the result if you children think that Mother is limited to this body. Always know that Mother is all-pervading. Have faith that Mother's Self and your Self are one.

Have the conviction, "I have power, everything is in me."

All human beings say "I, I." Therefore know that "I" is the same in all. That person is "I," this person is "I." Everyday some time should be spent in solitude. Soon after getting up in the morning, meditate for some time sitting on the bed. Then you will get alertness. It is not necessary to be concerned with purity and impurity at that time. At night before going to bed, contemplate on all the actions done that day and the things that you have thought. If you have committed any mistakes against someone, repent as you recollect all of them. This will be helpful so as not to repeat the same thing tomorrow. Many trees joined together are known as a forest. Many thoughts joined together are said to be the mind. Thoughts should be diligently controlled. Instruction should be given to the mind, "O mind, think only of good things today. You should not run after the objects that you see here and there. Many people will come to attract you. You should not even look at them. Stand firm in God alone."

Satsang should be done daily for some time. All of you children should gather together and discuss some spiritual subject. In this way, through various sādhanas, the mind should be concentrated on God.

Mother turned to Balu and asked, "Son, sing some songs."

O man, wandering around in search of worldly pleasure, have you peace of mind even for a moment?

*Without knowing the principles of virtuous living, you
are groping in the darkness of Illusion out of confusion.*

*Like the moth that rushes into the flame, you are
fruitlessly destroying yourself.*

Mother and the other devotees sang along.

Wednesday, 18 August 1982

The previous evening the *Bhâva Darshan* had ended
by 2 a.m. Due to the infrequency of bus services at night,
many of the devotees would leave the ashram early the
following morning at which time Mother would be in her
hut resting. Therefore, the devotees would stand outside the temple after the *Bhâva Darshan* had ended and
wait for Mother to come out, even after she had sat for
nine or ten hours continuously. Emerging from the
temple, the Mother would go to the waiting devotees
once more consoling them with a touch, word or look
until each one had been seen. Sometimes she would call
someone who had wanted to speak privately with her. Finally, she would walk around the grounds to make sure
that all her children had a place to sleep. Usually it would
be at least 4 or 5 o'clock in the morning before she went to
her hut to rest. This night was no different.

At 4 a.m. one devotee, Velayudhan Pillai, woke up and
called some other devotees as well: The Holy Mother had
agreed to visit his house that day and he was very happy.
Whether Mother had taken any rest cannot be known, as
she came from her hut at 5 a.m. ready to go. Some *brahmachârins*
and householder devotees joined Mother and set out for Velayudhan's house in Haripad, a village about 25 kilometres to
the north of Vallickavu.

His house and front yard had been so beautifully decorated to receive the Holy Mother that it seemed as if there
was a festival going on. Velayudhan's elderly mother and other

family members had come out of the house to receive the Mother at the front gate and lead her to the house.

It was a blissful day filled witn the reading of the *Srimad Bhâgavatam*, *satsang* and devotional singing led by Mother. After the *bhajan*, she got up in a semi-conscious mood and walked straight into the adjacent compound but did not stop there. Mother crossed that property and entered the next yard. Gayatri, Velayudhan's mother and several other devotees followed her. As she entered the second plot of land she said, *"Do not come."*

There was an old, small but beautiful Devi temple in that compound which belonged to one family. Mother entered the temple and sat there for a long time in deep meditation. Later, when she came out of the temple, she walked around it in a bliss-intoxicated mood for more than an hour. As she circumambulated the temple she raised her hands to the sky and sang:

> *O Mother, Supreme Goddess Kali,*
> *Today I will catch hold of You and devour You!*
> *Hear what I am saying!*
> *I was born under the star of death!*
>
> *A child born under such a planetary conjunc-*
> *tion devours it's own mother. So, either You eat*
> *me or I will eat You today itself!*

The family members were amazed as no one had mentioned a word about that temple to the Holy Mother. Later, while talking about that particular incident, Mother said, *"That temple is where many poojas (worship) were performed with concentration and devotion."* This was found out to be true when enquiries were made of the family who owned that temple.

Thursday, 19 August 1982

In the morning the Holy Mother was about to return to the ashram. As there was not enough space for everyone in the car, some were asked to go by bus.

One brahmachârin: *I will also ʃ by bus.*
Mother: Mother will neither say that you should or shouldn't go by bus because if she asks you to go, then you will say that she has no love for you. Son, you are too sensitive and are seeing Mother with the same attitude that you see the mother that gave birth to you. This Mother should be seen as the Mother of all. Then only can you grow spiritually.

The *brahmachârin* was about to get up and go in the bus when the Mother said, *"Son, you don't have to go by bus. Come in the car."* The Mother knew that even though he was boasting that he would go by bus, in reality, he didn't want to.

At 11:30 in the morning everyone returned to Vallickavu. After lunch while all the *brahmachârins* were still in the dining hall Mother came and told them,

Mother: Whatsoever Mother says, consider it to be for the good of the children. Sorrow arises because there is desire. There is no sorrow if you think, "Mother is my own." No one will make progress as long as there is selfish interest. You children should have the dedicated attitude of, "I have offered everything to my Mother, I have nothing of my own."

Today was a *Darshan* day and the devotional singing began at 5 o'clock as usual. Mother sang,

> Hare Kesava Govinda
> Vâsudeva   Jaganmaya
> Shiva Sankara Rudresa
> Nilakantha   Trilôchana
>
> Gopâla Mukunda Mâdhava
> Gopa Rakshaka Damodara
> Gauripati Shiva Shiva Hara
> Deva Deva Gangâdhara

Then,

> Parama Shiva Mâm Pâhi
> Sadâ Shiva Mâm Pâhi
> Sambho Shiva Mâm Pâhi
> Parama Shiva Mâm Pâhi
>
> Akshara Linga Mâm Pâhi
> Avyâya Linga Mâm Pâhi
> Akâsa Linga Mâm Pâhi
> Atma Linga Mâm Pâhi

Everyone became absorbed in the ecstatic singing.

Friday, 20 August 1982

The Holy Mother was sitting in her hut while Gayatri was serving her tea at 9 o'clock in the morning. The previous night *Darshan* had ended at 2:30 a.m. but Mother did not rest until 4:30 a.m. Even if she didn't sleep for days on end she was ever fresh and full of enthusiasm. The Holy Mother took the glass of tea from Gayatri's hand and after one sip, she put it down. With a frown on her face she turned to Gayatri and said,

Mother: Daughter Gayatri, you have not chanted even a single mantra while making this tea. If it was a householder who did this I would have forgiven them but you as a spiritual aspirant should be chanting your mantra at all times, especially when preparing something for Mother. Even the householder devotees are careful in chanting their mantra while making something for Mother.

Saying so, the Mother kept the tea aside without drinking it. Gayatri became dejected and stood there silently with her eyes downcast. It was true that she had forgotten to chant her mantra while preparing the tea, but that was only because she was in a hurry to make it while in the midst of numerous other urgent works. Realising the seriousness of her mistake, she felt repentant but took the incident as a good lesson to remind her that Mother was ever watching her inner movements.

At that moment, Venu entered Mother's hut and bowed before her. As she would do with everyone, she touched him and saluted.

Venu: *Mother, when somebody prostrates to you, why do you touch their body and salute them?*

Mother: Son, is not everything one and the same Truth? Mother bows down to the Truth. I bow down to my own Self.

Venu: *Didn't Mother tell me that the relationship between Mother and me is from a succession of several births? If so, I should have known the Truth in my previous birth, is it not? Then why was I allowed to lead a life in the world all these years?*

Mother: Light will be sought only if there is darkness.

One can renounce only if one understands the thing that is to be renounced. Must it not be known that such and such is untruth to understand that the Truth is God? For that, you should be in the world. *Jñāna* (Wisdom) will not be attained for individual souls within only one birth.

Brahmachârin: *Sometimes God will give everything to those who don't do any* sâdhana. *Yet He does not turn around and look even once at one who strives hard.*

Mother: God's nature is like that of a child. To some He will give. To some others He will not give. Goodness inherited from the previous birth should exist to become a worthy vessel for that. A Perfect Master is capable of seeing these subtle aspects which others cannot. God will become the servant of one who has innocence. However much they pay attention, no further progress will be there for those who do not have it. Do not worry about Grace as you have a Guru. It is enough if you do *sâdhana*. You children can know the Truth if you do *sâdhana* for four years as instructed by Mother. Many are not attaining anything even after doing years of *sâdhana*.

Brahmachârin: *Is God the servant of the devotee?*

Mother: Yes, He is the servant of His true devotee. A true devotee is one who takes everything as God's Will, both bad and good. In reality, there is nothing bad for him. Everything is seen as good and beautiful for a true devotee because for him, all is God so there is nothing to hate. Something is good and something else is bad only for a person who has likes and dislikes. But in the case of a real devotee, there are no likes and dislikes. He sees God's Divine Hand behind every experience and every act. For such a person, is there anything that could be called 'bad?' If he hates or dislikes something it is the same as hating God, which is unnatural to him. In his world there is only love. To such a devotee, God is his servant.

Mother suddenly entered an abstracted mood and as if from another world said,

Mother: Children, Mother is the servant of every-one of you. I do not have a particular dwelling place of my own. I dwell in the heart of all of you.

Brahmachârin: *Mother, you say, "Mother does not know anything; Mother is nobody" now and then. Why do you destroy our* sankalpa *(attitude that Mother knows everything) like this?*

Mother: Children, whatever Mother says, will there be a decrease in your *sankalpa*? Do you know what the attitude is of those who have reached Per-fection? It is, "I am everyone's servant." To say that "I am Brahman" is also movement. But there is no movement in Brahman. There is nothing to say when you reach there.

At this point in the conversation the Holy Mother got up and walked away towards the coconut grove.

It was after lunch and the Mother was lying on the bare ground in the dining hall. Her behavior was often strange and incomprehensible. There was no such thing as 'preference' and 'choice' for her. Most of the time she would do things as she felt. No one could insist that she do something or refrain from doing something unless she was in the mood of an innocent two-year old child. On such occassions, she would sometimes beg, request or do as someone bid.

One who closely observes Mother could distinguish the different moods and aspects which would manifest such as the Master, the Mother, the Father, an innocent child, the proficient administrator and organizer. But this same all-powerful Mother could at times be found lying in the muddy back waters, at other times in the scorching sun or pouring rain, in the sand or on the bare ground. Sometimes she would ask for a particular dish or edible and after it was brought she would taste a little bit of it and then stop eating it forever. Sometimes she would eat a lot, at other times very little. Sometimes it would happen that she would not eat any food at all for days.

Brahmachârin: *Mother, why are you so loving to small children?*

Mother: Previously, Mother would imagine children to be Krishna and talk to them, keeping them close beside her. Mother used to call them to come nearby saying that she would give them toffee. Playing and playing, she would see them as Krishna and get absorbed in meditation. Then Mother would completely forget about the children and after two or three hours would regain consciousness. Even at that time, those children would still be sitting there. As soon as Mother opened her eyes they would ask, "Auntie, toffee..." They were waiting for that.

Spending some time with children is a *sâdhana*. A child has all the signs of one who has reached Perfection. Children's innocence will reflect in us also. Forgetting everything, we will sit looking at them. *Vâsanas* are only in the seed form in them and have not yet manifested. Children have the eyes of one who has attained Perfection.

Brahmachârin: *Is it possible to verbally express the experience of reaching* Brahma Pâda *(the Absolute State)?*

Mother: Son, if someone were to give a beating to you, would it be possible to say how much your body pained? Just as a dumb person cannot speak about the taste of molasses after eating it, similarly it cannot be said that such and such is that experience. Mother has the conviction that all her spiritual children will have that experience. Other than that, there is no reason in telling all these things now.

Brahmachârin: *It is said that the mind of a Knower of the Self will always be fixed on the Truth. How is that possible?*

Mother: Son, a Knower of the Self has dissolved his mind completely through constant and intense spiritual practices as a result of which his mind is fully fixed on the Supreme. Because he is one with *That*, he can see everything as *That*. As is the mind, so is the man. When he sees an object, what he perceives is not the external appearance, but that which illumines it. For a goldsmith, all ornaments, in whatever shape, are nothing but gold. Likewise, for a Knower of *Brahman*, everything is nothing but *Brahman*. Even if he talks to someone, that person is also *Brahman*. He talks only for others, that is all.

The sun slowly sank below the western horizon. The auspicious twilight time arrived. The horizon remained red as if the

fire of separation from her beloved, the sun, was burning within.
The vibrations created by the poignant songs of the Holy
Mother filled the atmosphere with divinity and bliss. Her pierc-
ing voice transcended everyone elses as she sang,

> O Blissful One, O Absolute One,
> Whose form is of unsurpassed beauty,
> Crossing the six mystic centers, the yogis
> Come to know Thee, the Invaluable Treasure.
> Thy Glory, O Infinite Power,
> Is however, only slightly known to them...

The singing ended by 8 o'clock and was followed by
arati, the worship performed by waving burning camphor before the deity in the shrine. Afterwards, some
devotees sat inside the temple and others sat under the
coconut trees. Ganga and Madhu, two of the *brahmachârins,* went to the seaside. Mother was lying on the
southern side of the temple in the sand. After supper the
brahmachârins came and sat around the Holy Mother.
Gayatri was fanning her. The sound of the waves and the
blowing of the breeze from the sea made the atmosphere
calm and peaceful.

Venu: *Mother, what is the state of sleep like for one who
knows* Brahman?
Mother: Full awareness will be there. He knows
that he never sleeps. He will be a witness to the
sleeping state of his body. If you children try sincerely, you will have all these experiences.
Brahmachârin: *Mother, is it true that Brahma,
Vishnu and Maheswara (Shiva) exist?*
Mother: Due to the Primordial Resolve, vibration
arose in *Brahman.* From that arose the trigunas or
threefold qualities of Nature, *sattva* (goodness),

rajas (activity) and *tamas* (inertia). These three qualities are represented as the Trinity. All these are within
oneself. In this universe, all that we see is in fact existing
within. For example, sometimes a man will have the
cruel character of a tiger, sometimes the calm nature of
a deer, at other times, the forgetfulness of a lizard, the
changing colour of a chameleon and so on. All these
exist within. During a particular state of meditation,
we can grasp the essential principles from any object
we see. It will be possible for us to know the mind of
whomever we see. Those who are not under the super-
vision of a *Sadguru* will waste their time and energy to
measure others' minds during this state. This will obstruct their progress.

Brahmachârin: *Mother, Vivekananda did not have
the same amount of devotion to a personal God as Sri
Ramakrishna had, did he?*

Mother: Vivekanada had a *Sadguru* in Sri
Ramakrishna. He had firm devotion and faith in his
Guru. He who has a *Sadguru* does not have a par-
ticular God. The *Sadguru* himself is God.

Brahmachârin: *Mother, it is said that in order to test
Sri Ramakrishna, money was kept underneath his
pillow and he got up trembling. Why did he tremble
like that?*

Mother: If he trembled like that, it is felt by others
to be a weakness because then he would have seen
money as different from God. But for one who has
known *Brahman*, everything is *Brahman*. There is no
difference like good and bad. If difference arises, that is
duality. Truly there is no duality, is there? But that is
not the matter. Sri Ramakrishna was setting an ex-

ample to show how much distance a devotee and
sâdhak should keep from gold.

AVATAR AND JIVA
Incarnation and Individual Soul

Brahmachârin: *What is the difference between an Incarnation and an individual soul?*
Mother: Spiritual tendencies exist in a fully developed form in an *Avatâr* from birth itself whereas
others develop them through effort.

Do you know how that is? A great musician who
has the talent to sing from his birth will beautifully
sing any song within five minutes. An ordinary person cannot sing like that even if he works for five
hours at it. *Avataras* come with that inborn ability,
others have to develop that. Anyone can develop
spiritual qualities through constant practice.
Sâdhana should be done properly. Never become
lazy. Do not waste even a moment. In the olden
days Mother would not sit idle even for a moment.
She would always meditate. If someone would
come to talk, Mother would see them as the form of
Devi. They could talk as much as they liked.
Mother would not know anything. If one moment
was lost, Mother would feel terrible distress thinking, "O God, this much time was wasted." Then I
would do twice as much *sâdhana*. You will also get
the fruit if you try with an urgency like that. Being part
of God, all are incarnations. We call Perfect Knowers
of the Self, those who know *That*, as *Purna Jñânis*, as
Incarnations. Others whose knowledge is partial are
called *jîvas*.

Brahmachârin: *It is said that* Atman *is the root cause of everything. Therefore, it is* Atman *which causes the senses to function, isn't it? If so, why shouldn't* Atman *itself enjoy* karma phala *(the fruit of its actions)?*

Mother: In *vyavahâra* (the phenomenal world) there are two - *Paramâtma* and *jîvâtma*. It is the *jîvâtma* which experiences the *karma phala*. *Paramâtma* is only a witness to everything. *Paramâtma* is the platform or stage on which the drama of the world is being enacted. Without the stage there can be no drama but the stage still exists even without the drama. The Self is the Substratum on which all activities take place but It remains ever unaffected. It is inactive (*nishkriya*), (It) does nothing.

Brahmachârin: *Does one take birth even after attaining* Atmajñâna *(knowledge of the Self)?*

Mother: One may do so for the protection of the world by one's own will. Mother is ready to accept any number of births to serve the devotees and the suffering.

It was just past 10 o'clock at night. Mother told the *brahmachârins* to go to bed after meditating until 11 o'clock and went to her hut. One by one the *brahmachârins* got up and took their different places for meditation.

Saturday, 21 August 1982

At 6 o'clock in the morning the Mother, with some of the *brahmachârins,* was visiting a devotee's house in Quilon. About 25 people had come to see the Mother and to listen to the *bhajan*. Pai began by reading the *Devi Bhâgavatam*. Now and then the Mother also read a few lines. It was melodious to hear her reading. Sometimes she would abruptly stop reading and exclaim, *"Hey Mother! Everything is a play for You, but don't play your tricks with this one. Hey Kâli, You can't fool me. I am Your daughter, little Kâli!."* The devotees tremendously enjoyed this and laughed hearing the Holy Mother's recitation and seemingly light but significant utterances.

In the evening there was devotional singing led by Mother which went on from seven until ten followed by the chanting of the *Sri Lalita Sahasranama* led by Ganga. The whole house was filled with the bliss of devotion. Mother spent a great deal of time with the devotees after *the bhajan* had finished. The family members did all they could to serve Mother and the *brahmachârins* through their hospitality and great love and reverence.

KIRTANA IN THE KALIYUGA
Devotional Singing
In the Dark Age of Materialism

A group of devoted women were sitting around the Holy Mother. A few of them had taken a course on *Vedanta*. Mother said to them,

Mother: The goal is *Jñâna* and the means is *bhakti*. Children, *bhakti* is the path to *Jñâna*. Devotion with love for God should arise. In this age, more concentration is gained through *kirtana* (devotional singing) than through *dhyâna* (meditation). The reason is that the present atmosphere is always filled with different kinds of sound. Because of that, *dhyâna* will be difficult. Concentration will not be gained. This can be overcome if *kirtana* is performed. Not only that, the atmosphere will also become pure. Innocence will arise if one travels on the *bhakti marga* (path of devotion). All can be seen with the attitude of brotherhood.

A woman devotee: *Mother, isn't* jñâna marga *good?*

Mother: Daughter, *jñâna marga* is good, but very few can follow it correctly. If a real Guru is there, one can travel the path of knowledge. If the ego arises in the disciple, the Guru understands it and immediately corrects him. The disciple will not swerve from the path. If there is no Guru he will think, "I am *Brahman*. I can do anything; I have no attachment to anything," and he will be prepared to make any mistake.

A person who accepts the path of knowledge without having a Guru is like one who studies for an M.A. degree without attending the first grade. However, some will become followers of the *jñâna marga* by the inherited *samskâra* of the previous birth. From the beginning itself they will have the vision of light within.

A devotee will have *dâsatvam* (humility, servant-like attitude). The attitude that "I am nothing; everything is God" will come. Having this attitude, one will become a benefactor of the world.

Sunday, 22 August 1982

Mother started for Vallickavu from Quilon in the afternoon. On the way, she visited the homes of two devotees and blessed them. As the car proceeded to the ashram, Mother suddenly said, *"Son, stop the car. One son is lying prostrate crying in his house. Mother had told him that she would come. Quickly drive the car there."* Immediately the car headed for that house. Only after arriving did everyone understand why Mother was so particular about going to that house.

The head of the house was an ardent devotee of the Holy Mother. He was lying prostrate in the family shrine room weeping like a small child. His wife was standing near him totally dejected. Seeing the Mother approaching, he got up and burst into tears saying, "Mother, I thought that I must be a great sinner. Why should I live after coming to know that Mother had gone back to Vallickavu after she had told me that she would visit?" Mother replied, *"How could Mother go back when you were weeping so much, thinking of her? My son, your innocence and love stopped Mother from proceeding."*

With great affection, Mother consoled the devotee and sang a few songs in the shrine room and afterwards she did the *arati*. The devotee was very happy seeing all this. After taking leave of the devotee and his family, Mother again proceeded to the ashram.

It was four-thirty when she arrived and many devotees had gathered for the *Bhāva Darshan* that evening. Mother straightaway sat for *bhajan* and it was amazing to see her fully energetic even after the journey and the two days of outside programmes. All the others were quite exhausted.

Krishna and *Devi Bhāva* ended by 3 a.m. Afterwards, Mother came out of the temple and herself began spreading sheets and mats out for the devotees. Some of the devotees prayed for her to go and take rest. Mother replied, *"How can Mother be inside the hut when all the children are lying outside exposed to the cold? You children say that Mother should sleep. Likewise, Mother also thinks that you children should sleep comfortably."*

Monday, 23 August 1982

CONTROL OF FOOD

Mother was sitting in front of the temple with the *brahmachārins* at 5:30 in the evening. Venu asked, "Mother, what is the reason for dietary restrictions?"

Mother: In the beginning stages *sâdhaks* should observe such rules closely. Do not eat too much delicious food. As far as possible, avoid chillies and oil. Semen will increase if fat accumulates in the body. If the desire for tasty food increases, the passions in the body will increase. Diluted milk and fruit can be taken moderately. It is better not to take food in the morning. At night, only a little food should be taken. Half of the stomach should be for food, a quarter of the stomach for water, and the remaining portion for the movement of air. A little sweet can be taken. Salt should be decreased.

At a particular stage of meditation, one may feel terrible hunger. There are different kinds of roots and leaves in Nature. If those are eaten, hunger will not be felt. In the highest state of meditation, food can be given up altogether. One can live for any length of time on the *prâna* (vital force) taken from within. Tasty or otherwise, every food is the same for one who has attained Perfection. He can travel in any world. He will not have attachment to anything. He is beyond likes and dislikes.

EKAGRATA
One-pointedness

Brahmachârin: *Mother, what is the goal of doing sâdhana?*
Mother: One-pointedness alone, son. Always practice sitting in one *âsana* (posture). *Asana siddhi* (perfection in sitting unmoved) should be acquired. We should be able to sit three and a half hours

at a stretch. The spine will be held correctly if we sit in *padmásana* (the lotus posture). One must attain concentration somehow. Wherever a man of one-pointedness may go, he will have no problems. He can travel in any world. He will never swerve. One who has concentration can bring others to spirituality with only one look. Even other living creatures who touch the spittle of a Realized Being will attain Liberation. Even the mere ants creeping along his path will attain Salvation. A *sádhak* should meditate at least eight hours each day. External actions should be done during the remaining time. Sleep should be reduced. At a particular stage of meditation, sleep will spontaneously diminish.

It was dusk and the soul-stirring songs of the Mother resonated in the atmosphere sanctifying the whole village. She sang in a God-intoxicated mood,

> *O Mother Divine, the Eternal Virgin, I bow to Thee for Thy gracious glance.*

> *O Maya, Mother of the Universe, O Pure Awareness-Bliss, O Beloved Great Goddess, I bow to Thee.*

> *O Mind of the mind, O Dearest Mother, I am just a mere worm in Thy play...*

As the song ended, she became totally absorbed in a transcendental state. Alone in her own world, she got up from her seat showing a divine pose (mudra) with her right hand uplifted. She gently swayed from side to side in that mood of inexpressible divine bliss.

Those who stand on the shore can only see the flag of the ship which passes across the mid-ocean. The ship will be completely invisible. Likewise, we stand gazing at the moving image of the Holy Mother. Where is her real form hidden? Her divine nature is concealed from us beneath the layers of this ocean of ever-changing Illusion.

Saturday, 28 August 1982

The time was 9:30 in the morning and the devotees were preparing flower petals for the *Devi puja*. Mother was also there and joined them in the preparations. She told the devotees,

Mother: Fixing the mind in each external action, we should proceed with attention (*sraddha*). *Sraddha* is most necessary. Every action should be done as an offering to God. Without external alertness, internal alertness is not possible. If *samatva buddhi* (equal-mindedness) is there, *shânti* (peace) will arise. Everything should be seen as One. There is nobody to be hated if we see that others and oneself are one.

DHYANA AND BRAHMANUBHUTI
Meditation and Experience Of the Absolute

After the worship was completed, Venu came to sit near the Holy Mother and asked, "Mother, however much I try, I am not getting my *dhyâna rûpam* (one's form of meditation) clearly. Why is it so?"

Mother: Son, at least a minimum of four years is needed for the form to become full within. In the beginning stages one should try to attain concentration by sitting and looking at the form. If you sit with closed eyes for ten minutes, then the next ten minutes should be spent looking at the picture of one's form of meditation. First external alertness is what is necessary. If there is no alertness in one's external nature it will not be possible to conquer the internal nature *(antarika prakriti)*. There is nothing else to know once one knows that one is *Brahman*. There everything is full.

Brahmachârin: *Mother, what is the state of* Brahmânubhûti *(experience of the Absolute)?*

Mother: *Anandam* (bliss). No happiness or sorrow. No "I" and "you." It can be compared to deep sleep, but in that state complete awareness will be there. In deep sleep there is no awareness, is it not? In sleep there is no "I" and "you." Once we wake up there comes I, you, yesterday, today, etc. *Sahaja samâdhi* (the natural state of abidance in the Absolute) is *pûrnam* (fullness, perfection). There the mind attains complete absorption.

Brahmachârin: *Sri Ramakrishna used to pray, "O Mother, do not make me mad with Brahmajñâna (the knowledge of Brahman). It is enough for me to become Your child." Why was that?*

Mother: Form is a ladder on the path of devotion. The devotee loves to be God's servant even after attaining *Brahmajñâna*. A true devotee's wish is to continue as such even after attaining the supreme state of *Brahmajñâna*. In order to drink the sweetness of devotion, he will again come down and will intentionally retain the devotional attitude. No one would be satisfied once they had enjoyed the *rasa* (essence or sweetness) of *bhakti*. Didn't Sri Krishna Himself incarnate as *Gauranga* just to know the *rasa* of *Râdha bhâva*?[55] Children, the sweetness of devotion is something unique.

Brahman has no name or form. It is infinite like the sky. Knowledge is eternal. When we are in name and form we are in the non-eternal. With his *sankalpa*, the devotee can again do *rûpa dhyâna*, that is, meditation on the form of his Beloved Deity even after becoming one with the Absolute.

As described by the great sage Narada in his classic work on devotion, *Narada Bhakti Sutras*, all the signs of *parâbhakti* (supreme devotion) are manifest in the the Holy Mother. For instance, in the days when she was performing *sâdhana* to realise the Divine Mother, she would suffer excruciating pain of separation from God. If she happened to forget the Divine Name even for a single moment she would feel extremely dejected thinking of the lost time. To make up for that, she would chant or meditate with more intensity. Mother would also see everything as Devi and in that mood she would embrace the trees actually feeling them to be Devi. Sometime she would sit for a long time on the banks of the backwaters touching her nose on the surface of the water as if kissing the ripples. If she happened to see any women or girls dressed in sarees at this time, Mother would run to them and embrace them calling *"Amma, Amma!"* Now the Holy Mother was sharing her own experiences with her children and devotees. She told, *"Even now I am struggling hard to keep my mind down, especially while singing bhajans. It is always shooting up."*

Mother continued by explaining,

Mother: While taking each flower into your hand

---

[55]Gauranga or Chaitanya Mahaprabhu of Bengal had the attitude of Radha, Sri Krishna's Beloved, His greatest devotee.

to offer during the *archana* (the chanting of the Thousand Names of the Divine Mother), the Beloved Deity's form should be remembered within. Then it should be imagined that the flower of the mind is being offered to God. Alertness *(sraddha)* is what is necessary. It is enough if you have *sraddha, sahôdhara buddhi* (brotherly attitude) and complete faith. Progress will occur by and by. If there arises one iota of ego in the *brahmachârin* children's hearts, Mother will rub it and remove it that moment itself. Mother is ready to take any number of births to serve the devotees, but Mother cannot become the servant of ego.

The bell was rung for lunch. There were no visitors today, only *brahmachârins*. Mother came to the dining hall and laid down on the floor. Calling aloud, "Shiva...Shiva...Shiva...," she playfully pummeled those who were sitting nearby. Some of the children would purposely sit close to Mother simply to receive these playful beatings when she was in that mood. They considered it a great blessing.

As the *brahmachârins* watched Mother, her mood took a sudden change and she began rolling on the ground with her hands showing a divine *mudra*. Her mind soared to some unknown plane. Her eyes were closed in an absorbed state and her body became still. Gayatri fanned her. Some of the *brahmachârins* closely observed her and others sat for meditation. It was almost one hour before Mother returned to this world of appearances. When she opened her eyes she said, *"I am thirsty, bring some water."* The Holy Mother would say, *"If Mother expresses a desire it is only to give you a chance to serve. It will also help me to keep the mind down."*

Wednesday, 1 September 1982

Today Mother was visiting *brahmachârini* Vimala's house in

Vallickavu. From the very beginning of the Mother's divine moods that family had been extremely devoted to her.

Mother was sitting in the backyard of their house. It was 5 o'clock in the afternoon. The atmosphere was calm and quiet. Their family deity was the snake god and there were small shrines situated randomly in the yard. On the western side of the old style Kerala house, there were bushes, flowering plants and creepers. On the whole, the property looked like a hermitage. Pai, Ganga, Balu, Venu, Ramakrishna, Gayatri, Vimala and the elderly mother of the house were sitting near the Holy Mother. Venu asked about his Sanskrit studies.

Mother: Venu is a bit crazy about Sanskrit but fascination for anything except God is dangerous.

Pai: *Mother, for one who leaves his body after reaching the Supreme State, is there another birth?*

Mother: Only if he wishes. Even after giving up the body, he can maintain a subtle, separate existence according to his own *sankalpa*. He will not completely dissolve in *Brahman*. By his own self-will he will again accept a body. This coming back is for the benefit of the world.

SARVATRA SAMADARSHINAHA
Seeing all as One

Venu: *What kind of actions are you expecting from me, Mother?*

Mother: Son, selfless service, even-mindedness, seeing good even in the mistakes of others, these are things which Mother likes. If you children love Mother, you should love and serve all these living beings that are seen. Then only can it be said that

you children love Mother. Do not think only about
your own comfort. Do not think even for a moment
about the body that "This is my body." See everything as your own *Atman*. Whatever others tell you,
listen carefully and observe even-mindedness *(sama
chittata)*. Talk to them only after they finish speaking
to you. Aversion should not be felt towards anyone.
Like a river flowing without hindrance, let your mind
flow with the sound *"Hrîm."* Unbroken remembrance
of God should be there like the links of a chain. That
cool air will give freshness to everyone. Whomever
you see, remember God's Form. Then everything will
rise up from within.

Son, there is only one Self. That is omnipresent and
omnipotent. When our mind becomes expansive we
can merge with the Infinite. Then there will be no selfishness nor ego because Infinity means vastness. There
everything is equal. Serve others without wasting
even a moment. Help the suffering. Do not expect anything from anyone mentally or physically. For a *sannyâsin* there is no particular God dwelling in the sky.
Both heaven and hell are on earth alone. There is only
one thing he has to do, which is to see God in everything. For a true seeker, the Guru is everything. In fact,
the Guru and God are one and the Guru's will is God's
Will.

Usually the Guru will give the ochre cloth to the
disciple only when he has reached an advanced
spiritual state. That is, when the disciple does not
pray for any selfish things anymore. God has no
form nor taste. He is infinite. When our ignorance
is removed we can see everything equally in any
circumstance.

Ganga was also sitting nearby listening to all that Mother was saying. He was looking down hanging his head. Turning to him, she said,

Mother: Son, you had a desire to wear ochre cloth. You believed that it would help you to overcome worldly desires. Mother has caught you because during the time when you came here, goodness was already obscure. You always talked about *Brahman*. As far as you were concerned, there was no God. You thought that only Ramana Maharshi was great and that no one else had any greatness. Even then, you did not try to understand who Ramana really was. You have seen that "person" alone. You did not try to study him. You did not think about his equal vision, selfless service and devotion. You were only convinced "I am the greatest." Darling son, at least now, correct that ignorance.

5 September 1982

GURU MAHIMA
Guru's Glory

A woman named Mahatti from Tamil Nadu who was doing her doctoral research came to see the Holy Mother. From a very young age Mahatti had been interested in spiritual matters. *Brahmachârin* Madhu from Reunion Island had told her about Mother. She needed an interpreter, so Mother sent for one of the *brahmachârins*.

However, that *brahmachârin* had been scolded that morning by Mother for not milking the cow at the usual time. He replied, "I can't" in a tone as if he were talking to his biological mother. Mother calmly replied, *"Son, you can tell anything to Mother. Mother will forgive. But at that moment itself Nature has recorded your words and you will not get forgiveness from that. Such words should never come from one who meditates."* Mother called another of the *brahmachārins* and the talk began.

Mahatti told Mother about certain spiritual experiences which she had and sought her instructions regarding her path for further spiritual attainment.

Mother: Daughter, do you have a personal deity?

Mahatti: *No, I don't. I have no inclination at all towards any form of God or Goddess. But I have an intense thirst to realise the formless Self.*

Mother: Daughter, name and form are ladders to reach the Formless. We who are limited cannot conceive of the Unlimited. A form is needed to reach the Formless. Another thorn is needed to remove the thorn which has pierced our foot. Once the thorn is removed, both can be discarded. Likewise, after reaching the Ultimate Goal you can abandon all names and forms if you want. Child, even when you meditate on the formless Self you need a pure conception which is nothing but a thought. That is also a concept, is it not? Even when you meditate on the form of a God or Goddess, you are not meditating on an external object but only on your own Self.

Mahatti: *That is a convincing point but can't Mother suggest another method which suits my mind?*

Mother: Mother can understand your difficulty in following meditation on a form. Therefore, you can do one thing. Whenever you feel like it and have the time, sit in solitude and try to visualise everything as pure light. Look at the vast sky and try to merge in that expansiveness. Look within and observe the thoughts and trace them back to their source. Give instructions to the mind such as, "O mind, why do you crave for unnecessary things? You think that this will give you happiness and satisfy you. But it is not so. Know that this will only drain your energy and give you nothing but restlessness and unending tension. O mind, stop this wandering. Return to your source and rest in peace." Try this, daughter. This will enable you to gain peace and tranquillity.

Hearing the words of the Mother, Mahatti's face became bright and her smile revealed her inner contentment. "Mother, I am so happy to hear such an instruction befitting my mental constitution. I am very grateful to you for this valuable piece of advice which will help a lot in my search to realise the Supreme." Mother affectionately patted her back as she prostrated.

Mother came out of the hut to see the other devotees who were waiting. She sat in front of the temple on the verandah. The devotees one by one prostrated to her and sat nearby. A few of the *brahmachârins* were also present and one of them seemed to be dejected. Mother enquired about the reason. Even though she is aware of everything, she also knows the soothing affect of her motherly enquiry on the hearts of her children.

Brahmachârin: *Mother, before seeing you I was a devotee of Lord Krishna, but now there is nothing like that. Everything is Mother alone.*

Mother: Son, one who has a real Guru will have no other particular God. One can say that God and I are one, but a disciple will always have a higher place in his

mind for the Guru than for God. Son, don't think that
the Guru and one's Beloved Deity are two. In reality,
they are one and the same.

Brahmachârin: *Mother, what are the books suitable
for us to read?*

Mother: The *Srimad Bhâgavatam* is good. All the
inner principles are explained in it. A storyteller
will not start telling the story from the very beginning.
At first, he will amuse the people by telling certain
other incidents. Once they start paying attention then
he will begin the real story. Likewise, in the *Bhâgavatam*. Many interesting stories are told. Telling and telling these stories, they will gradually enter into discussing the Real Principle. It is enough to read the eleventh
chapter only. All principles are contained in it.

In the beginning stages aspirants should only read
books like the *Bhagavad Gîta,* the *Bhâgavatam* and the
life and teachings of great saints and sages. Devotion
must be developed first and then *jñâna.* Otherwise
egotism will develop. After reading the *Advaitic* book,
"I am That," Venu is imitating certain things without
understanding the real principle of the things which
were said in it. What Nisargadatta Maharaj says is that
he served his Guru with faith for three years. He had
perfect devotion to his Guru. It was in the end that he
said, "I am That, the Brahman."

Brahmachârin: *Is meditation on a form necessary,
Mother?*

Mother: Son, when we meditate on a form, it is not
the form but we who get peace and concentration.
In *rûpa dhyâna, laya* (dissolution of the mind) will take
place. In reality, even then we are meditating on our

own self. Form is a ladder. After some time it will be felt that form is a mere shadow. All experiences will be gained from this.

Wednesday, 8 September 1982

Today, Mother visited Srimati Mohanan's house in Quilon. She was an ardent devotee of the Holy Mother. The *brahmachârins* also came. In her excitement, Mohanan was running here and there, not knowing how to welcome and serve Mother.

It was 10 o'clock in the morning. Mother sat on the front verandah conversing with Mohanan. She asked, "Mother, while in the state of *Krishna Bhâva*, will you return to your normal state now and then?"

Mother: No, only Krishna alone. There are many who are still not aware that Mother is assuming *Krishna* and *Devi Bhâvas* by self-will nor that Mother and Krishna are one. Even then, they have a special love and reverence for Mother. Mother will only strengthen the faith of those who believe her to be two. Mother would say that is helpful for the progress of their devotion. The feeling that both are one will shake their devotion. *Bhaya bhakti* (reverential devotion) will go. Mother will play with them and crack jokes, is it not? That is why they also will think that "This innocent child (the Holy Mother) cannot be Krishna or Devi." How many things each one tells to Mother during *Bhâva Darshan* which they would not tell to Mother at ordinary times. These people's belief is that after Devi and Krishna have heard, they will go away and nobody will know anything that has been told.

The *brahmachárins* felt a little sad at heart to hear Mother's reply. When Mohanan went to the kitchen, Mother turned to them and said,

Mother: You believe that everything is Mother, but do not try to make others, who see Mother and Devi or Krishna as two, understand this thing. They get great benefit from the attitude of two.

It was afternoon and Mother was lying on a cot in the inner apartment of the house. Mohanan was fanning her while her two children sat near Mother with her head and feet on their laps. A few of the *brahmachárins* were sitting on the floor. Mother told them,

Mother: If one practices celibacy for 12 years, a new nerve will be created in the body. The power of the seed which ordinary man throws away for the sake of trivial enjoyment is what is changed into nectar in a yogi. As concentration deepens, the length of the tongue will increase and then, bending back, it will rise towards the top of the head through a hole in the uvula (palate). During a particular state of meditation some will drink this nectar by slightly severing the tendon that joins the tongue to the throat. Thus, if a single drop is imbibed, they become immortal. This is the inner meaning of the saying that the gods used to quaff nectar. Remember that it is this power which is lost each time a drop of semen is lost. Such discharges will take place both in men and women after the age of fifteen. Sometimes this loss will occur while dreaming also. This will not happen if we are alert during sleep. Do not use much oil. Wherever you go, try to overcome any attraction to women by seeing everyone as your Mother. If a lustful woman passes by, that is enough to make a lustless man become lustful. We can experience real liquor and ganja if the power of celibacy is acquired. Just like a good drunkard, we will experience an intoxicated state at certain stages of meditation. That experience is lasting whereas the happiness gained from liquor and ganja is fleeting.

Brahmachârin: *Even though I have done intense sâdhana for this many years, my mind is not becoming still. It is due to the lack of Mother's Grace. Therefore I am going to commence a vow of silence and fasting from tomorrow onwards.*

Mother: Son, how will you get Grace as long as you think "I am doing?" On the contrary, you do not have the attitude of surrender characterised by the feeling that "I have offered everything to Mother, Mother will save me." This is not *sannyâsa*. Mother will not let you walk along whatever path you like. Your thought should be, "I am doing *sâdhana* not for my own selfish purposes but for the world." Son, do your *sâdhana* sincerely with utmost care. Don't waste your energy thinking of the fruit. It must come if your effort is sincere and intense. One must forget the fruit of the action if one really wants to get the full benefit of it. Patience and self-surrender are very necessary for an aspirant.

Friday, 10 September 1982

It was the occasion of Sri Krishna's birthday and the ashram and its surroundings were being prepared for the auspicious celebration. The reading of the *Srimad Bhâgavatam* was going on. The Holy Mother also participated in the recitation by reading and listening.

Uriyadi began in the evening. *Uriyadi* is a folk custom typically celebrated on Lord Krishna's birthday. It depicts the childhood sportings of Lord Krishna, in particular His escapades of stealing butter, milk and curd from the houses of the *gopis*. First, Mother herself would dress the young village children like Krishna and the *gopas* (cowherd boys) and they would carry a staff in their hand. A clay pot (containing butter, milk and curd) would dangle from a rope slung over a bamboo pole some thirty feet high. As the boys came dancing up to the pot so as to break it with their staff, it would be pulled up and down and swing like a pendulum. At the same time, two of the *brahmachârins* standing on either side would splash water in their faces as they ran by, jumping to break the pot. This game went on until 7 o'clock in the evening. The Holy Mother, like a small child, was laughing and clapping her hands as the play went on. Altogether the bliss enjoyed by everyone present was inexpressible.

Later in the evening there was a long *bhajan*. In between there was an old-style Kerala folk dance called 'Tiruwâtira Kali' performed by the women and young girls while the praises of Sri Krishna were sung. Afterwards, Mother sat in the front yard of the ashram with some of the *brahmachârins* and householder devotees.

Venu: *Mother, what is experienced in* samâdhi?
Mother: Bliss. No happiness or sorrow. There is no "I" and "you." This state can be compared to deep sleep, but there is a difference. In *samâdhi* there is full awareness. Not only that. After sleep, when we wake up, no gñâna has been gained. Instead "I", "you" and the world emerge again. In reality, because of our ignorance, we feel that "All this is." To remove this ignorance, constant practice should be done fixing the mind on one object.

Ganga: *The* Puranas[56] *say that Vishwamitra was a Realised Soul, but he was sometimes seen as hot-tempered. Why is it so?*

Mother: Son, whatever a Perfect Being does is for the good of others. In reality, Vishwamitra was testing the devotion of Harischandra. All the quarrels made by the sage Narada were for the benefit of others.[57]

Ganga: *That reveals a lot. If Mother's Grace is there, I can do many good things in this world.*

Mother: Son, you should have your own power. Mother is telling you that she and you are One. The all-pervading Truth cannot be seen due to ignorance. Therefore, try to see everything as Mother's form.

Do not become angry with anyone. If somebody gets angry with you, immediately think, "The thing which is called 'I' is one in me and in him also. That is the *Atman. Atman* is only one. So with whom shall I get angry?"

ONE-POINTEDNESS

Brahmachârin: *Mother, how can concentration be gained?*

Mother: Son, if intensity to reach the goal *(lakshya bodha)* is there, one-pointedness *(ekâgrata)* will arise. There was a boy who had never done any work in

---

[56]Ancient scriptures written in story form by the sage Vedavyasa.

[57]Vishvamithra was a sage who deprived King Harischandra and his wife of their kingdom and put them through other intense and prolonged trials. Likewise, the sage Narada has been depicted as doing similar things.

his life. His father was a coconut tree climber by profession. One day the boy's father died. After his death, all the people would still come and call the son to pluck the coconuts from their tree. But, what could he do? He did not know coconut tree climbing. This boy could find no other way to earn a living so he decided to try to learn to climb coconut trees. This has to be learned with great care. If he happens to fall, his arms and legs will be broken. Afterwards it will not be possible to climb any coconut trees. His life will also be wasted. Therefore, with great care he tried to climb a coconut tree. Placing each foot with utmost care and embracing the tree tightly, he would climb a little ways and then come down. The next day he would climb little higher. As a result of several days effort, he learned coconut tree climbing. Through practice, he was able to ascend and descend the tree very quickly.

A *sâdhak* should be like that. God alone is Truth. Only if this is realised will life be fulfilled. Only God- Realisation is life's goal. That alone is the food for all eternity. But there are obstacles in the way of reaching this goal. If immense care is not taken, we will slip and fall. One's life will be wasted if one falls down. This kind of attitude should be there in the beginning stages. Then only will concentration be gained. Try for that, children.

While singing *bhajans* the Holy Mother rejoiced and danced blissfully like a small innocent child, which made all the devotees feel that Lord Krishna had once again taken birth on this earth. Everyone was very happy and content.

At around 10 o'clock the *Srimad Bhâgavatam* was again read, especially the chapter describing the birth of Krishna. At midnight, *bhajan* and *arati* were performed as a token of celebrating the auspicious occasion of Sri Krishna's birth.

Wednesday, 15 September 1982

GUDAKESA
Conqueror of sleep

At quarter past five in the morning, *Bhâva Darshan* was just ending. Even after sitting for 13 continuous hours without moving from the seat, the Holy Mother was very energetic. She did not go to her hut but remained with the devotees and began talking to them.

Ramesh Rao was a young man from Haripad who wanted to stay in the Holy Mother's presence. He had been forcibly taken by his family and friends to a mental hospital in Trivandrum to undergo a series of treatments for mental abnormality. Pai, a close friend of Rao's and a spiritual son of the Mother, told her what had happened. Mother sat quietly for a long time deep in thought.

Besides this, *brahmachârini* Gayatri had been admitted to a hospital in Quilon after symptoms of cancer had been detected. Today was the day she was to undergo surgery. In fact, it was Mother who had first pointed out that Gayatri was suffering from cancer and had instructed her to immediately get medical care. After the diagnosis, this fact was found out to be perfectly true. It was not a wonder to anyone, as Mother knows everything. Yet the news of Gayatri's operation had created a feeling of sadness in everyone's mind.

Now and then devotees would invite the Mother and the *brahmachârins* to their homes and the day would be spent blissfully singing, reading the *Bhâgavatam*, conducting the *archana*, etc. The previous night, a woman had come to the ashram to invite Mother to her house the next day. However, it was not the right time to leave the ashram as Mother had many things to do in connection with Gayatri's operation and Rao's matter and other things of concern. Mother explained to the devotee that she was unable to visit her house on that day and the woman had left with a dejected and disappointed mind.

As mentioned before, some devotees who saw the Mother and Devi as different would approach the Mother with silly matters. For the past two days Mother had neither slept nor rested even for a moment. It was at about 6 o'clock in the morning and she was getting ready to visit Gayatri in the hospital. One *brahmachârin* requested, "Mother, please sleep a little." To this Mother replied, *"It is not for sleeping that Mother has come here. All of you can sleep. Mother has to take care of so many people's matters."*

Saturday, 18 September 1982

MOTHER OF THE HOUSE

Today all the ashram work such as sweeping the grounds, cooking meals for everyone and cleaning all the vessels and utensils was done by Mother herself as most of the *brahmachârins* were bed-ridden with a severe fever. As if she were their natural mother, she made hot gruel and went to each one making them drink it. Even in the midst of all this work, she noticed the dirty dress of a *brahmachârin* who was about to go outside for some purpose. She lovingly scolded him for wearing it and asked him to change. It should be pointed out that even at this time Mother found the time to give spiritual instructions.

Talking to a *brahmachârin* about how an aspirant should control his diet, she said,

Mother: At first, food should be controlled. A *sadhak* should not eat much tasty food. Due to the attraction towards taste, it will become difficult to overcome many other things. However tasty a thing is, it is not possible to know the taste once it goes down the throat. Tasty food will cause more and more increase in the quantity of semen. Because of that, lust will increase. Both tasty and tasteless food should become the same. Practice eating bitter things. Not only the tongue but all the sense organs should be overcome. Going to places that stink, try to overcome one's aversion by sitting there for some time.

In the evening, Mother cooked tapioca for everyone. On certain days the Mother would do all the ashram work including cooking while the *brahmacharins* sat for meditation and japa. She would bring rice gruel and bananas to the place where they were sitting.

At about 4:30 a devotee named Srinivasan from Bangalore came to see the Holy Mother. Though he was working as a doctor in the United States for the last ten years, his deep rooted devotion to Lord Krishna which had been there since his childhood still remained with the same intensity. He arrived on the previous day from the States. He came to see the Holy Mother inspired by a dream which he had. Balu, whom he met first in the ashram, was curious to know more about the dream, but did not ask thinking that it would not be proper to do so before he saw Mother.

At five the doctor was called to the Mother's hut. Balu noticed his face blooming and shining when he beheld the Mother's form. His whole body was trembling and his eyes were getting filled with tears. Mother tenderly welcomed him and made him sit near her. After some formal enquiries Mother asked him, *"Son, tell Mother what you want to say."* Controlling his emotions, Srinivasan said,

Srinivasan: *It was a vision rather than a dream. I had not even met or heard about the Mother then. The most striking aspect of the vision was the place where I was when it occurred. It took place in the airplane, yes, the same flight on which I was traveling to India this time. I had a window seat. For a long time I gazed at the sky and chanted my mantra. As I was chanting the mantra I slowly glided into a semi-sleepy mood. Then, in the sky appeared a strong effulgence which slowly assumed a form. To my wonderment I found that it was the beautiful form of Krishna, my Beloved Deity. I was really thrilled and felt that each and every cell of my body was dancing in bliss. As I was drinking the beauty of my Lord there appeared just beside Him another equally radiant and splendid glow. That also assumed a form but was that of a lady wrapped in pure white clothes with a beaming smile on her face. Her nose ring sent forth rays which blinded my eyes. It seemed as if two suns had appeared up in the sky at the same time. My mind soared up to the heights of supreme bliss. Actually I could not contain the tremendous amount of bliss which was generated then. Both of them, dark blue in hue, smiled at me. A few moments passed thus when Krishna turned to the woman who was still smiling at me, and pointed His index finger towards her. As He remained in that position, both of them vanished from my sight. I suddenly woke up. I was still enjoying the bliss and was quite sure that it wasn't a dream but a vision. Even the semi-sleepy mood was felt to me as a created circumstance for this divine drama to take place. I knew that it was a hint asking me to do something. But who is this woman, I thought? My eagerness to know the significance of this dream became so intense that I could not eat or sleep dur-*

ing the whole trip. All my thoughts were focused only on the vision. Nothing else entered into my mind. It was a sixteen hour flight. This 'divine drama' took place just four hours after the departure of the flight from the New York airport. Twelve more hours were left. I became very restless.

The next morning at eleven o'clock I reached home. My parents and my older brother warmly welcomed me with open arms. In spite of all their love and affection, my mind was not at rest. The vision became more and more clear in my mind, especially the smiling face of the woman. I thought, 'What is this?' I'm a devotee of Krishna, but instead of being attracted to His divine form, this lady's face was overpowering me. My parents and elder brother noticed my strange mood. I was really confused and therefore could not give a satisfactory answer to them. I was doing everything more or less mechanically. Eventually, when I entered the room which was arranged for me, the first thing which caught my attention almost made me dumb with wonderment. Pasted on the wall was a picture of the same woman who appeared in the dream. Overwhelmed with joy I turned to my parents and asked, "Who is this lady?" "People say that She is God," answered my elder brother. He continued, "I found this picture in one of the newspapers and felt a strange attraction to it. This room was occupied by me until yesterday evening. For your convenience I moved to another one." Rejoiced at heart, I requested him to tell me more about her.

Thus I am here, Mother. Please tell me what am I to do? I am yours, please guide me. Bless me by giving implicit faith and devotion.

Mother: Mother is really happy to see your innocence. This is something very difficult to get. Even though you had been living in the midst of worldly pleasures son, you were able to maintain devotion and faith. It is that innocent devotion and faith which caused all this. Keep up this attitude, that is enough for your spiritual progress. Child, Mother is always with you.

He cried like a small child keeping his head on the Mother's lap. The Mother with great affection and love caressed him. He left the ashram at 7 o'clock having paid his homage to the Holy Mother while requesting her to be in his heart always.

Wednesday, 22 September 1982

Today the Mother left in a boat with all the others for *bhajan* in a nearby place. It was twilight time. The blue expansive sky, the coconut trees growing on either side of the backwaters, the gentle breeze caressing the water's surface, all made for a really inspiring scene.

The Holy Mother rose from her seat and started dancing. Unable to control the bliss, she cried out, *"Hoi, Ho, Hoi, Ho..."* and raising her hands upwards she sang:

> *The Sea of Compassion art Thou and if Thou art not compassionate to me, who else is there to give me refuge?*
>
> *My heart keeps on waiting for Thee. Will this day also be lost in vain, O Mother? Will this day also be lost in vain?*

Everyone responded to the Mother's song. Taking water from the river with her cupped hands, she threw it in the air calling *"Devi, Devi..."* All of a sudden she went into *samádhi* and stood still in the boat with uplifted hands. After a couple of minutes she slowly opened her eyes and asked Venu to sing a song. He sang:

> *O ever youthful Mother, because Thou art not showering mercy on Thy children, grief if intensifying in their hearts.*

> *O ever youthful Mother, allow me not to fall and sink down due to delusion like the sun that gets covered by clouds.*

When the song was over he asked, "Mother, this time is good for meditation, isn't it?"

Mother: Yes son, Nature is calm. Dusk is a suitable time for *sâdhaks* to do *sâdhana*. More concentration will be had by those who meditate then. At this time the mind will get more one-pointedness in the thought which predominates then. But in worldly people more worldly thoughts will occur because their minds are immersed in that. Twilight is the confluence of day and night, is it not? Two different natures are present here. The mind won't stay in anything at that time. All living beings will be in a haste to sleep. All will be thinking of their day to day lives. This is a time when there are alot of worldly vibrations. If all of that is breathed in, worldly waves will be created in us also. It is because of this that it is said to chant the Divine Names loudly at dusk. Leaving off bad thoughts, the mind will become concentrated on God. The atmosphere will become pure. Don't eat or sleep during twilight. Because the atmosphere is impure it will affect us through food. Just as changes are taking place externally in Nature at that time, changes will occur within us also. There is a special relationship between the body and Nature. Just as there are planets in the external universe there are subtle planets within us also. They are rotating as well. Solar eclipses, lunar eclipses and everything else is within us also.

In the olden days Mother used to cut grass for the cows from the shore of these backwaters. With friends, Mother used to bathe here, and standing in the water, Mother would meditate.

Brahmachârin: Mother says that *sraddha* is needed. What is *sraddha?*

Mother: Son, suppose somebody is talking to us angrily. Listen to everything with patience. Don't feel angry at him. Anger comes when we think that we are the body. No anger or hatred will be felt if you think, "I am not the body but the Supreme Self." At whom to be angry with then? There is only one Self that is all-pervading. It is in everyone. We must perfectly understand that we are not the body but the *Atman.* All this together forms sraddha. Using discrimination is *sraddha.* Faith and detachment are signs of *sraddha.*

Brahmachârin: *Mother, why am I not getting any experience even after doing so much meditation?*

Mother: Son, due to lack of *sraddha* there is no concentration. Experience will come only if *sâdhana* is done for at least four years with proper *sraddha.* Meditation should be done always. Don't waste even a moment. To one who has a Guru, complete faith in the Guru is enough.

Brahmachârin: *Mother, even after experiencing* brahmânanda *(absolute bliss), do you feel that the* *time you spend talking with us is wasted or that this is insignificant compared to that?*

Mother: In the olden days when Mother talked with someone, she used to feel that the time was being wasted but today Mother sees all the children as part of God *(Iswara amsa)*. Just as a weaver goes on spinning thread even while talking to those sitting nearby, Mother's mind is fully immersed in That even while she talks to her children. Mother sees nothing but God. Therefore, where is the question of wasting time? Mother's dwelling place is in her childrens' heart.

Brahmachârin: *On certain occasions it is seen that Mother is worried while thinking of her children. In reality, does Mother have any attachment to anyone?*

Mother: Children, in the innermost core, Mother is not attached to anything. She feels neither sadness nor sorrow. But the vibrations emanating from her children when they are sad will reflect in her. Then, for their peace of mind Mother also will grieve.

If there are no desires then there will be no sorrow. We must be able to love without expecting anything from anyone. Always think that we are the servant of all.

23 September 1982

THE GURU AND DISCIPLINE

One *brahmachârin* was not well. He expressed a wish to go home and take rest for a couple of days.

Mother: Today is a Darshan day and Nealu will have to do all the work alone if you go. Not only that. This is an ashram and having settled down here, Mother does not like for you to wander out. If your body is trying to make you its slave you should not easily give in to it. Overcome it by applying strength of mind. There is nothing that faith and courage cannot accomplish.

The *brahmachârin* gave up his idea of going home. Because it was a *Bhâva Darshan* day, devotees started coming from noon onwards.

Mother: (To one brahmachârin) The *prema bhakti* (loving devotion) of these householders is very deep. They are very innocent. Some days ago Mother became oblivious to the world while singing bhajans. Crawling on all fours, she went to the other side of the yard and sat under a coconut tree. There was no external awareness at all. It was not until she regained consciousness that Mother knew where she was sitting. Do you know why Mother did that? The daughter who lived in a nearby house one day had an intense desire to see Mother. She could not come here. That daughter was crying and crying, looking over to this side. It was then that Mother unknowingly went over to that side. So intense is the love and devotion of some householder devotees.

Brahmachârin: *Why is Mother always creating sorrow in our minds?*

Mother: Son, it will be like this until complete surrender and refuge is sought. Complete surrender and discipline under the Guru's guidance is needed. Is it not a life of renunciation? It is not possible to get closer to

God if there is no sorrow of some kind. Therefore, God will create some kind of difficulties through Mother. Having heated the iron in the fire, the ironsmith beats it. It is not possible to beat it into a shape without heating it up properly. Reformation won't happen if the iron thinks, "I will not allow myself to be heated in the fire." The Guru will create obstacles and sorrows for the disciple. The disciple should overcome all that with intense *sâdhana*. Spirituality is not for idle people. The difficulties of the subtle level are hard compared to the sorrows of the external world. There is nothing to fear for one who dedicates everything to a *Sadguru*.

Brahmachârin: *Mother, why is it that sorrow comes to me now and then?*

Mother clearly knew that the thought that Mother had less love for him was the cause of his sorrow.

Mother: It is due to the lack of complete faith. If there is faith, you won't be sad thinking, "Mother has more love for them; she has less for me."

Brahmachârin: *What do you mean by faith, Mother?*

Mother: Complete obedience to the Guru's words. In front of a Guru, a disciple should be like a servant in front of his master. The servant has no opinions of his own, only complete obedience to whatever the master says, no opinions at all. When obedience awakens in the disciple, the Guru's grace will unknowingly flow to the disciple. Grace will be there when the servant-like attitude that "I am nothing" is held. The Guru's heart will be filled

when he sees the disciple's innocence. One's goal will
be realised by worshipping God and serving the devotees of God with a servant-like attitude.

Thurday, 30 September 1982

It was the time of Navarâtri.[58] All over India the
Durga *pooja* was being celebrated. From early morning
onwards the neighbourhood children came to the
ashram to place their books in front of the Goddess Saraswati, the Goddess of Knowledge, in order to get Her
blessings for success in their studies. Also present were
many devotees with their sons and daughters. Mother
was playing and cracking jokes with the children. She
was cutting sugar cane and making them eat it. Mother
herself seemed exactly like a small child. One would be
amazed watching her. Some people present remembered the
Holy Mother's words, *"God has the nature of a small child. God
won't even look at those who do tapas with ego but He will shower His
grace on the innocent-hearted ones who do not do anything. This
may be due to His childlike nature."*

The Holy Mother continued playing with the children. The
devotees' hearts and eyes took delight in watching the Mother's
innocent sports. Knowingly or unknowingly they also partook
in the bliss.

Friday, 1 October 1982

COMPLETE FAITH & LIBERATION

Today the *brahmachârins* along with Mother went to
visit Sreekumar's house. Even after waiting a long time
for a bus at Vallickavu, it did not come. The Holy Mother

---

[58]Nine days festival and worship of the Divine Mother.

would not permit a taxi to be taken either. The Mother said, *"Spiritual people should not spend money unnecessarily."* Finally, a bus came and they reached their destination. As Mother was walking from the bus stop towards Sreekumar's house, she said to one *brahmachârin,*

Mother: The old enthusiasm is not seen in your meditation nowadays. After one hour of physical work, meditate the rest of the time. Don't spend time looking after Mother's needs. You children will become weak-minded if you think Mother is sick or weak. If you think Mother has power, you children will also get power. Unshakable faith is needed. None of you children have full faith in Mother. Complete faith means Liberation. What is necessary for you children now is a regular routine.

About eating food prepared the previous day, Mother said, *"The food which we eat will influence our character. Don't eat the food cooked on the previous day. It is tamasic (conducive to dullness or inertia)."*

Next, the discussion turned to *kirtana*. Somebody said something about Unni's songs. Mother said that some of Unni's *kirtanas* had come from his meditation. It is possible to cry to God when the mind becomes pure enough through meditation. At that time, songs can be composed without effort.

Brahmachârin: *Mother, will the mind subside of itself?*
Mother: The mind can be controlled by constant practice.

All of a sudden the Mother stopped. An elderly lady sitting by the side of the road was looking at Mother. The Holy Mother approached the old woman who, with great difficulty, tried to prostrate to her. The Holy Mother with great affection lifted the old lady up holding her by the hand and gave a kiss to her hand. The Mother then continued walking. The previous day the woman found out from Sreekumar's father that the Mother was coming and so she had waited by the side of the road to see her.

The Holy Mother continued: Until yesterday we were living thinking, "I am the body." In the beginning there will be some waves in the mind. Through practice they will go. It is to control these waves that *sâdhana* should be done sitting steadfastly in one place. The waves will not subside simply if you read some books. Instead, they will only increase. In the deep sea there are no waves. It is on the shore that the waves strongly break because there is little depth. Peace can be experienced when the mind becomes expansive and deep through *sâdhana*.

Many people had come to Sreekumar's house to see Mother and listen to her *bhajans*. After supper all the children gathered around the Mother. The Holy Mother said, " *The passing of time is not known when I am with these children.*" Catching hold of her hands, the children were walking with the Mother, following her wherever she went. They were fighting with each other to be able to sleep with the Mother that night. The Mother made each one of them lay down beside her for five minutes. When they see the Holy Mother they do not want their own mother. They would come and gather around Mother on their own. When she would sit somewhere they would also sit around her. If the Mother happened to sit quietly, these children would also sit near her gazing at her face.

Many times when Mother sat in deep meditation they would also sit with their eyes closed. This natural attraction of the children towards the Mother is proof enough of her unconditional love. This pure love, ever radiating from the Holy Mother has remolded and transformed many lives which were about to be ruined. If pure Love is God's nature, then why can't we call such a phenomena as God?

Monday, 4 October 1982

Gayatri was recuperating at *brahmachârini* Vimala's house after her operation. She had been staying there for a few days. Today Mother decided to visit her. Accompanied by some women householder devotees, the Holy Mother started from the ashram. Even though it was only a short distance away, the *brahmachârins* felt very sad. With great emotion they stood watching Mother as she walked away. Some of them sought Mother's permission to follow but Mother left saying she would return soon. The *brahmachârins* would feel pained at heart even if Mother left the ashram for only half an hour or an hour. That experience is beyond words. In those days, it would cause unbearable agony for the residents to be away from Mother even for a moment. Those who were happy and smiling would become like living corpses when separated from the Mother.

Sometimes when the Holy Mother left the ashram, she would only take a few *brahmachârins* with her. But before reaching the bus stop she would stop all of a sudden and say that a particular son or daughter was crying and send someone to fetch them. When the person who was sent reached the ashram, he would find that what the Mother said was correct. As the Mother said, he or she would be seen crying with a broken heart. The Mother would proceed only after that boy or girl reached her. Only those who are very close to the Holy Mother can understand the intensity of that pain. The heart will pain like the wringing out of a wet cloth. At that time they

would neither eat nor sleep. They would sit in a corner crying like
a small child who has been separated from its mother. This mental pain of the residents was like the excruciating pain of the
Gopis of Brindavan who were separated from their beloved
Krishna.

Tuesday, 5 October 1982

At 2 o'clock the Holy Mother returned from *brahmachârini* Vimala's house. Everyone prostrated to the
Mother and then she summoned all the residents and distributed sweets to all. It seemed as if the ashram regained
its lustre and glory after Mother's absence. Bhargavan,
an ardent devotee from Mother's village, came before the
evening *bhajan* started. He believed that Mother was
only divine during the *Bhâva*. He had much love for Sri
Krishna and owing to this, he would take a little freedom during
Krishna Bhâva by playing with Mother. Mother would really
glorify his innocence. When she saw him, the Mother said,
"Krishna has come." She then told the others,

Mother: Father Bhargavan's innocence is really
deep. During *Krishna Bhâva* he would say,
"Krishna, this man behaved in such and such a way,
that man behaved in such and such a way. I went
there, I went here." His attitude is that Krishna is
his own. Having told Him all this, he would simply
look at Krishna and laugh. He could easily go up if
the real path were known.

The Holy Mother's birthday was the following day.
Many devotees started arriving. Some were decorating
the ashram and its surroundings. The *Bhâva Darshan*
went on until 5:30 a.m. The Mother sat for twelve hours on the
peetham, receiving the devotees without moving from there. On

certain days she will sit for fifteen or sixteen hours and will be full of energy and ever cheerful. Tirelessly working for the well-being of the world, she puts new light and life into their meaningless lives, instilling faith and restoring peace.

Wednesday, 6 October 1982

BIRTHDAY

Today is *Trikártika*, the Holy Mother's birth star. Having gotten up early and taken their baths, all the devotees waited outside the hut to receive the Holy Mother and offer their salutations. The *brahmachárins* chanted the *suprabhátam*.[59] After many requests and prayers, the Holy Mother sat on the seat which was especially prepared for her. One by one the devotees offered their salutations, some putting garlands on her while others offered flower petals. The *brahmachárins* worshipped the Mother's feet and Pai did the *arati*. All the time the Mother was absorbed in deep *samádhi*. When she finally became somewhat normal, the Mother got up from the seat and distributed *prasád* to everyone. With her own hands she gave sweet pudding, rice gruel and clothes to the village children. The reading of the *Srimad Bhágavatam* and the singing of *bhajan* took place at the same time. As part of the celebration, in the evening a folk dance known as *Koladi* was performed by some girls. They would stand in a circle rhythmically beating two small wooden sticks which they held in both hands as they moved dancing to the music sung by others. The song glorified the Holy Mother, highlighting her great and beneficent qualities and asking how to repay her for the transformation which she had brought in the lives of so many.

> *Today is the Kartika star*
> *Which is my Mother's birthday,*

---

[59] A song requesting the Divine Mother to wake up during the early morning hours.

A day shining forth with beauty
Causing us to overflow with joy.

You have made us blessed
And liberating us from worldliness,
You have made us devotees
And given us peace.

You have showered immense love on us and we
drank it forgetting everything. O Mother, we
have nothing, nothing to repay You with for this
divine love which You have showered on us.

How many births have I done tapas
To gain this, Your Divine Presence?
I bow at Thy Holy Feet millions of times for mak-
ing this life fulfilled.

One child was watching the *Koladi* with great attention. Seeing that, the Mother said,

Mother: Look, have you seen the concentration of
that child? This kind of concentration and desire
should be there for God. Not even a moment will be
wasted if we have love for God. All-encompassing
bliss is there for him who dwells close to God.

After the evening *bhajan* the chanting of the Thousand Names of the Divine Mother took place. The residents and *brahmachârins* decided to offer the worship to
the Holy Mother. When everyone requested, the
Mother finally agreed to sit. The worship started. All the
brahmacharins sat around Mother forming a circle.
Brahmachârin Unni led the chanting of the mantras
while the others responded. One by one lotus flower petals were offered at the Mother's feet. The Mother entered into

samâdhi. At a particular stage of the worship the Mother started offering flowers to her own body and then to other's bodies also. She sees the same Consciousness pervading everywhere. The ashram was saturated with concentration and devotion. Everyone was at the peak of bliss. When the *archana* was over, there was a big heap of lotus flower petals around Mother. The Holy Mother looked like Mother Durga sitting on a large lotus. The sight was a feast to the eyes and devotional ecstasy to the heart. At the end, all the devotees again saluted the Holy Mother.

WHAT IS THERE AFTER DEATH?

An ardent devotee of the Holy Mother died in the beginning of October, 1982. This incident inspired *brahmachârin* Venu to ask Mother about life after death.

Mother: There is a very subtle sheath covering our gross body. All our thoughts are imprinted in this layer. Like a tape recorder, this covering will record all acts which we do mentally, verbally and physically while we are alive. This forms a covering of thoughts. After death, when we leave the body, the thoughts and covering will rise up with the individual self. According to the actions done, each *jîva* will go to a particular plane. In that state, the *jîva* has no gross body. Even then, the *jîva* will feel hunger and thirst. Due to the actions done in their previous birth, they will feel as if they are in the mid-ocean. They will have a lot of unfulfilled desires but cannot fulfill them. Some *jîvas* will attack other living beings in order to fulfill their desires. Entering within them through their breath, they will destroy the other beings' consciousness. After that, they will make them eat according to their will, but they cannot give life to a dead body. This attack is possible only on those who have no mental power. The next birth will be according to the thoughts one has at death. The *jīva* will go on accepting bodies until all desires are eliminated. Usually it is through the breath and food materials that a *jīva* enters into other bodies. Some *jīvas*, without much delay after death, accept other bodies according to their karma. Some others will wander around. It is for those that wander that the rituals are done by the relatives who are still living. By chanting certain mantras with concentration, it is possible for the wandering *jīvas* to get a higher birth and stop their wandering.

But the case is different as far as a Liberated Soul is concerned. He will merge with the Absolute just as the air in a soda bottle rises up and dissolves in the atmosphere on bursting open.

Thursday, 7 October 1982

The Holy Mother was sitting by the side of the back-waters looking at the water. A few minutes passed. Afterwards, she said to those sitting nearby,

Mother: Our mind is like this canal. Due to the stagnant water, how many people are smelling the foul odour produced from it. Make this water flow and unite with the ocean and there will be no more odour. Likewise, at present the mind is dirty owing to accumulated tendencies. It should be cleaned by making all the thoughts flow towards God. Then the mind will become expansive.

One of the brahmachārins: *Mother, why do you behave*

*differently and in an incomprehensible way to different
people?*

Mother: For some time Mother will deliberately
slacken the hook and let you nibble. Then when you
are fully hooked, Mother will catch hold of you.
You children have been living in the illusory world
since birth. One day you come to Mother calling
"Amma" but she cannot suddenly discipline you in
the beginning itself. The disciplining should be
slow and steady, properly understanding the mental constitution and assimilating power of the student. The Guru must have patience and forbearance to train the disciple. Above all, selfless love
must be the basis of everything. A *Sadguru* will
have all these qualities. You children will throw
everything away and leave if Mother manifests the
Guru bhâva (attitude of a Guru) at the very beginning.

Mother got up and went to the hut. At that time Saraswathi Amma, a householder devotee of the Mother, arrived. Whenever she came she would bring food for the
brahmacharins as well as for the Mother. Saraswathi
Amma was waiting outside the Mother's hut with a
packet in her hands. Seeing her, the Holy Mother smilingly said, *"Ah, you have come. Today Mother thought of
you. Everything is straightened out, is it not?"*
Hearing this, Saraswathi Amma started weeping,
falling on Mother's lap. Her eldest son was in great difficulty due to not having a job. With Mother's permission
and blessings he went to Bombay and was appointed to a
good post. She received a letter from him on that day informing about his appointment. Before she could utter a
word about it, the Holy Mother smilingly revealed that

she knew it already as if telling Saraswathi Amma that nothing happens without her knowledge. This is what made her cry.

The *brahmachârins* also waited for a chance to sit in the presence of the Holy Mother and to listen to her nectarean words. Taking this as an opportunity, some of the *brahmacharins* entered the hut. At this time, Venu tried to stealthily take some of the edibles which Saraswati Amma had brought. Watching the Mother's face, he slowly pulled the packet towards himself, pretending as if nothing was happening. Just at that moment, the Mother glanced at him and catching hold of his hand said, "*You little thief! Are you trying to steal from the Greatest Thief? Aren't you Mother's son? She knows your nature very well.*" Everyone laughed and Venu blushed from embarrassment on being caught.

Shortly after, a *brahmachârin* asked, "Mother, is scriptural knowledge necessary?"

Mother: Didn't Sankaracharya and other great souls study the scriptures? Knowledge of the scriptures is a must. Study is a *sâdhana*. It should not be to inflate your ego but to get rid of it. The scriptural statements and dictums will act as weapons to fight against mental conflicts and weaknesses which might arise during the course of *sâdhana*. While studying the scriptures, one should feel, "I am studying divine mantras."

Venu: *Mother, why is* Bhagavân *(Sri Krishna) not coming in front of me?*

Mother: Definitely He will come if you have such a wish. Some more alertness should be there externally. Patience should be instilled into the mind. *Asana siddhi* (being able to sit three hours in one posture without moving) should be there. Today, if you sit two hours in one *âsana*, tomorrow you

must try to sit five more minutes. Afterwards it should
be made ten minutes. Like this you should be able to sit
three or four hours in one *âsana.* Thus, when patience is
there, everything else will come of its own accord. We
should imagine that the form of our Beloved Deity is
walking beside us and smiling at us while we walk,
bathe, sit, etc. Cry to your Deity imagining that your
Beloved is standing in the atmosphere. More time
should be utilised in the night for meditation.

In the olden days, without wasting any time at all,
Mother would do *sâdhana* in the night without even
sleeping. Whatever we see, we will feel it as our *dhyâna
rûpa* when innocent devotion arises. Mother, when
she was very small, would imagine while plucking
grass or sweeping the ground that Krishna was playing
and dancing with her.

One *brahmachârin* had an intense desire to meditate
sitting on the seashore during the night time but sometimes he would feel fearful. Hearing this, one among the
brahmachârins asked, "Mother, do ghosts and evil spirits really exist?"

Mother: Son, Mother won't say that there are no
subtle beings. But they cannot do anything to
spiritual people. A meditator's proximity will give
them much happiness. They will easily attack us if
we don't have mental power. At a certain stage,
subtle beings can be seen while meditating in the
graveyard.

Brahmachârin: *Is there any harm in showing siddhis?*

Mother: If the laws of Nature are transgressed, it is harmful. Not only that, others will also be fascinated by such displays. As far as possible, a Perfect Man will avoid showing *siddhis*. But, by manifesting such psychic powers, he has nothing to lose because he is already full. If the energy which is used in showing *siddhis* were to be used to instill renunciation into one, that would be more beneficial to the world. One will only get diverted from the goal if one is deluded by *siddhis*.

Brahmachârin: *Mother, I have committed many mistakes. What is the redress?*

Mother: Nothing particular is needed. It is enough if you meditate well. Mother has sought forgiveness from God for your faults.

Just like Sri Ramakrishna's devotion to Devi, you children have devotion to Mother. You realise this when you stay away from Mother for some time. Many children have come and told me, "Mother, when we are away, whichever woman we see we will feel that they are Mother only, especially those who wear white clothes." When Mother is near, the children will think, "Mother is near, so why should we meditate?" That is why in the beginning itself Mother told you not to meditate on her form. Not only that, once you believe that Mother is one with God, then your mind should not falter even for a moment. Such firm faith is needed. Don't think, "Mother has more love for him and she has less love for me." All this shows lack of faith.

Friday, 8 October 1982

It was morning, soon after dawn and the ashram premises had still not been swept. The Holy Mother came to the scene with a broom in hand to do the sweeping herself. Seeing the Mother, the *brahmachârins* also started cleaning the compound. Within a few minutes the ashram and its surroundings were clean. Rather than taking the easy way and telling others what to do, Mother sets an example herself although it means exertion on her part. In her eyes, no work is low, all is sacred and a means to reach God.

CONTROL OF FOOD

Almost all the *brahmachârins* were from wealthy families and had led comfortable lives. Sometimes, due to their old habits they would eat something at odd times. The Mother, if she saw them doing so, would scold and correct them accepting no excuses. She would always remind them, *"Children, without giving up taste, you cannot progress spiritually."*

One day Mother noticed one *brahmachârin* eating some titbits taken from the cabinet.

Mother: This son is only thinking of food. That is very bad. In the beginning, food should be controlled very much. Everything is excreta once it goes inside the body. If you sit thinking of food, then where is the time to remember God? Just experiment and see what happens after taking plenty of tasty food one day. You children will lose your semen at least in the dream state. It won't happen like that if you eat only *sattvic* food. When your seed is lost you will be angry with Mother. The complaint is that this happened because of the lack of

Mother's Grace. What does it matter if you get angry with Mother without controlling your food? Those who are intent to reach the goal will control themselves.

The *brahmachârin* felt ashamed and became a little offended. He said, as if like a son to his mother, "Am I the only one who eats everything?" He then left the room. After a couple of minutes, this *brahmachârin* with great remorse approached Mother and confessed his mistake. He sought forgiveness for his indiscriminate act.

The usual evening *bhajan* was over at eight. One *brahmachârin* had been meditating and did not attend.

Mother: This is an ashram. A general routine should be followed. Everyone must come during the *bhajan*. One person meditates, another one does *pranayâma* and some others do *bhajan*. All these are not right.

Though she gives such general instructions, there also are exceptions. The Mother will exempt those who can meditate well from all other works and from the general routine. The Holy Mother will allow them to spend as much time as they can in meditation. They don't have to come even to the *Vedanta* classes or *bhajan*. The Holy Mother says, *"I am ready to serve them and look after their needs myself."* But Mother is very particular that the others who cannot do meditation for long hours should actively participate in the daily routine of the ashram, which also includes a total of six hours of meditation done at different times of the day.

9 October 1982

MAKE ME INTOXICATED WITH YOUR LOVE

Today at 3 o'clock in the afternoon and the Holy Mother was sitting on the front verandah of the temple. Calling *"Sreekumar!"* the Mother then started singing a song. Sreekumar came with the harmonium and sat near Mother. The Mother gave certain instructions to him about the song and it's music. She herself set the music to it and began singing each line. In between, she told certain things to Sreekumar about the beat of the song. She clapped her hands according to the rhythm. Balu, Pai and Ganga came and sat near Mother and Venu came and played the drums. Such occasions, when Mother with her spiritual children compose and sing music, are really blissful moments. Unforgettable and unique are these times.

Eventually the Holy Mother sang the song which created an overflow of devotion, bliss and love which engulfed everyone there.

> *O Mother, make me mad with Thy Love! What need have I of knowledge or reason? Make me drunk with Thy Love's wine.*
>
> *O Thou Who stealest Thy devotees' hearts, drown me deep in the Sea of Thy Love!*

Intoxicated by the song, Mother got up and started moving round and round. She was in an abstracted mood. The speed of her circling increased and in that state of total absorption, the Holy Mother now and then burst into blissful laughter. No sign of an end was to be seen. Sugunanandan, who was watching the whole scene, became very anxious about his daughter and in great consternation caught hold of her calling "My child!" and made her lay down on his lap. He didn't stop

there. Before anybody could prevent him, he poured water on
the Mother's head. Totally transported to a world unknown to
those of gross intellect, the Mother burst into an uproarious
laugh. It became louder and continued unabated. Half an hour
passed as the laugh of uncontrollable and overflowing supreme
bliss continued.

All the family members gathered around the Holy Mother.
The Mother's sisters started crying and Mother Damayanti also
cried calling the Divine Mother. Owing to their spiritual ignorance they thought that the Holy Mother was going to lose
her mental balance. It took a long time for the Mother to come
down to the normal state. Afterwards, it seemed as though she
was struggling to keep her mind down. Her eyes went up and got
fixed at the point between the eyebrows. About three and a half
hours later Mother regained her external awareness. She got up
from her father Sugunanandan's lap and told him, *"Father
Sugunanandan, hereafter don't touch my body on such occasions."*
The *brahmachârins* as well as some learned people several times
had told Sugunanandan and the other family members not to
disturb the Mother during such times. But they could neither
control their emotions nor could they understand the situation.
Later, the *brahmachârins,* as instructed by the Mother herself,
would sing *bhajans* during that time. In those days Mother
would lose her external awareness almost every day. It would
take a long while, some times even hours, for her to come down.
As the number of *brahmachârins* increased, the Holy Mother
controlled herself from getting totally absorbed. About this,
she said one day, *"If Mother always lets herself get into that mood of
supreme bliss, then the very purpose of taking this body will be de-
feated. Mother has a lot to do including the raising of the*
brahmachârins *which is very important."*

11 October 1982

Today Mother was going to a devotee's house in
Quilon. At 7 o'clock in the morning and everyone was
preparing to go. Having noticed the dirty *dhoti* worn by a *brahmachârin*, the Mother said,

Mother: Son, go and come back wearing a good dhoti. Cleanliness is what is necessary. Even if there is only one set of clothes, wash it daily and wear it. Bathe, at least scrubbing with sand. External cleanliness is what is needed first. Wherever you go, take your own seat for meditation. You children should not use things which are used by others. Things which are urgently needed should be taken along. Henceforth, a vessel for eating will be purchased for each one of you.

SADHANA AND VASANA

When the Holy Mother reached the devotee's house, she became like a small child. Everyone took delight seeing the Mother's childlike innocence and sportings. The Mother danced as she was eating peanuts given by a devotee. Like a child she said, *"No, I won't give this to you."* It was an unforgettable day for the members of the devotee's family. They watched the Holy Mother as if they were looking at something very attractive and precious. The next moment, the Holy Mother, leaving the peanut packet, which she said she wouldn't give to anyone, walked towards the family shrine room and entered it. This act of the Holy Mother's reminded the *brahma-chárins* of Mother's own statement that God's nature is like that of a child. He is not attached to anything. After entering the shrine room and looking at the portrait of the Divine Mother, the Mother said in a childlike way, *"Hey Grandma, look after the needs of these children."* Afterwards, she went to the terrace and lay down on a mat which was spread there. All the family members were sitting around her. Mother was eating ice cream fed to her by the youngest girl of the house. It was quite obvious that she was eating it only for their happiness. When she had three spoonfuls she said, *"Enough. It was only for daughter's satisfaction that Mother ate it."*

The head of the family who was a spiritual aspirant asked, "Ammachi, why do more *vâsanas* rise up as we do *sâdhana?*"

Mother: When we clean a room all the superficial dirt will go first. The room will seem as if clean but when wiped harder we can see all the mud coming out. The *vâsanas* lying subdued within come up when we do *sâdhana*. They come up only to get exhausted. Those are all illusions *(mithya)* and ever-changing.

The next day when the Holy Mother was about to return to the ashram, the little daughter of the house expressed a wish to go with Mother in the car. But saying that her classes will suffer, the parents did not take her. As the car started and moved away, the little girl cried aloud looking at the Mother, "Ammachi...Ammachi!" As the parents were very much interested in her studies, the Mother thought that it would not be fair to say anything. The car moved forward but suddenly stopped after going five kilometers. There was more than enough fuel. The driver checked the car but couldn't find any trouble. However much the driver tried, the car would not start. After some time, the Mother who was keeping quiet until then said, *"The car will start if you try to go back to the house."* They obeyed Mother's words and the car immediately started. There was no trouble at all. They were amazed when they reached the house and saw the little girl who wanted to go with Mother crying aloud lying in the shrine room. When the girl saw Mother, she came running to her calling aloud "Ammachi!" and embraced her tightly, crying and crying. Returning to the ashram with the girl at her side, the Holy Mother said, *"It is this daughter's sankalpa that caused the car to stop. There is nothing which cannot not happen with a pure and innocent sankalpa. Small children can get it easily."*

13 October 1982

Mother was talking with four year old Shakti Prasad, a child born out of Mother's blessings.

Mother: Son, you must become the *sannyāsin* teacher of this entire world. You should teach everyone.

Shakti: *I will become a teacher by studying in the school.*

Mother: Son, sing a song. Let Ammachi hear it.

Shakti Prasad sang with great concentration folding his hands on his chest,

> *Through my mind, speech and actions*
> *I am remembering You incessantly.*
> *Why then are You delaying to show*
> *Your mercy to me, beloved Mother?*
>
> *I am a miserable destitute.*
> *I have none but You, Mother.*
> *Please stop Your tests and*
> *Extending Your hand, pull me up...*

Someone walked nearby and Shakti Prasad looked in that direction. Mother said, *"Don't look at whoever comes. You must sing with concentration."* Shakti again sang. When the song was over, Mother made him repeat the English alphabet.

Mother: Mother's son should learn Sanskrit. Son, show how you meditate.

Shakti sat in a perfect posture and meditated. Seeing this, Mother and the others all rejoiced at his innocence.

THE MOTHER WITHIN

It was 3 o'clock in the afternoon. Gayatri, Nealu, Venu and Ganga were sitting near Mother.

Question: *Mother says not to look at the external Mother. No spiritual progress will be gained if we sit looking at Mother's external form. What is the meaning of this?*

Mother: Son, Mother said that so that you children will look inside. If you don't have strong faith in Mother, doubts will crop up in your mind regarding Mother's actions. You may feel, "Why is Mother talking to that person for such a long time and not even looking at me." Such doubts will create many obstacles in your spiritual path, due to your seeing only the external Mother. This will not happen if you enshrine Mother within. You must also have the strong conviction that "Mother is not the body but the all-pervading Consciousness." Staying with Mother for some years, you will have to fight. Only then can you win wherever you go. Children, the ignorance of ego should be pulled out and thrown away with its roots. Sincerity towards the Guru will come only if the disciple stays with the Guru for some years.

Question: *Mother, what should be done to control lustful feelings* (kâma vikâra)?

Mother: Through constant association with the *Sadguru* all those will be automatically removed. Desireless love also will help to attenuate lust.

Just before the *bhajan* the Mother was talking about the ashram affairs.

A new brahmachârin: *Mother, how are the ashram needs being met?*
Mother: Children, whenever there is a lack of something, then and there God will have it sent. Mother has given everything to Him. He will look after everything. Mother doesn't need anything. For Mother, her children are everything. Mother's heart will become full when she sees each child growing spiritually. Now what is necessary is for you children to do spiritual practice. You don't have to pay attention to anything else. Somehow the things will come. Mother doesn't like anybody serving her. You should meditate. It should go on very well. That is what is necessary.

Thursday, 14 October 1982

TAKING ON DISEASE

Today was a *Bhâva Darshan* day. The *Devi Bhâva* was over by 4 a.m. At the end of *Devi Bhâva* the Holy Mother sucked blood and pus from the head of a leper. On certain days, due to accepting the illnesses of many people, the Holy Mother would become sick but would recover within a few minutes. The Mother says,

Mother: A perfect person is filled with compassion when he sees a leper or such other persons; he will not feel disgust or aversion. Through concentration and divine power he can absorb the disease into himself. The sick people who are coming here might have been carrying around their disease for the last ten or fifteen years, undergoing different kinds of treatments and still not finding any cure. If Mother accepts that, she will have to suffer only ten or fifteen minutes and those poor people will be saved from any more suffering.

The time was three in the afternoon. The Holy Mother was lying on the cot in her hut. Some of the residents were sitting down on the floor.

Question: *Mother, no improvement is seen in my* sådhana. *What should be done for that?*
Mother: Children, don't worry. All that will come. It is enough if you try. While sitting in an airplane as it is flying across the sky, we will not feel that it is moving, but once having reached the destination, we understand that we had been travelling all along. Likewise, we are progressing but it is too subtle for us to understand. After reaching the goal, everything will become clear. Concentration, that is what is needed. One who has concentration can conquer this entire world. Anyone will feel an attraction if his voice is heard. One look at him is enough to bring one to the spiritual path, however wicked one may be. Concentration should be increased somehow. It is possible through practice.

Question: *Mother, can meditation be done imagining oneself as the form?*
Mother: No, that is not necessary. The ego will come if meditation is done on oneself. Not only that, it is always better to choose a Perfect Being as your form of meditation. Whichever form you meditate on, eventually we will come to the understanding that we and *That* are one. During the period which Mother meditated she saw herself as Devi.

Friday, 15 October 1982

FAITH IN THE GURU

Mother was in Quilon at a devotee's house. In the evening there were *bhajan, satsang* and chanting of the Thousand Names of Devi. Many people were there to see Mother and to participate in the *bhajan*. A great soul, Nisargadatta Maharaj, had left his body recently. One devotee brought it to Mother's attention.

Devotee: *Mother, it has been said in the book "I Am That" that Nisargadatta Maharaj met his Guru at the age of 34 and had known the Self at the age of 37. He had reached the goal within three years only. Is that possible?*
Mother: Son, there is one thing. Has it not been said that he had complete faith in the Guru? If such faith is there, then there is no difficulty at all. It is not enough to consider only time for the attainment of the goal. Faith, disposition inherited from the past birth, and practice are all applicable.

Wednesday, 20 October 1982

In the afternoon at 3 o'clock, the Holy Mother was sitting in front of the *Vedanta Vidyalaya* (*Vedanta School*) surrounded by the residents. There were some visiting devotees as well.

One devotee: *Mother, is there any harm if there happens to be a break in the* pooja *performed to a particular form of God or Goddess?*

Mother: Son, when we do worship to a form, it gets power. It is we who transmit life to it. In fact, when you children salute someone with concentration, power will flow from you to him and from him to you. However, if the worship is discontinued, the same power can do harm to you.

Question: *Mother, it is said that there is godliness in human beings. If that is true, can a human become totally identified with God or can he become God?*

Mother: He is God. There is nothing to become. But at present, he is not aware of this great Truth because of his accumulated tendencies. Son, even if it is said that God is in man, there is a Power that transcends everything. That is the Supreme Reality. That power is unique. That exists even beyond a Liberated Soul. The waves and the ocean are not essentially different, but the wave does not contain the ocean. The ocean stands as the substratum of the wave. There is no tree that touches the heavens and no root that reaches to the netherworld. This means that all names and forms are limited.

THE CAUSE OF THE MANGO TREE
AND THE SEED

Brahmachârin: *Will the atheists agree that there is a God?*

Mother: You should ask the atheists, "Which came into being first, the mango tree or the seed?" If it is the mango tree then a seed should be there and if it is the seed than a tree should be there. Therefore, beyond both, there is a Power which is the cause of everything. That is God. As we progress in *sâdhana* we will understand everything. There is no meaning in unnecessary dispute.

The topic suddenly changed to the narration of her own experience during Mother's *sâdhana* period. The Mother continued,

Mother: In the old days Mother was not even able to say "Krishna." Body-consciousness would be lost immediately. If concentration was not gained in meditation I would angrily jump towards Devi's portrait shouting at Her. I used to beat my head on the wall. But what to say about other times! I would embrace Devi's picture with overflowing love and crumble it into pieces. In those days, Mother would only see Devi in whoever came. If I happened to see any good-looking girls nicely dressed up, I would leap and jump out of bliss. I felt all of them to be Devi.

About her spiritual children, the Mother said,

Mother: All the children have that kind of devotion. Children, if you see someone who looks like Mother, don't you stand gazing at them? When you are away from Mother, won't you cry if you see someone who has a face which closely resembles Mother's? That devotion will help a lot. If you stay away from Mother, you will be able to cry and call to Mother. In however much an elevated state a disciple may be, he will have a kind of selfishness when he comes in front of the Guru. Children, don't you have the feeling that Mother should have more love towards you than towards others?

At that time one *brahmachârin* returned who had gone out of the ashram for some purpose. He had waited a long time at the bus stop without being able to catch a bus. Having prostrated to the Mother, he sat near her.

Mother: Son, haven't you gone?
Brahmachârin: *I couldn't catch a bus. I waited nearly one hour.*
Mother: Is it a *brahmachârin* who is saying this? Hasn't God given you good health? Don't you have hands and legs? Can't you walk? If you had walked during the time you waited for the bus, you could have returned having accomplished the thing for which you went, is that not so? Will the time be wasted if you chant your mantra while walking? On the way, if the bus comes you can get in as well, is it not? Hereafter, you children should not waste time waiting in the bus stop. While you are stand-

ing there, people of different calibres will come and you will talk with them. All that will be the cause for creating new *vâsanas*.

Monday, 25 October 1982

INACTION IN ACTION

In the morning Mother, all of a sudden, came to the kitchen and began doing all the work. She sent all the *brahmachârins* from the kitchen saying, *"Go and do meditation."* Some still stood there hoping to help.

One brahmachârin: *Shall I simply stand looking on while Mother is working?*
Mother: Children, Mother does not feel that she is doing anything. It would have been enough if you would have stayed at home if it was simply for doing work that you came here. Otherwise, think over whether you can do work with an attitude of dedication to God. Mother doesn't think that you can do so, and therefore, you children should meditate without breaking the daily routine. That is enough for Mother.
Venu: *Mother, how many days are still needed to attain Truth?*
Mother: Children, you work. Don't be sad thinking of time. God will give everything.
Brahmachârin: *However much work I do, if Mother's Grace is not there, there is nothing. If Mother's* sankalpa *is there I will be liberated this very moment.*
Mother: Son, don't talk like that. That is weakness. If you work you will get the wages. God will not

simply give anything to anyone without their working for it. Self-effort and grace are interdependent. If *tapas* (spiritual discipline) is performed sincerely, you can then see God's Grace flowing into you. Sitting behind the closed doors of a room saying "The sun is not giving me any light" is foolishness. Open the door and light will enter. Likewise, open the doors of your heart by removing the obstacles of egoistic thoughts and by developing such qualities as love and humility. That needs effort. Prepare your mind to become a befitting instrument of God's Grace which flows in a never-ending stream.

You should pray to God to always be given work. You should not feel that "Having done this much, I still did not get anything." God is to be loved without desiring anything. Wishing for a vision is also a desire. This is what God said when He was approached, "To overcome the mind is more difficult than finding Me. See everything with an attitude of equanimity. Overcome the mind."

Don't unnecessarily argue with others. Tell them, "I don't have time to waste talking unnecessarily. My Mother has told me 'Truth is God. That is in you also. It is everywhere. When you find *That*, you will know your Self.' Mother hasn't said even to have faith in her." Also tell them, "I am trying to know myself, to love and serve all with a brotherly attitude. My aim is not to attain Liberation."

Brahmachârin: *Mother, what is the nature of At-man?*[60]

Mother: No attributes at all. Changeless like the sky. It cannot be said what *It* is. There is no motion at all. There is no "you" and "I" there. It can be known only through experience.

MAHABALI[61]

Venu: *Mother, why did Vamana push down Mahabali to the nether world? Why was he not sent to the heavens?*

Mother: Son, even heaven is not permanent. When the merit which was responsible for sending one to heaven is exhausted, one will come down again. In fact, Vishnu was testing Mahabali's devotion. He asked for three feet of land. After Vishnu measured two, when there was no other place, Mahabali offered his own head. Mahabali's devotion was revealed then. It was Eternal Liberation that Vishnu gave to him. Whether in heaven or hell, there is no change for *Atman* at all. The *Atman* has no trouble even if pushed down to hell.

Marriage celebrations were going on in a house related to the Idammanel family.

One brahmachârin: *Mother, do we have to go to the marriage at the other house?*

60The Self Absolute.

61Mahabali was a king of ancient times who was approached by Vamana, the dwarf Incarnation of Lord Vishnu, who asked for three steps of land. Vamana showed His Universal Form and covered the entire cosmos with the first two steps. In order to remain truthful to his promise of giving three steps of land, Mahabali offered his head as the third step.

Mother: Don't ask such questions. What does it matter for us? *Sâdhaks* should never participate in such functions. Help them, but only if they ask for help.

Thursday, 28 October 1982

UNSTEADINESS

One *brahmachârin* had a wish to go somewhere to practice meditation in solitude.

Mother: Mother will not allow you to do that. You want to escape without confronting and defeating the obstacles rising within you. After two days you will come back. If you go somewhere, *sâdhana* should be performed staying there at least for a month, without moving around. But you won't do that. You would say that staying with the Mother is the best. Go and meditate after changing your clothes.

The Holy Mother was sitting in the ashram library after lunch.

Brahmachârin Balu: *Can a* Jñâni *(Knower of the Self) bestow Liberation on one by mere* sankalpa?
Mother: Certainly, but the disciple should have alertness and faith. One who has faith will not ask any questions of the Guru. He will obey the Guru's words implicitly. That is service to the Guru. There is no benefit if one who does service has no *'visâla buddhi'* (expansive vision). Obedience and

proper discipline are necessary. The Prime Minister entrusts each section to the other ministers. What if they walk around to serve the Prime Minister without doing their job? Is that correct? Will he be happy? The same is the case with the spiritual Guru. God doesn't need anything, neither service nor flattery. Devotion, faith and obedience is what is needed.

SRADDHA
Alertness

The Holy Mother was working in the kitchen. It is interesting and at the same time amazing to watch the Mother's kitchen work. She works very quickly but she is very careful and alert. She can cook rice and the necessary side dishes using less spices and still they are tasty. Within an hour and a half, she can have the meal prepared for all the residents.

As the cooking was going on, the Mother told the *brahmachârini* who was assisting her,

Mother: You have burnt the mung beans by not pouring in enough water. While doing one thing your full attention should be in it. Then only *sraddha* will come. Do not distract yourself by chewing things or talking to anyone while doing work. Your mantra should always be chanted within. We should always be centered within. A person may be rowing the boat for some time and then he sits and rests on his oars without rowing for awhile. Even then he is alert as to whether the boat is going straight or not. In the same way, we must have inner alertness whether we are doing external work or taking rest. Even if the Guru scolds, beats or kicks, offer everything completely at the Guru's feet thinking that everything is for our own good."

The Holy Mother noticed that the *brahmachârin* had not removed a banana peel which was laying on the floor for a long time.

Mother: (To the *brahmachârin*) So, you haven't removed that banana peel until now even though you have seen it lying there. If it lies there, unknowingly somebody may step on it and fall down. Are we not the one at fault for not removing it even after seeing it?

Understanding the mistake, the *brahmachârin* removed the banana peel.

Mother: Likewise, you should also be alert while walking along the road. If there are any stones or pieces of glass, they should be removed. The egoistic ones won't care about that. We should care that they also should not slip and fall.

Brahmachârin: *Why is it said that one should stay with the Guru?*

Mother: Son, the Guru alone can remove the *vâsanas*. Otherwise, if one doesn't have a Guru one should at least have a very strong spiritual disposition. Sitting in one corner of the jungle, the fox may decide, "I won't howl at the dog henceforth." But it will be the same old case when he sees one. Same is the case with *vâsanas*. When we are alone we may feel that all the *vâsanas* have subsided, but when a circumstance arises, we can see all of them rising up. If there is faith in the Guru, *sâdhana* can be done sitting somewhere. Wherever he sits, he will get the Guru's Grace. Faith is what matters. Those children who stay at a distant place will have intense longing when they think of Mother with concentration. They will get what they need even without Mother's knowledge.

Brahmachârin: *Mother, sleep comes during meditation. What should be done to remove this?*

Mother: Son, it is due to the lack of *sraddha*. You should be alert. When sleep comes, you should know that sleep is coming. Then you won't sleep. At that time you can either repeat the *mantra* with eyes open or get up from your seat and repeat the *mantra* walking to and fro. The mind is very tricky, don't let it enslave you. Not only that. In the beginning stages all the dullness will come up. But if you have alertness and enthusiasm you can overcome all this in due course.

Sunday, 7 November 1982

At seven in the morning, the Holy Mother was sitting in the front yard of the temple where the coconut trees were growing. She was in an abstracted mood. After half an hour she got up and walked around as if intoxicated. Some times she turned around with eyes closed showing a particular gesture *(mudra)* with her right hand. At other times, she uttered certain words as if to an unseen person, still showing the *mudra* but at a different angle.

She roamed around for some more time fully absorbed and then all of a sudden broke into a rapturous song,

*O Mother, for the satisfaction of my life, give a drop of
Thy love to my dry burning heart. Why O why dost
Thou put burning fire as fertilizer to this scorched
creeper?*

*O Devi, chanting the Name 'Durga, Durga' my
mind has forgotten all other paths. O my
Durga, I want neither heaven nor Liberation. I
want only pure devotion to Thee...*

Hearing the song, the *brahmachârins* who were
watching from a distance, slowly gathered around the
Mother. As she sang, tears of bliss and devotion rolled
down her cheeks. When the song was over, in a semi-
conscious mood, the Mother slowly sat down and remained still for a while. Then turning to the *brahmach ârins,* she
softly said,

Mother: Children, the sweetness of devotion is in-
comparable. Once you taste it you will never like to
taste the objects of the world. Children, don't
speak about *Brahman* to worldly people. Tell them
only about pure love and devotion. To those who
are a little educated and rational say "I am searching for my Self."

THE MEDITATION OF A JNANI

Brahmachârin: *Mother, does a* Jñâni *who has attained
Perfection need to meditate?*
Mother: No, son, it is not necessary for them to
meditate. Once Perfection is attained they will not
perceive anything as separate from themselves. Even
then, in order to set an example for others, they will

meditate. Now, if Mother sits idle without meditating, you children will imitate her. That is why Mother meditates. Even after attaining Perfection, many *Mahâtmas* did *sâdhana,* did they not? That was not for their own sake but for setting an example for others to follow. In the *Srimad Bhâgavatam*, even Sri Krishna is said to have practiced meditation.

Brahmachârin: *While living as a householder, can one attain salvation?*

Mother: Certainly, but one must be a real householder. All one's actions must be performed with full dedication. One must always discriminate thinking, "Everything is God's, nothing is mine. He alone is my true Father, Mother, friend and relative." A *grahastâshrami* should always be careful not to get too attached to his wife, children, parents and other relatives. Attachment will cause sorrow. In the past, everyone had faith. At the time of birth itself, a mantra would be chanted in the ear of the child. The child would grow up leading a chaste and austere life. After finishing his studies in the hermitage of his Guru, he would enter into the life of a householder by marrying. His wife also would have been brought up in the same spiritual way. While she is pregnant, she would take a vow of silence and perform rituals in remembrance of God for the first six or seven months of pregnancy. The husband would also do the same. Therefore, the child born to them would be pre-eminent. The child's nature would evolve according to the nature of the woman's thoughts during the time of pregnancy.

Brahmachârin: *Mother, I am not getting concentration during meditation.*

Mother: Son, in the beginning for at least three years, you should keep looking at the form of meditation. Then only the form will be properly fixed within. While looking at the middle of the forehead or the tip of the nose, you must try to achieve concentration. Then you must control food. Otherwise the food will control the mind. You should be careful about that. Good food and bad food, these are all just delusions of the mind. It is possible to live eating only grass. As we attain concentration in meditation, we get all the essence of food from within. There should be the desire to meditate. It is because of the lack of detachment that one doesn't feel like meditating.

Friday, 12 November 1982

THE TASTE OF WORK

The *brahmachárins* were building their own huts in which to live. The Holy Mother was helping them. No one wanted to let Mother do the work, but whatever one may say, it would be of no use as Mother would definitely work.

Mother: The difficulties of life will be understood when we do all these things. When this much work is done we feel tired. Therefore, what must be the weariness of those who work day in and day out? Only if we work like this will we develop compassion. Actually this is nothing. Still, Mother has to make you children carry more of the burden.

Food is to be taken after having worked. Only then will the taste of work be known. What happens in most of the ashrams? Some books will be read from which the knowledge to speak will be gained. My children, Mother won't allow that. She will make you work hard.

One *brahmachârin* asked permission to go home.

Mother: Until yesterday Mother gave you children that freedom. Hereafter it will not be possible. This is an ashram. There is a discipline here. You should live here observing it. Be careful while associating with worldly people. When you get home, your mother, grandmother and all the others will come and tell you many worldly things. You will also get immersed in that. New *vâsanas* will be created as a result. If you go to any worldly house, sit silently. If they ask anything answer with a few words. What you children need is the removal of ignorance.

Thursday, 18 November 1982

The building of the *brahmachârin's* huts was still continuing. There was not any water to mix the cement for the floors. Mother herself was bringing water in a big pitcher. As she was carrying the pitcher on her hip, one of the *brahmachârins* who had just finished washing clothes was about to throw away the remaining detergent water from the bucket after taking his clothes out. This was for washing just one *dhoti*. The Holy Mother noticed this and said to the *brahmachârin,*

Mother: You children have no *sraddha* at all. You have not been through any difficulties. You are wasting things like this because you have not known what suffering is. You must have alertness in each and every thing. Don't waste this much detergent for only one *dhoti*. This can be used to wash other clothes as well. *Sannyāsins* should not waste anything. Then the value of work will be known.

One *brahmachārin* was about to go out wearing a big black rudraksha rosary over white clothes.

Mother: Son, remove that rosary or people will stare at you. We don't require any external show. Devotion is not in wearing that. In this *Kaliyuga* we must wear good clothes and comb our hair. It should be without any external show that we must teach spirituality to others.

Another *brahmachārin* came near Mother and said, "Mother, I am not getting the full form of the Deity during meditation."

Mother: In the beginning it is difficult to get the full form. Therefore try to visualise the feet of the Deity and focus your mind on them. Once the form gets absolutely clear, we become *That*. For this, continuous practice is needed. All that is seen should be imagined as the form of your Beloved Deity. Everyone is to be seen with a vision of equality. Imagine "I am the servant of everyone." If everything is the Self, then who is there to hate? A real devotee's heart must pant for God just like a fish taken out of water. He won't waste even a moment. Some cannot meditate for even two hours. Therefore, they should learn Sanskrit or study scriptures. Knowledge of the scriptures is also necessary. Others can then be taught, can't they?

Brahmachârin: *Mother, why have you come down? Do you know what your real nature is?*

Mother: Son, it is the body that is coming and going, the Self remains unchanged. It is all-pervading. From birth itself Mother knew that God alone is the Truth and that all that is seen is not true. She could see her own reflection in each and every object as if in a mirror. Mother would constantly remember God and would cry singing God's Name. In the nighttime she would sing loudly. I always had the strong feeling that without realising and becoming one with Him I could not live. Worldly pleasures and all other objects were meaningless and equal to poison for me. How many said that Mother was mad! Even the family members would always say, "She is giving a bad reputation to the family." But Mother did not care. Mother has not come just to do something and go. Mother has a clear goal and will not go leaving in the middle without fulfilling it.

Thursday, 9 September 1983

A NEWCOMER

A college professor visited the ashram for the first time just after Mother's birthday. The big decorated shed still remained. He had seen the Mother's picture and the article about her birthday in the newspaper. When he saw her photo he felt strongly attracted to her and felt inspired to see her immediately. He sat waiting for the

Mother on the front verandah of the temple. It was around noon and one *brahmachârin* told him that the Mother was in her hut reading the day's mail and would come soon.

The professor, who later compiled the *Conversations of the Holy Mother* in Malayalam, experienced inexpressible peace and divinity in the atmosphere. He later related, "I was certain even at that time that there must be a highly evolved spiritual personality as the heart and soul of this divine centre."

In a few minutes the Holy Mother came. Without blinking his eyes, the professor gazed at her. Full of cheer and vigour, the Holy Mother came and sat on the verandah as the professor prostrated to her.

The Holy Mother smiled at him with a smile that registered deeply in his heart. Whoever has met the Mother will never forget her smile. A few moments passed silently then the Mother asked,

Mother: Have you eaten anything, son?
Professor: *Yes.*

The Mother again smiled followed by another silence. Now and then, the Holy Mother seemed totally absorbed. She whirled around her right hand showing a *mudra* and uttering *"Shiva, Shiva."* The professor watched in amazement. "Where am I sitting?" he thought. "She is not only an *Avadhuta* or *Paramahamsa*[62] but something transcending both. What a tremendous peace in her presence." As such thoughts passed through his mind the Holy Mother said, *"Say something, son."*

Professor: *Mother, please speak. I will listen.*

Mother: No, son, you say something. Let Mother hear.

Professor: *I came to hear Mother's words. That is the tradition, is it not?*

---

[62]A God-Realised soul who has gone beyond the necessity or observance of all the rules and regulations of spiritual life.

Mother: Son has read a lot. Enough. Now you should perform some *sâdhana*.

The professor could not but wonder. From an ordinary standpoint he was a total stranger to the Mother but that was not at all reflected in the conversation. He was quite convinced by the aforesaid statement of the Mother's that she knew everything about him because it was a fact that he had studied much but had practiced little.

Mother: Son, everyday you must meditate for some time.
Professor: *While seeing you, on whom else could I meditate with eyes closed?*
Mother: That is all right, but even then, the Vision of God is also needed within so that no trouble will occur. If you only see the external form, sorrow may come.

One *brahmachârin* came and sat down on the sand near Mother.

Brahmachârin: *Mother, some devotees have an idea to bring out a souvenir about you. Would you agree, Mother?*
Mother: Darling son, this Mother of yours does not need any publicity. Son, don't be in a haste. All the wealth of this world is Mother's. Don't hurry for anything. Everything will take place at the correct time when it is needed. Children, you go and meditate without thinking about all this.

The professor then cherished a desire to know about the ashram. The Holy Mother, as if understanding his thoughts said,

Mother: Son, it is only two years since the ashram was registered. So many obstacles were there! Especially since Mother's form is that of a woman. There was no freedom. Different people had different doubts. Father Sugunanandan of this house had no faith at all in me.

Professor: *(Hesitantly) About the needs and necessities of the ashram...*

Mother: Look son, here in this ashram there is nothing. Some times there will not even be a penny. Forty or fifty people need to have their livelihood met with also. The children would come and ask in the beginning, "Mother, what should we do for tomorrow?" Mother would sit quietly. Whatever was necessary would come here the day before it was needed. When things went on like that, the children stopped complaining to Mother.

Some devotees just arrived and prostrated to the Holy Mother. They offered apples, mangos and other fruit at the Holy Mother's feet. The Mother distributed them to all the devotees present as *prasâd*.

One devotee: *Having not seen Mother for so many days, my mind became restless. Therefore, I came today.*

Mother: Son, Mother is there within you. She is always with you. Sorrow will result if you think

Mother is only this body. Mother is everywhere and within everyone. Therefore, don't worry.

Hearing these words of the Mother, the devotee's eyes were filled with tears. The Holy Mother is always simple and humble in her statements but there are occasions when she unequivocally and precisely would declare her total identity with the Supreme. Such declarations spring forth spontaneously and unexpectedly when there arises a suitable situation.

Devotee: *What should we do, Mother?*
Mother: Chant God's Name. Repeat the mantra while making each step. That is enough.
Devotee: *Pranayâma...?*
Mother: Breath control is not necessary. *Kumbhaka* (retention of breath) will come by chanting the Divine Name itself.
Devotee: *Mother, even the so-called believers in God abuse us for coming here. How can they give an opinion without having come here and seen for themselves?*
Mother: Don't blame them, children. It is most difficult to remove egoism and jealousy. These are seen even in advanced *sâdhaks*. We should not give importance to what those ignorant children say. Don't get angry with them. We would only lose our power by doing so, that's all.
Another householder devotee: *What should I do, Mother? My desire is to join the ashram as soon as possible.*
Mother: Son, for the time being you stay in your home. The egg will hatch when the time is correct. Don't break it open before that. The bondages of

the family will fall off in due course of time when your desire to realise God becomes stronger.

Professor: *What are Mother's plans for the future activities?*

Mother: Mother's aim is to raise these *brahmachâri* children who are now here by making them do spiritual practices and discipline them to become good *sannyâsins*. They will propagate *Dharma* in the future. Mother has given a regular routine for them. As there are no hired workers here, all the ashram work is done by the *brahmachârins*. A *brahmachârin* should not cling to anything or anyone. He should be free. The habit of self-dependence is needed.

The Holy Mother was sitting in the front yard of the ashram where there was a small coconut grove. A song exemplifying the oneness of Lord Shiva and Lord Vishnu filtered through the small speakers in front of the temple,

> *Hare Keshava Govinda*
> *Vasudeva Jaganmaya*
> *Shiva Sankara Rudresa*
> *Nilakantha Trilochana...*

A householder devotee came and sat silently near the Mother. She opened her eyes after some time, saying, "*Shiva, Shiva.*" Moving her head sideways with the rhythm of the music, the Mother was enjoying the singing. At the same time, she looked at the devotee and smiled at him most naturally. After some time, the devotee asked the following,

Devotee: *Please tell me what I need spiritually, Mother.*
Mother: What does Mother know, son? She knows nothing. Mother is just telling some crazy utterances, that's all.
Devotee: *Mother is playing tricks with me.*
Mother: (In a low tone as if to tell a secret) Now, now son, Mother will tell you something. One day when the three gods Brahma, Vishnu and Shiva came to see Goddess Saraswathi, the Goddess of learning, they saw Her sitting holding a book. When they asked, "What are You doing?" Devi replied, "I am studying." Son, that is how infinite knowledge is. Won't humility come when we remember that? Even Goddess Saraswathi is studying. Then, what about Mother? Never let go of humility.

Understanding that the Mother was asking him to always be humble, the devotee said,

Devotee: *Mother has understood me correctly. Humility, that is what I lack. I have never been able to yield to anyone.*

BHAVA DARSHAN

Outside the ashram compound, on the other side of the canal, fisherwomen were beating coconut husks to make rope. Seeing that, one devotee said, "It is amazing that the Mother felt to take birth in this place where coconut husks are beaten."

Mother: Son, look at that rotten coconut husk. How black and dirty it is. Have you seen them refining

it by beating it again and again? Likewise, the mind
should be made pure through intense *sâdhana*.

Devotee: *Mother, isn't this ordinary mood enough for
you? What is the purpose of the* Devi Bhâva *and* Krishna
Bhâva?

Mother: Maybe it is *Iswara's sankalpa* (God's Will).
If Mother sits in the ordinary manner many will not
speak out their heart. They have no hesitation to
tell anything to Mother during the *Bhâva*. Then
they are talking to the *Bhagavân* (Lord) and the
Bhagavati (Goddess), aren't they? The people
think that afterwards Mother cannot remember
anything. Thus, so many people are consoled by
unloading their burdened heart before God.
Therefore, is not the *Bhâva* beneficial for others?
Everything is His Will. Infinite and multifaceted is
God's play.

One *brahmachârin* who went home for some purpose
just arrived and prostrated before the Mother.

Mother: Son, why are you late?

Brahmachârin: *It was late when I got the bus, Mother.*
Mother: It is not good for *brahmachârins* to go home
during the period of *sâdhana*. Don't stand at bus stands
and such places. There people are of different character. Walk, having the destination in mind. When the
bus comes, you can get in. We will reach the place
where we have to go even if we cannot catch a bus.
Something can be purchased and given to beggars with
the money which we saved on the fare as well. That is
real and selfless service. We serve others by renouncing

our own comfort. What if we would have waited for the bus? Sometimes we may have to wait four or five hours. We will have to go back if the bus does not come. We will be disappointed also. This is not proper for one who wants to lead a spiritual life. Therefore, you must walk without waiting for the bus.

Mother looked at the householder devotee. Even though Mother had told this to the *brahmachârin* it also seemed applicable to householder devotees who do *sâdhana*.

Mother: Similarly, a *brahmachârin* should not take food from a shop. The shop keepers are business-minded. While taking each and every ingredient, the shopkeeper's only thought will be how to make more profit. While making tea he would think, "Is this much sugar necessary? This much milk is not needed, oh, the tea powder is a little too much." In this way he is doing each and everything in a miserly and calculating way just to gain profit. His mind is not concentrated but filled with vacillating thoughts. It will affect those who eat the food as well.

A *sannyâsin* dreamt about newspapers although he was not in the habit of reading them. The newspaper and news appeared clearly in front of him during sleep. He thought about the reason and an inquiry was made. It was then discovered that the cook was reading the newspaper while cooking. Due to carelessness, the fire in the oven would get extinguished while he read the newspaper. Again he would light the fire and read the paper. This was the way the servant cooked the food. The vibration created by his habit reflected in the *sannyâsin*.

Different types of characters come to the shop. We will hear different things there. The thought vibrations of the atmosphere will affect us as well. If control is not maintained, it will become a habit to eat from shops immediately when hunger comes. It is not possible to study ourselves without *tyâga* (renunciation). Plantain fruits and lemon juice can be taken while traveling. If it is necessary, milk and water can also be taken. In the beginning stages an aspirant should be very careful. The plants should be very carefully raised until the roots are firmly fixed. The same is the case with a *sâdhaka* also. When his roots are firmly fixed, then he won't go astray.

Hearing the reading of the *Srimad Bhâgavatam* from a distant place through the loud speakers, one devotee asked, "Mother, is it right to read the Srimad Bhâgavatam and accept money for it?"

Mother: Son, it is not wrong to receive a *dakshina* (offering) if a householder does not have any other means to earn his livelihood. But reading the *Bhâgavatam* desiring money is not correct.

The devotee: *Mother, what is the meaning of the saying that God is of the nature of Love* (prema swarûpa)?

Mother: It simply means that He can give nothing but love. In fact, He is the only One who truly loves us, without expecting anything. Children, even if all the creatures in the whole world love us, that cannot equal an infinitesimal fraction of the love we experience from God in one second. There is no other love which can compare to God's love.

A child stricken by illness was laying in a hospital. The doctors and nurses treated the child with great care. Seeing their expression of affection, the child was also very interested in them. When the illness was cured the parents made ready to take the child home. The child said to the father, "How loving these people are." Before he could give an answer the nurse handed over the hospital bill to the father. The child wanted to know what that was. The father said, "This is the bill for which they have loved and served you. A separate amount is shown for each and every thing they have done. Their love was selfishly motivated." Whoever loves you in this world will have a selfish interest in it. We will get real love only from God. Real love is selfless. Unconditional love will be seen only in God. What else can such a God be except the embodiment of Love? But, how many know the glory of that selfless love? Those who have known at least a little taste of that love won't run after worldly happiness.

Friday, 7 October 1983

The beginning of *Navaratri* celebrations were taking place in the ashram. A big oil lamp was lit in front of the portrait of *Vidya Devi* (the Goddess of learning) for the first day of worship. The reading of the *Srimad Devi Bhágavatam* had already begun. Worship with the Thousand Names of the Divine Mother would also be performed. The Holy Mother and the *brahmacharins* were preparing margosa (*bilva*) leaves for the worship and Gayatri was sitting near Mother helping prepare the leaves.

One brahmachârin: *Mother, all these leaves are damaged by worms. They are not good for the worship.*

Mother: Oh, that doesn't matter, son. It is enough if we give importance to the devotion. We can do the worship with these leaves. It is not the leaf but the innocent mind (heart) that we are offering at the Feet of the Lord through the leaf. It is enough if we take care of our minds so as to not be destroyed by worms.

A newcomer who had never had the opportunity to learn anything about the Mother asked, "Mother, do you have a Guru?"

Mother: (While preparing the leaves) Mother has neither Guru nor *sishyas* (disciples). Mother salutes (bows down) to everything in the world. All are Mother's Guru. Mother has learned everything from Nature. At a particular state of meditation we will get knowledge about the essential principles from any object in Nature.

The western horizon was very cloudy and showed signs of a heavy downpour. The roaring sound of the ocean could be heard.

Mother: There, did you hear the roaring sound of the ocean? The sound will be louder in places where there is no depth but calm where it is deep. The evil-minded people will walk around making a commotion. Personalities with profound ideas will be calm in any circumstance. They won't be moved by anything.

Devotee: *Mother, which is better, the philosophy of non-duality or the path of devotion?*

Mother: Son, the path of devotion suits the majority of people. Can the majority be discarded for a few non-dualists? Sri Sankara, the exponent of *Advaita Vedanta,* propagated *bhakti,* didn't he? Didn't he compose many poems glorifying gods and goddesses and installed idols of the same? He knew that the path of devotion is what is needed for ordinary people.

Ganga told me that Ramana Maharshi was a *jñāna margi* [63] and did not accept *bhakti.* Mother did not agree with Ganga and he argued saying that *bhakti* is a weakness. Without reading any books, Mother said that Ramana Maharshi approved of *bhakti.* How could Ganga agree with my point of view? Soon after, Ganga went to Tiruvannamalai. The first book which he took to read from the Ramanashram library gave Ganga a surprise. It was a text written by Ramana Maharshi glorifying *bhakti.* That finished son Ganga's doubt. Ganga believed that Mother was speaking through Ramana Maharshi in that book.

Saturday, 8 October 1983

GOD'S GRACE

---

[63]One who follows the path of knowledge.

It was 8 o'clock in the morning and the worship through the Thousand Names of the Divine Mother was about to be completed. The Holy Mother entered the temple and sat near the holy seat. One *brahmachârin* began to get up immediately after the worship.

Mother: Don't get up immediately after the worship is over. Sit still for a while; the taste should be enjoyed at least for some time. The effect of taking a medicine may not be felt immediately. It must be given some time to pervade the system. Likewise, the energy gained by doing *japa* and meditation must be given some time to take effect by sitting silently for a while.

The Holy Mother sang,

> *O Divine Mother, Mother of the world,*
> *O most courageous Mother,*
> *Giver of Truth and Divine Love,*
> *Thou art the Universe Itself...*

All joined in. The singing reached the peak of devotional heights. It seemed as if the Holy Mother was carrying all the others with her and soaring high in the vast expansiveness of infinite bliss. Now and then the Mother burst into an ecstatic laughter, followed by her calling "*Amma, Amma!*" which penetrated into the hearts of the *brahmacharins* and other devotees, surcharging their minds as well as the whole atmosphere with spiritual energy.

The singing went on for about 45 minutes and ended with the *arati*. After a while the Mother came and sat in the front verandah of the meditation hall. A few householder devotees and some *brahmachârins* were also there.

Brahmachârin: *What should be done to get God's Grace?*

Mother: Son, if the load of ego and desires are there, the wind of God's Grace won't lift us. The load must be lessened. In her youth Mother never thought about anything other than God. When the wind blew, having touched her body, she would call aloud crying, "O Mother, are you running away having touched my body? Mother, why are you not taking me also with you?" One will certainly get God's Grace if that kind of devotion is there. It is not possible without reducing the weight of worldliness in the mind.

Devotee: *Is there a particular posture for* sâdhana?

Mother: It does not matter if you cannot sit in one posture without moving for a long time. Assuming any sitting posture, you can repeat the *mantra* or meditate. *Japa* can also be done while walking. But you must sit and practice *japa*. That will teach us patience. Sitting in one posture comfortably without moving, is *âsana siddhi*. This is good for meditation.

ASTROLOGY AND IT'S RESULT

Devotee: *It is said that one's horoscope cannot be changed. Is that true Mother?*

Mother: What is said in astrology is the result of the actions done in the past. The fruit of actions can be obstructed through other actions, i.e., actions dedicated to God. A stone which is thrown upwards can be caught before it falls down. Likewise, the course of the fruit of actions *(karma phala)* can be changed before fructifying. A horoscope will give way before God's Will *(sankalpa)*. It may show in one's horoscope that he will marry. But the horoscope will change if he does spiritual practices and happens to get *satsang* (the company of sages) at a young age. Thus he might be able to become a *sannyāsin*. It will certainly change, provided there is a good spiritual disposition and *satsang*. Self-effort also is indispensable, doing spiritual practices like worship, *japa* and meditation.

OBLATIONS TO THE DEPARTED

Devotee: *Are oblations to the deceased ancestors necessary?*

Mother: Mother will narrate an incident. Here, the son of a person who lives nearby was a vagabond and a doer of wicked deeds. Seeing his son's bad ways, the father would scold him. Even then, the son did not care and continued in his ways. Therefore, one day the father said, "After I die, don't let him perform my death ceremonies. If he does, his sin will also come to me. I won't accept the offerings even if he does do the ceremonies after my death." When the father died, the son performed the ritual saying, "I must see for myself whether or not he will accept the offerings." Even though he performed the ritual several times, at the conclusion when the balls of rice which he offered for his deceased father were offered to the crows to eat, they would not even touch them although they would peck at everyone else's. Thus the wicked son's offerings were not accepted.

Just as the correctly addressed letter will be received unfailingly by the addressee, the benefit of

the rituals performed by chanting *mantras* with concentration will reach the soul of the intended person
wherever he is. But as far as a real *sâdhak* is concerned,
he does not have to do any of these *karmas*.

Sunday, 9 October 1983

SRADDHA AND NISHTHA
Alertness and Discipline

More devotees than usual were present because it was
the time of *Navaratri*. Some were newcomers. It was 8
o'clock in the morning when the Holy Mother came out
of her hut benignly smiling at the devotees. All present
prostrated to the Mother. She touched each one and saluted them with all humility. Calling everyone, the Mother went
to the front yard of the temple where the coconut trees were
growing. Some devotees spread a mat under one tree where she
sat and started meditating, asking everyone to join her. About
thirty people were present. All of them sat together and began to
meditate. Seeing this unusual sight, the passersby could not
help themselves from stopping and gazing for at least a moment.
Shortly after the Mother closed her eyes, the devotees opened
theirs and remained gazing at her. After some time when the
Mother opened her eyes, she found that everyone was sitting
there looking at her. An elderly man who was a retired doctor
softly whispered to his friend sitting nearby, "On whom can we
meditate when the personification of love is sitting right in front
of us? But the Mother is simply playing games with us. What do
we know about this divine play?"

The Holy Mother asked raising her voice, *"What are
you saying doctor son?* (Turning to the other devotees)
*Doctor son is of the opinion that doing meditation when this
crazy Kali is sitting here is not correct."*

The doctor was struck with wonder when he heard Mother repeating the sentence that he said a few moments before. He was sitting in the rear which was too far away for the Mother to have been able to hear their conversation. He exclaimed, "How did Mother hear it?" Saying this, he got up from his seat, and having approached the Mother, he prostrated at full length before her.

The Holy Mother caressed him with great affection but did not say anything but *"Shiva, Shiva."* The doctor shed tears of joy which the Mother wiped with her own hands as they rolled down his cheeks. Greatly moved by this show of love, he cried loudly, calling out "Amma Saranam Saranam..!" (Mother is my Refuge). Everyone silently shed tears. After a few moments he returned to his seat. An unusual peace pervaded everywhere. The atmosphere was extraordinarily calm and serene. A few more moments passed in silence. Everyone seemed as if they were in a contemplative mood. All of a sudden, a young man broke the silence by raising a question to the Mother.

Young man: *Mother, why has God given happiness to some and sorrow to others?*

Mother: God is not making anyone sorrowful. It is the demon which makes us sorrowful.

Young man: *Is not God in the demons also?*

Mother: Son, it is the character of the person that is said to be like a demon *(asura)*. It is the *asura svabhâva* (the demoniac nature) which makes us sorrowful.

Young man: *How is that?*

Mother: Suppose there is a blazing fire. Someone tells you not to jump in it. Without listening you jump and burn yourself. If fire is *Brahman,* the person who told you not to jump is also *Brahman.* In the beginning use your discrimination; only do things which are needed. But usually when a circumstance arises, we will lose our discriminative power and do as our ego tells us. The ego and its products are *asuric* qualities. It will spoil our life and personality. In the olden days both men and women would get the training at a young age to control the demoniac forces and become masters of their minds through scriptural studies and practical application in their lives.

A child will study out of fear of his father. But later when he becomes aware of his place in the world and the society, he studies by himself. In the beginning, guidance and discipline are needed. Don't blame God for your not obeying these things and then having loaded yourself with sorrows by acting as you liked. Alertness *(sraddha)* is needed. Nothing is possible without that.

Sraddha and *nishta* (alertness or faith and strict observance) are necessary. Once two fishermen went fishing in a river. Standing near a canal with thick vegetation the first man said, "See, I am going to catch fish here by making a bund around this vegetation. Would you like to join me?" The second man said, "No, if I join you I may have to work until evening and if I don't get any fish my children will starve today. I shall go somewhere else and try." Thus saying, he left. Now the first fisherman started to build a bund with mud and grass which was at hand. He had no tools with him and so he started to bail out the water with his hands. With patience, and faith, without even a slight change in his attitude, he continued his work. Not being strong enough, the bund broke in many places and water started to gush out. But with a steady mind and firm faith he went on repairing it and continued his work. At last in the evening he succeeded in his task and got plenty of fish. At that time the other fisherman, after wandering here and there, returned to the place empty- handed. The first fisherman supplied him with fish and made him happy. Because of his un-shakable faith and perseverance he could save himself and the other man as well. The one who had no faith did not achieve anything at all. Not only that, his whole time was wasted and he unnecessarily dissipated his energy for nothing. Dear children! Wherever one may be, if one has strong faith in God, he will succeed in everything. This is what we have to understand.

GURU

Young man: *Mother, is a Guru necessary?*
Mother: Son, a Guru's presence is unique. Even though wind is everywhere, nowhere but under a tree will we find coolness. Doesn't the breeze that filters through the leaves of a tree give soothing coolness to those who are living in hot climates? Likewise, for us who live in the scorching heat of worldly existence, a Guru is necessary. A Guru's presence will give us peace and tranquillity. One whose goal is Self-Realisation must have a Guru. Without a *Sadguru*, Realisation is hard to attain. The dormant subtle *vâsanas* can only be removed by a Perfect Master. Even for gaining worldly knowledge a teacher is necessary. What can be said then about spiritual science, the subtlest of all branches of learning?

Devotee: *It is said that* satsang *is good for spiritual uplift. What is your opinion about this, Mother?*

Mother: Yes, that is true. If there is *satsang* it is not necessary to do *sâdhana* in the beginning stages. But the only thing is that it must be real *satsang*. Real *satsang* is the yoking of *jîvâtman* and *Paramâtman*. God or Guru represents the *Paramâtman*, disciple or devotee is the *jîvâtman*. Yoking happens when the disciple or devotee applies the Guru's teachings. Scriptural discussion is also a kind of *satsang* because it remind us of the Truth with which we are trying to have a companionship.

CUSTOMS AND DISCIPLINE

Young man: *Mother, is a discipline necessary for* sâdhana?

Mother: A road is required for the buses, cars and cycles. Traffic rules are also necessary; otherwise, accidents will happen. Likewise, ordinary people should have a discipline. There are no traffic rules for the wind and the bird. In a like manner, a Knower of *Brahman* does not need any discipline.

One devotee: *It is said in the Bhagavad Gita,*

> *Abandoning all dharmas, take refuge in Me alone; I will liberate thee from all sins; grieve not.*

Mother: What does that mean? Is it so that everyone should abandon their *dharma*? The Lord won't say so. Other *dharmas* are not needed for those who have the attitude of complete surrender. Not that *dharma* is unnecessary. Beginners must perform their duties but in a Godward direction.

The questioner was surprised on hearing Mother's interpretation of the Sanskrit verse. He might have wondered how Mother, who has no knowledge of Sanskrit and has not read any books at all, could give an explanation about a particular verse taken from the Holy Gita.

Young man: *Mother, I have no peace of mind. What is the way to get it?*

Mother: Son, this attitude of yours to know the way itself opens the door to the path. Now what is needed is *sâdhana*.

Devotee: *Mother, some people say that the knowledge of* Brahman *is enough and that idol worship is not necessary.*

Mother: Son, ordinary people need idols and temples and other such aids. When we are about to go to the temple we remember God and after reaching the temple we remember God. Thus the temple awakens the remembrance of God in us. There is yet another thing. The *âtmachaitanya* (consciousness) of the devotees will be reflected by the idol. There is a special power in the temple where the devotion and concentration of the people remains saturated. By going to temples we will get concentration and devotion.

Young man: *Mother, there are those who say that temples are not wanted because of the crimes committed by people who believe in religion.*

Mother: If that is so, medical treatment and hospitals should also be done away with because of the mistakes committed by a few doctors. Instead of trying to correct the mistakes, should one be obstinate in saying that to right the mistakes is unnecessary?

Young man: *Is not applying sacred ash to the forehead simply a custom?*

Mother: It is very good if you apply ash baked out of cowdung. First grass will be transformed into cowdung. Then, after drying out in the sun, it will be slowly burnt in a fire made from paddy husk. Having removed all the dirt (sand) through purification, one gets ash. Then, after going through several changes, this ash becomes an infallible medicine. It will destroy the bad germs in the hair pores. When we see ash, we should remember the end of our life (death). Ash reminds us that at some time, this body will turn into ash. Ash from a burnt corpse is the best.

It was lunch time. The Holy Mother took everyone to the dining hall. She asked the *brahmachârins* to serve the food quickly. The Mother said, *"All the children may be feeling hungry."* The devotees said, "Mother should also eat." *"Mother doesn't need to now. Children, you eat. Mother will sit here."* The Holy Mother sat in the dining hall. Everyone ate but Mother didn't, even though all requested her to. The *brahmachârins* begged, "Mother, you haven't eaten anything at all till now. Please eat at least a little rice." Mother kept quiet. She lay down in the dining hall itself. It was 3 o'clock. At that time a devotee of the Mother named Karunakaran came running to the Mother. He was carrying a bag. He saluted the Holy Mother but soon marks of sadness appeared on his face. Seeing the devotee the Holy Mother, like a small child, snatched the bag from the devotee's hand saying, *"What were you doing until now? My head is spinning due to hunger."* The bag contained rice and other dishes especially cooked by his wife to offer to Mother. The devotee's joy knew no bounds when he came to know that Mother had not eaten anything until now. With tears in his eyes he said, "I knew that you would not eat because my wife was constantly uttering your name while preparing it."

Having finished cooking early in the morning, the devotee, cherishing the desire to feed the Holy Mother, set out from his house intending to reach the ashram before noon. But, unfortunately he missed the bus and did not reach there until 3 o'clock. It was quite obvious that the Holy Mother was waiting to fulfill the devotee's pure and innocent wish.

After lunch the Mother lay down on the sand under some trees. Some *brahmachârins* and householders insisted that she lie on a mat, but the Mother didn't agree. A devotee who had not visited the Mother for many months came to see her at that time. Pointing to him, one *brahmachârin* said, "Mother, an old son has come."

Mother: Are there old and new sons?

Those devotees who were sitting at a distance came closer and sat near Mother when she began talking. The Holy Mother got up and sat down next to one devotee. He said, "I have visited several times but never brought my wife and children. Until now Mother has not asked anything about them. Sometimes I feel sad about it."

Mother: They are Mother's children even from before, aren't they? Doesn't your wife cook Bengal gram and keep it in the shrine room in front of Mother's picture every day before the usual evening bhajan? Whenever you scold your children, don't they say, "We will tell Vallickavu Amma that you have scolded us and she will scold you!"

The devotee, hearing these words from the Mother's own lips, was overwhelmed with joy and wonder. He said, "Yes, I am a fool to think that the all-knowing Mother is not knowing or caring about my family." He bowed down at the Mother's feet and chanted the following verse with tears in his eyes.

O Annapurna Devi, the Ever-Perfect,
The Beloved and Life of Lord Shiva,
In order to get Wisdom and Dispassion
I am begging of Thee, O Mother Parvati.

My Mother is Goddess Parvati,
and the Great Lord is my Father.
The devotees of Lord Shiva are my relatives
and the three worlds are my home.

Devotee: *I heard Mother saying that in the Kaliyuga (the present age of materialism) concentration is gained more by singing devotional songs than through meditation. Therefore, can meditation be wholly given up?*
Mother: Children, what Mother said was that nowadays the atmosphere is filled with a lot of bustle and sound and therefore to attain concentration, *kirtana* (devotional singing) is better than meditation. A silent and peaceful atmosphere is needed for meditation. Other sounds can be overcome by singing devotional songs loudly, is it not? Even beyond concentration is *dhyāna* (meditation). *Kirtan* - concentration - *dhyāna*, this is the progression.
Devotee: *It seems that in Kerala, devotees of Krishna and Devi are more. Why is that, Mother?*
Mother: In each place the custom is different. It depends on the mental disposition inherited from the previous birth. (Humourously, with a smile) Whoever they might be, they will be in trouble if they have not pleased Devi. In the olden days the Guru, after initiating the disciple, would give him a

Lalitasahasranam book (Thousand Names of the Divine Mother) as well. Only then would he be sent to do *tapas*. The disciple would be asked to chant it everyday.

Only one endowed with the spirit of renunciation can realise Sri Krishna. The reason is that in order to please Krishna, the Embodiment of *Suddha Sattva,*[64] one must himself become like Him. Feelings of doership, self-importance and other such egocentric qualities should not be there. Whoever it may be, without renunciation one cannot realise God. A devotee, during his course of spiritual practice, may have to undergo different kinds of trials and tribulations. Destroying your sense of "I" and "mine," He may deprive you of all your wealth, and even then, only if you catch hold of His Feet will He give His *Darshan.* Sri Ramakrishna said that he had undergone great difficulties to realise Krishna. But the bliss that you experience will be infinite and inexpressible compared to which the sufferings are nothing.

In olden days, a *Lalitasahasranam* book would also be given to the person getting initiated into Krishna's *mantra.* Do you know why? So that the initiate should not be in want of food and clothing. Devi will look after that. Motherhood is predominant in God as the Divine Mother. Children will have a natural attraction towards their mother and a mother will be naturally loving and compassionate towards her children and will look after their needs. So also is the case with the Divine Mother. To get your bread, Devi should be satisfied. That is why She is known as *"Bhukti-Mukti-Pradáyani"* or the

---

[64]Absolute purity or pure sattva.

One who bestows both material happiness and Liberation.

Devotee: *Mother, what is the meaning of the verse "Without doing anything, She does everything?"*

Mother: Mother doesn't do anything. That She does everything is only seemingly so. The sun does nothing but without him, nothing can continue. He stands as a witness, yet he does everything. Likewise, Mother in only a Witness. Though doing everything, She is not bound or attached to it. Therefore, She does nothing though doing everything.

One householder devotee: *What is to be done for gaining mental peace?*

Mother: Son, daily you should give some solitude to the mind. God's Name should be chanted. Have faith in a Perfect Guru. A ladder is needed to climb a coconut tree. The Guru is the ladder. When children are young, they study mainly out of fear of their father, mother and teacher. Therefore, it is clear that in the beginning stages, *bhaya bhakti* (devotion endowed with reverence and fear) is necessary. Thus, mental peace can be gained if one moves forward adhering to the Guru's words.

Devotee: *In order to gain mental peace, I have gone to several sannyâsins but I got nothing from them. All were fakes.*

Mother: Son, *shânti* (peace) will not be had if you search outside. It should be sought within. God dwells within. He should be known by becoming introspective.

Son, you have abused *sannyāsins,* haven't you? You should not do that. Look at Sri Sankara, Swami Vivekananda and others. You can see that it was *sannyāsins* alone who did lasting good to the world. Siddhartha, who was an emperor, became the *sannyāsin* Buddha and did so much good to the world. Then too, there are fake *sannyāsins,* aren't there? But is that only among *sannyāsins?* Do the virtuous ones become worthless because there are also impostors? When going to the market, if you find that one of the shops is illegally selling goods does it mean that all the shops there are doing the same?

A young man: *I feel that there is no meaning in temples.*

Mother: Son, that is not the case. When we see an artificial apple we are reminded of the real one. When we see temples and divine images, we will be reminded of God, is it not so?

Young man: *That is right.*

DISCRIMINATION

Mother: It is not enough if you simply agree with everything. You should do *sādhana.* Sweetness will not be had if you write on a paper 'sugar' and lick it. You must eat sugar. Studying books alone is not enough. *Sādhana* should be performed. If you want to get inspiration to do *sādhana,* life should be understood after having observed it closely. After all, what is marriage nowadays but another bondage? It is a relationship of two bodies. It has nothing to do with the relationship of the soul without which there will not be any essence in it. In the olden days marriage and married life was considered as divine and was another means to attain Self-Realisation. Their spirits were united rather than their bodies which as a result led to peace, tranquillity and eventually culminated in God-Realisation. Nowadays it is nothing but another means to satisfy lust. There is no real love in it, only selfishness. Who will listen and contemplate deeply if it is said that the body is a bag of stools and urine! Children, don't think that Mother is telling to completely discard worldly life. What Mother is trying to say is that you should use this life in a more intelligent way so that this world and your life will become more joyful and beautiful. Discriminate and see. Is the love that we get from our relatives, wife, husband or children real? Is it not for fulfilling their selfish ends that men love women and women love men? What will happen if she or he runs away with another man or woman? Then the attitude becomes just the opposite. You will be ready even to kill her or him. Is this love?

Mothers will say that they love their children. In fact, do they? If they love, why are they not loving the children of the neighbouring houses? Therefore, what they really love is "mine." Mother would say that even the birth of a child is accidental which occured during the course of the parents effort to satisfy their lust and other selfish motives. If the parents really love their children, they should make their children understand and assimilate spiritual truths which would give mental strength and control in order to confront the challenges of life, instead of throwing them into this world without giv-

ing proper spiritual education and forcing them to lead
the same kind of life as themselves.

We say that we love our children. But would any of
those who love their children be willing to die for
them? It is not seen or heard of that someone is ready to
save their child's life by sacrificing their own at the time
of the child's death. Do you know how many are telling
Mother this? A woman was watching when her child
fell into a well with seventeen rings (depth measure-
ment of wells). That mother was not ready to jump into
the well and save her child from death. She cried and
shouted aloud. The child was already dead by the time
he was taken out by a diver brought by a neighbour.
Rare are such people who are ready to save another life
by sacrificing their own. To be frank, worldly pleasure
is equal to a dog's excreta. From one drop of semen we
are losing energy equal to a hundred drops of blood.
For a spiritual aspirant, *brahmacharya* (celibacy) is his
wealth. As far as he is concerned, worldly life is indeed
equal to a dog's excreta. For a dog, human excreta is
like nectar, but for human beings it is an object of detes-
tation. For a spiritual person, worldly life is something
to be loathed. Only if he has this attitude can he attain
the goal. Otherwise, his energy will be dissipated by
the objects of the world.

Real *vairagya* (detachment) will develop if one dis-
criminates like this. Then it will become possible to
perform intense *sådhana*. A *sannyåsin* should acquire
inner wealth by doing *sådhana*. *Sannyåsa* is not child's
play. It needs tremendous courage, courage born out
of sense control. It is enough for a married person to
look after his wife and two children, but a *sannyåsin* has
to carry the burden of the whole world.

In the middle of the conversation a lawyer, a devotee of the Holy Mother, also arrived and sat with the Mother having offered his salutations to her. Hearing Mother's words, he raised a question concerning his own mind and life.

Lawyer: *What is our fate, Mother? We are walking around getting involved in court cases, quarrels, lies, etc.*

Mother: That is all right son, it is the *dharma* (duty) of a lawyer to argue for his party in a suit. That is not wrong. A lawyer is only performing his duty when he argues for a murderer. Even then, accept only truthful cases as far as possible. The sin does not go to the lawyer if the criminal is saved by the arguments put forth by him. The criminal is only saved from the court of law. He cannot escape from God's court. One must bear the fruit of one's actions.

Anyhow, like others, a lawyer can also come to spirituality, abandoning worldly life after the dawn of real *vairagya* has risen in him. Until then, *svadharma* (one's own *dharma)* should be performed dedicating everything to God.

Mother took the fruit offered to her by the devotees, and having made them into small slices, fed the devotees with her own hand. Everyone was happy with their hearts overflowing.

Tuesday, 11 October 1983

It was 11 o'clock in the morning. The Holy Mother was sitting in the front yard of the ashram in the coconut grove. A group of householder devotees from Trivandrum arrived. They saluted the Mother and sat near her. Some *brahmachârins* who just finished their meditation also came and prostrated and sat with the other devotees. She expressed a wish to hear devotional songs. Sreekumar brought the harmonium. The Mother sang with full devotional fervor,

O Devi, O Ambika, Beauty Personified, O Thou Who art affectionate towards devotees, may Thou dwell here in order to end the sufferings of the devotees.

Since how many days have I been desiring to see Thee? I am praising Thee without losing even a moment. Did some mistake happen on my part or is it that Thou hast no mind to end my sorrow?

The *brahmachárins* sang along with the Holy Mother. Tears of bliss rolled down the Mother's cheeks as she called out, *"Amma ente Amma"* (O Mother, O my mother). All the devotees were immersed in the Mother's songs. Some shed tears of devotion and others sat with closed eyes. The atmosphere was calm and quiet except for the singing of the fishermen which could be heard as they pulled the fishing nets from the ocean nearby.

Half an hour passed before the Holy Mother opened her eyes. A young man asked, "Mother, what are the signs of a person who has conquered his mind?"

Another devotee interrupted: *It is enough to look at Mother!*

Mother: This crazy one? Very good! Children, those who have conquered the mind are like a child. They have no attachment to anything. If a child sees gold it will take it. Then throwing the gold away, it will grab a charcoal if it happens to see it laying nearby. This is a child's nature. They do not have

attachment to anything, no bondages. There will not
be any ego at all.

One devotee: *(Humorously) Mother is a very egotis-
tic person. Mother is the All-Witness and therefore
everyone's ego is Mother's. The ego in me is also not
mine, it is hers.*

Mother: That is the attitude that is needed, son.
This is the perfect way of thinking. But you should
apply it in your life also.

Devotee: *But in Mother not even a speck of ego is
found.*

The Holy Mother laughed like a child.

NAME AND LOVE

A woman householder devotee came. She saluted and
kissed the Mother's feet.

Mother: It is a long time since this daughter has
been seen!

Devotee: *It is one year, Mother. There has been no time
available to come here.*

Mother: There is time to go to the hospital if the
child is sick. However long it might be, there is
enough time to stand waiting in bus stops. There is
also time to stand in the long queue in front of the
movie theatre even in the scorching heat. But there
is no time to go to temples and to come here. You
will go running to the place which you like and to
gain objects that you love.

The woman devotee: *What should be done to develop
love, Mother?*

Mother: Daughter, when the Divine Name is chanted constantly, spiritual hunger will come. Consequently, a taste for the Name will arise followed by love for God *(Isvara prema)*. We are saved if love is obtained.

Devotee: *How can one repeat the Divine Name while working?*

Mother: You can chant during leisure times, can't you? Then, through chanting and chanting during those times, the constant chanting will become a habit. At that time, even when we are doing worldly things, our breath will go on repeating the Divine Name. Thus, a state will come when we can do *japa* as well as worldly activities simultaneously.

A devotee sought Mother's permission to go and prostrated to her while taking his leave of the Mother. Touching his back, Mother saluted him in return. This is Mother's usual way, bowing down to the Indwelling Truth.

THERE IS NO MATTER, EVERYTHING IS CONSCIOUSNESS

One man who heard about Mother came to see her in person. He went on babbling about his own glories and achievements. Later when he left, the Holy Mother jokingly said about him,

Mother: Son, once the tape starts playing, shouldn't the song finish? Is it possible to easily wash away the tough stains that have accumulated over many years?

A science student who was interested in spiritual matters as well asked, "The *rishis* (seers) declare that everything is Brahman. Modern science also says that everything is energy. Is there any connection between these two?"

Mother: Son, when we enter into the higher states (planes) of *sâdhana* we can hear all these stones and wooden pieces talking to us. They are not inert but conscious. Then it will become clear that they are also talking. What is known as matter is only at the empirical level. In reality, it is not there. Everything is one and the same Consciousness.

An aspirant: *Mother, why is it that the circulation of the blood through the veins is not felt?*

Mother: At a particular stage of meditation, when the mind becomes one-pointed, we can hear the sound of the harmonious flow of the blood through the veins. It can be experienced. It will be felt as if water is rushing through thousands of small pipes. Such experiences are not born out of any physical disorder. There is nothing to worry about. Several experiences of this kind will occur when we progress in meditation. (Hugging a small girl) See, look at this daughter. She is only seven but meditates like a great yogi. This daughter asked Mother, "Mother, where does the body go while meditating?" When I lie down, she would fan me as she sits in the lotus posture repeating the *mantra* with her eyes closed. If Mother has her eyes closed, thinking Mother is asleep she would embrace Mother's feet and start crying and shedding tears. What kind of girl is this, O God?

Mother laughed loudly like a small child. Everyone joyfully laughed with her. The little girl also expressed her joy, smiling and embracing the Holy Mother.

Wednesday, 12 October 1983

Mother with some other devotees were preparing *bilva* leaves for the *archana* at 8 o'clock in the morning

One devotee: *Mother, what happens if all these ants die getting entrapped in the* bilva *leaves?*
Mother: Children, you don't have to worry about it. All those will return to where they came from. Prepare the leaves chanting the Divine Name *(mantra)* endowed with sraddha *(faith)*.
Devotee: *Do the* brahmachârins *practice* prânayâma?
Mother: A little bit. It shouldn't be practiced too much. *Kumbhakam* (retention of the breath) will automatically come when concentration is attained through chanting of the Divine Name. The *kundalini* (the serpent power) will awaken. For that, no particular breath control is needed. How is it possible to practice *prânayâma* during this age when even pure air is not available? *Prânayâma* should be practiced with discipline under the guidance of an experienced Guru. It is a dangerous path if not done correctly. *Japa* is more than enough.

One *brahmachârin* came and made some complaint about another one.

Mother: Son, *brahmachârins* should not even think anything which is against *sâdhana*. All the power that is acquired through *sâdhana* will be lost. Anger should not be there at all. It is more difficult to remove jealousy. Always the mind should be vacant. Son, go and meditate.

The *brahmachârin* retired having offered his salutation.

One householder devotee: *Mother, can a* grahastha *take* sannyâsa?
Mother: (Laughingly) Oh, have you attained that state? (All laugh) A *grahastha* should look after his family. Don't abandon them. But you can give them up, if there is complete detachment. Then you can leave the house. After relinquishing that, not even a thought about the house should enter into the mind.

It was time for lunch. The Holy Mother went to the hut after instructing the *brahmachârins* to feed the devotees.

STORY OF SANDEEPAKA

After lunch Mother narrated the following story to the *brahmachârins*:

Mother: Angiras was a great sage endowed with immense spiritual power. He had many disciples. One day, summoning all of them he addressed them as follows,

"Due to the fruits of past karmas my body will soon be afflicted by the terrible disease of leprosy and blindness. I would like to spend those days in Kasi (Benaras). Now, I want to know who among you is willing to follow me to Kasi and serve me during those days of suffering?"

Looking at each other, the disciples all stood silently. At that time, there stood up Sandeepaka, the youngest among Angiras' disciples. With all humility he said, "Respected Guru, I am ready to come with you."

The Guru replied, "You are too young. Also, you don't know what service is."

Sandeepaka said, "Revered Master, I am ready and will certainly come with you."

Angiras explained, "It is easy to undergo suffering oneself but to serve the one who suffers is much more difficult."

But Sandeepaka was determined. Such was the intensity of his desire to serve his Guru. Thus, the Guru and his young disciple went to Kasi.

Soon after reaching there, Angiras was afflicted by the fell disease and lost his eyesight. Sandeepaka sincerely and devotedly served his Guru day in and day out. He would never go out leaving his Guru alone except in order to beg for their food or to wash his Guru's clothes. He was constantly engaged in looking after his Guru and took the utmost care to meet even his slightest needs. He would say, "My Gurudev is himself Kasi Vishvanath (Lord Shiva presiding over the city of Kasi)."

In spite of little Sandeepaka's unshakable devotion and utter dedication, the Guru would severely chastise him and accuse him of having made mistakes which he had not done. Some times he would scold Sandeepaka, saying that the clothes were not properly washed or that the food was sour and so on. At other times he would show great affection and love to him and would even comment that he was putting Sandeepaka to so much trouble.

One day, Lord Shiva appeared in front of Sandeepaka and said, "I am very pleased with your devotion and dedication to your Guru. Please ask for a boon." But Sandeepaka was not willing to ask for a boon without first having the consent of his Guru. He therefore ran back to him and after prostrating to Angiras, asked him, "O Revered Guru, may I ask a boon of Lord Shiva to remove your disease?"

Angiras angrily replied, "You are not my disciple but my enemy. Is it your wish to make me suffer more by having to take another birth? Don't you wish that I become liberated in this birth itself?"

Sandeepaka sadly returned to the presence of Lord Shiva and said, "O Lord, forgive me! My Guru doesn't like that I ask for the thing which I would like. As for me, I do not want anything for myself."

Years rolled by and Sandeepaka, the embodiment of devotion to the Guru, still continued to serve his Guru with the same amount of love and surrender. One day, while he was going to the town to beg food, Lord Vishnu appeared before him and said, "My child, I am very pleased with your devotion and dedication to your Guru. I am ready to give whatever boon you ask. You did not ask anything of Lord Shiva but this time you should not disappoint Me as well."

Struck with wonder, Sandeepaka enquired of the Lord, "Even though I haven't served You or even remembered You once a day, how could it be that You are pleased with my service?"

Vishnu smilingly replied, "Guru and God are not different but are one. It is your service to your Guru which has pleased me."

This time also Sandeepaka went to seek his Guru's permission to ask for a boon. The Guru said, "Sandeepaka, if you want some boon for yourself go ahead and ask. Don't ask anything for me."

Sandeepaka returned to Lord Vishnu and said, "O Lord, give me more wisdom and knowledge so that I can understand how to serve my Guru according to his wishes. Most of the time, due to my ignorance, I am not able to understand what he likes. Therefore, O Lord, grant me the knowledge to serve my Guru properly." Lord Vishnu was very pleased and saying, "So be it," He disappeared.

When Sandeepaka returned from the presence of Lord Vishnu, Angiras asked him what was the boon that he sought from the Lord. Sandeepaka told him everything that had happened. Immediately, all the symptoms of leprosy disappeared from the Guru's body and his sight was restored. He stood smiling at his disciple and hugged him. The leprosy and blindness had been self-imposed by the Great Master Angiras in order to test the devotion and dedication of his youngest disciple. Being established in the Supreme Truth, he had no karma to work out. Graciously blessing Sandeepaka, the sage said, "I am very pleased with your devotion. No harm or danger will come to those disciples who serve their Guru with as much devotion and dedication as you have served me with. May all of the disciples and their disciples for coming ages be blessed because of you."

Children, this is real *bhakti*. If such devotion is there, then nothing else is needed.

Thursday, 13 October 1983

MITHYA MEANS CHANGING

A person belonging to the neighbouring house had epilepsy. The relatives of the patient came to see the Holy Mother. The Mother was sitting on the front verandah of the old temple facing east.

The Great Mantra (Mahâmantra) *"Hare Râma Hare Râma Râma Râma Hare Hare, Hare Krishna Hare Krishna Krishna Krishna Hare Hare"* was echoing in the ashram atmosphere.

Mother told the relatives of the sick man, *"For diseases like epilepsy and hysteria, practicing meditation is better than medicines. Those who have practiced meditation according to Mother's instructions have received a cure for such diseases."*

A young man sitting near Mother asked, "How does one meditate, Mother?"

Mother: Children, it is not the same path for everyone. Son, you should meditate on the form of your Beloved Deity and chant the mantra of that particular

Deity. While meditating, you can fix the eyes can either in between the eyebrows or on the tip of the nose. If you find it difficult to concentrate on one of these, then visualise your Beloved Deity's form within the heart lotus. As far householders are concerned, it is better for them to meditate in the heart. The mantra can be chanted at any time irrespective of time and place. Chanting the mantra while using a rosary will help to attain more concentration and to maintain alertness.

Young man: *Mother, how is it possible to remove sorrow?*

Mother: We have been thinking that the body is eternal. That has created sorrow. Now it should be thought in the opposite way, i.e., *Atman* (the Self) is eternal. It should be realised as well. In order to convince ourselves that the body is non-eternal, we must train the mind using the weapons of discrimination and detachment. Look here son, if you put your finger in the nostrils, mucous will come out, from the eyes dirt will come out and from the ears the same. Now, if you do not brush your teeth for a day, your breath will smell terrible. If a wound gets infected with pus, a putrid smell will emanate. In a similar manner, take every part and every organ of the body. What is it after all except a bag of stools, flesh and blood? This is the thing that you dress with beautiful clothes and golden ornaments. Try to pierce through and see the Real Thing which makes it beautiful and shining. That is the Supreme Consciousness. This is how you have to discriminate and detach yourselves from the body and the world of objects. Once you are convinced of the ephemeral nature of the so-called pleasure-giving objects, then you won't desire them. There ends sorrow.

Young man: *This is really useful for any practice. Mother, some say that there is no God.*

Mother: Children, it is like saying with the tongue that I have no tongue. It is with the power given by God alone that one denies God. Not only that. When one denies the existence of something, he is actually affirming its existence. In order to reject something, one must first have a general idea of that particular object. For example, when somebody says, "There is no book," it is quite certain that he had an idea of a book which he saw formerly. Likewise, with God. Above all, the existence of God or the Self is a matter of pure experience. It is not a subject for argumentation.

Young man: *Is there any difference between the mind and the* Atman?

Mother: Pure mind alone is *Atman*.

Young man: *It is said that the world is* mithya *(an illusion).*

Mother: Son, *mithya* only means changing. It doesn't mean that it is non-existent, it means that it is not permanent. If rice is ground, first it becomes powder, then it transforms into edibles and finally into excreta. There is only transformation. The object is still there. There is no change for *Brahman* (the Absolute), but there is change for the world. *Brahman* alone is the Truth, the world is illusory. To understand *Maya* (illusion) and *Brahman* (the Absolute) is very difficult.

Young man: *Mother, is not* Kurukshetra[65] *within ourselves only or is it outside also?*

---

[65]The battlefield where the Pandava and Kaurava armies arrayed and fought the Mahabharata War in ancient times.

Mother: The battlefield of *Kurukshetra* is there both outside and inside. Symbolically, it is the constant war which is fought within each one of us between righteousness and unrighteousness, vice and virtue, untruth and truth, evil and good, the demons and God. We cannot deny the fact that this *Kurukshetra* battle was also historical truth. If you simply interpret everything symbolically, all these happenings which occured long ago will lose their splendour and significance. People will become egoistic and arrogant, thinking, "Oh, everything is inside, then why and whom should I fear?" It must not be interpreted in that way. Rama, Krishna, Buddha and Christ were historical personalities who led a perfect life in every way, setting an example for the entire human race. You cannot simply say that *Dvaraka* (a city where Sri Krishna was living) is the *Sahasradala Padma* (the thousand-petalled lotus chakra in the head) and Krishna is the Supreme Power who dwells within and similar esoteric interpretations. That is foolishness. Suppose after a hundred years a grandfather tells his grandchild, "Child, you know what Mahatma Gandhi did? He fought against the British without any weapons. His weapons were truth and non-violence. He stood smilingly in front of the machine guns of the Britishers without thought of revenge or enmity. Indians arrayed behind him and obeyed his words with utter submission. Even when he was shot dead he didn't cry but uttered the name of Lord Rama. Above all, physically he wasn't a striking personality. He always dressed like a peasant." The boy would tease his grandfather saying, "Grandpa, that was a beautiful story even though it is a fabricated one." Later, somebody else may say that Gandhiji is an inner state. Children, it is foolishness to interpret things like this.

Young man: *Mother, is there life after death?*

Mother: Yes, there is. During our life time, all our thoughts and actions will be recorded by a subtle sheath which functions like a tape recorder. According to the impressions gathered during one's life time, the *jīva* (individual soul) will take another body during which the recorded impressions will be replayed. Children, we can see some people very talented in music, mathematics or in science since birth even though they haven't undergone any special training in those particular fields. Neither their parents nor any of their family members or ancestors might have been a musician or a mathematician or scientist but this particular boy or girl would manifest these qualities even from a very young age. This is where we have to agree with certain mysteries connected with our past birth. Anyhow, it is difficult to convince everyone about these things, even though it still remains a fact.

DETERMINATION TO REACH THE GOAL SHOULD BE THERE

Young man: *Mother, what is to be done to attain the goal?*

Mother: Be intent on the goal. To be first in the class is the aim of a student who studies for a degree in engineering. He won't go to movies. He won't waste time making friends or spend too much time with them. Even while travelling, he would study while sit-

ting in the bus. Circumstance will not obstruct one
who is intent on reaching his goal. If the intense desire
to reach the goal should arise in one, first, he must have
discrimination of what is proper and what is improper.
He should have the awareness, "How meaningless are
the things of the world." Bliss is not in all those things.
If we want to have peace, Truth should be enquired
into. Mother doesn't tell her children to worship God
or Mother but she says to know "who you are."

Worldly relationships are like the relationships at
the bus stop. All will get down at some stop. You alone
will remain. Therefore, what Mother says is to search
for the Truth without getting engrossed in dreams.

Saturday, 15 October 1983

It was the day of *"Poojayeduppu,"* part of the Navaratri festival. Already at 6:30 a.m., many children were already present. Many parents brought their kids for initiating them into learning the first alphabets. As a con-
cluding ceremony of the worship, all, irrespective of
age, are supposed to sit down crossed legged, considering themselves as beginners sitting in front of the Goddess Saraswathi writing the first alphabets either in the
sand or in rice, praying to Her to shower Her grace upon
them. The Holy Mother made all of them write each of the
first syllables in the sand and asked them to respond as
she herself repeated each one of the syllables in a loud
voice. Truly a blissful moment, everyone was overwhelmed with joy. There were women, men, elderly
people, young men and children all gathered together.
All were initiated into learning by the Holy Mother.

All of a sudden a young man, a medical student from
the northern part of Kerala, who was only twenty-five or
so, started crying, laughing, dancing and rolling on the

ground. It was the first time he came to visit Mother. He called out, "O Goddess, O Saraswathi, O Amma Saraswathi, here is your child, teach me, teach me, O Saraswathi!" The Holy Mother smilingly went near him and caressed his forehead and chest with her hand and said, *"Calm down, child, calm down, Mother is here."* In a couple of seconds he became normal. He got up and seeing Mother standing in front of him, prostrated at her feet with tears of joy in his eyes.

Later, when asked, the youth in a voice choked with emotion related, "I was gazing at Mother's face as I wrote the syllables as instructed by her. All of a sudden, even while my eyes were wide open, the Holy Mother's form transformed into that of Goddess Saraswathi seated on a beautiful white lotus holding the veena, Vedas and the rosary in Her four hands. She was dressed in pure white. But I could easily recognise Her face because it was the Holy Mother's enchanting countenance. Tremendous light was emanating from all over Her body as if a thousand suns had risen up together. I could not control the bliss which I experienced. I became totally oblivious of the surroundings." Before he could finish the sentence he again burst into tears.

By this time the *bhajan* started with all accompaniments. The Holy Mother sang:

> *O Kali, the Holy Consort of Lord Shiva,*
> *Parvati,   Sankari,*
> *My only refuge is Thy beautiful Lotus Feet.*
>
> *Hail, hail to the Goddess of Knowledge,*
> *Hail to the Mother of the Universe,*
> *Hail to the Mother who bestows*
> *Auspiciousness on Her devotees.*
>
> *Victory, victory to the Goddess of Sound*
> *Who holds the veena in Her hands,*
> *Victory, victory to the Goddess of Speech*
> *Who is the Ruler of the Universe.*

O Lalita, the Power contained in the
seed letters,
The Embodiment of Knowledge and the
Liberator of the Universe, I humbly bow down to
Thee praying for Thy Grace...

The singing lasted for two hours but passed like five or ten minutes; such was the bliss radiated by the Holy Mother.

Monday, 17 October 1983

The Holy Mother was sitting in the front verandah of the meditation hall facing east. Many devotees were sitting on the steps as well as on the ground. Now and then a few of the residents came to seek Mother's opinion on certain matters concerning the administration of the ashram. Some others came with a question or a doubt so as to find a way to come near Mother and hear a word or two from her.

One devotee: *Mother, how could you attract these children when they were still very young?*
Mother: I haven't attracted anyone. On the contrary, they were attracted by something in this crazy girl. It is their *samskâra* (latent tendencies) which brought them here. Anyhow, it is better to turn to spirituality when you are young. The more you live in this world, the more will be the worldly experience and *vâsanas* (resultant habits). Each experience is an addition to the already existing one. It will become more and more dense. A tender stick can be easily bent but a dry one will break if you try to bend it. Likewise, training young people is easy because they have comparatively less concep-

tions and ideas about life in their mind. Whereas, others have many and most of them are misconceptions. Still they cling to them strongly believing that they are right. However, the case is different if they have self-surrender and devotion.

Son, attraction is the nature of a magnet. In reality it doesn't attract anything but iron filings get attracted to it by it's mere presence. The magnet simply is.

Devotee: *Mother, how is it possible for you to behave equally towards all?*

Mother: Children, a spiritual person is not seeing the external appearance but only the Essence or God. The sculptor, when he sees a rock, beholds the beautiful idol which he can carve on it, not the rock. Likewise, a *sâdhak* should see only God which is the Essence in everything. Then only equanimity *(samatva bhâvana)* will come. The electricity which comes through a fan, bulb or refrigerator iis one and the same. The difference is only in the medium. Likewise, it is the same Consciousness which dwells in all living beings. We will not feel hatred or anger towards anyone when we think that the Consciousness which dwells in him is the same as in me.

SCRIPTURES ARE BILLBOARDS

Devotee: *Mother, can one attain the goal through scriptural studies?*

Mother: Son, suppose there is a billboard on the roadside saying that there is a jewelry shop at a certain place. You won't get gold if you ask the billboard for it, will you? If you want gold you must go to the jewellery shop. Scriptures are like billboards. They are pointers. They point out the goal. That is the only use for them.

We cannot get coconuts from the picture of a coconut tree. Scriptures are like the picture. Having drawn the blueprint of a house, we cannot possibly live in it. We have to build a house according to the plan, only then we can live in it. Scriptures are like the blueprint. We ourselves have to work and attain the goal.

One *brahmachárin* was making scrawlings in the sand with his fingers. The Holy Mother noticed it.

Mother: Children, don't move your legs and hands unnecessarily. Movement shows the vacillation of your mind. Wherever you sit, sit with concentration without moving your hands and legs unnecessarily.

A devotee just arrived to offer *dakshina*[66] to the Holy Mother. The Mother declined to accept it. When the devotee insisted, Mother said, *"Mother has not given* dakshina *to anyone. Then how could Mother accept it? Mother has neither Guru . or disciples."*

GURU BHAKTI

A householder: *Mother, some people say that a Guru is not necessary. Is that correct?*
Mother: Consecration is not needed for a *svayambhu linga* (a self-manifest idol). Discipline

[66]A gift to a revered person like a preceptor in connection with an auspicious occasion.

under a Guru is not necessary for those who are perfect from birth. Even such people might accept a Guru in order to set an example. Sri Krishna had studied in a *gurukula* (Guru's residence), didn't He? Whereas, those who haven't attained perfection need a Guru. Is it proper to say that only for *Atma Vidya* (Self-Knowledge) one doesn't need a Guru when a Guru is needed for all other arts? He who says that a Guru is not necessary is an egoistic person who is not ready to bow his head down in front of another. He will not make any progress unless he serves a *Sadguru* who will help him remove his ego.

Suppose someone wants to learn carpentry. First he must find a master carpenter. Then he must listen with patience and attention to the carpenter. After that, he must reflect on all that has been learned and try to assimilate it. Then follows the practical application of that by making a door, table or window. The same is the case with spirituality as well. The Guru's words must be listened to with great attention and devotion. Next comes discriminative reflection followed by application in one's own life. Without a Perfect Master and His Grace, Realisation is most difficult.

The Guru will test the disciple in different ways. Only one who is endowed with strong determination can withstand all those tests and proceed on the spiritual path. But once those tests are passed, then the infinite Grace of the Guru will flow towards the disciple unimpeded.

There was once a Self-Realised Guru who had a single disciple. One day, the Guru summoned the disciple and told him to sculpt an idol of the disciple's Beloved Deity, Sri Krishna. Seeing that it was his Guru's wish, he made the idol applying all of his skill and talent. On seeing it, the Guru smashed it to pieces and said, "What is this? How ugly! Make another one." The disciple patiently and silently obeyed his Guru's words and made another idol with even more care.

This time the Guru severely scolded him saying, "You are not sincere and do not obey my words. This idol is even worse than the first one. Make another one." He smashed the beautiful idol of Krishna which the disciple for the second time.

The disciple made nine idols, all of which met with the same fate. Yet, he accepted the Guru's words and actions submissively without getting impatient or angry. Only he felt sad that he could not please his Guru. Finally, when he brought the tenth idol his Guru hugged him with overflowing love and said, "Now you are fit enough." Upon saying this, he touched the disciple on the fore-head. Immediately, the disciple experienced the ecstasy of *samâdhi*. By his Guru's Grace he was able to sustain that high experience.

Children, there is nothing that the Guru cannot give. Guru is the Supreme Consciousness Itself. Selfless service and utter dedication are the two things which make one fit to receive the Guru's Grace.

After staying in the ashram during the *Navaratri pooja* and performing his spiritual practices in the presence of the Holy Mother, a devotee from Kottayam[67] came to

---

[67]A town which is about 65 kilometers away from Vallickavu.

take his leave. He saluted the Mother. While patting him on the back the Mother said,

Mother: Son, go happily and return, Mother is always near you. You have stayed here this many days. Even after going home, reflect on the memory of this experience. Remember the Divine Mother while walking, sitting or working.

Devotee: *Mother, please give me some instructions.*

Mother: You should get up early in the morning. Having washed your face, hands and legs, do *japa* for some time. Then, after finishing your nature calls and bath, chant *the Lalitasahasranam*. Don't chant it for namesake. Do it sincerely and with devotion. Visualise the enchanting form of the Divine Mother standing in front of you and offer flowers at Her Feet. It is enough to offer mental flowers if flowers are not available. Son, if you find it difficult to visualise the full form of the Divine Mother, try at least to see Her Feet. Meditate for a few minutes when the chanting of the *Sahasranama* is over. Try to repeat your mantra even while at work. You should sing *bhajans* at dusk. Control your food and sleep. Meditate for some time every day.

The Holy Mother took the rosary which the devotee was wearing on his neck. The Mother meditated for some time keeping the rosary in her hands. Putting it back on the devotee's neck the Mother said,

Mother: Chant your Beloved Deity's mantra on this rosary. Avoid mingling with people too much. Speak softly and behave sweetly towards your wife and children. If they are not interested in spiritual practice, slowly try to make them understand the importance of it and try to make them participate in the practices that you are following. When you return home after work, talk moderately about absolutely necessary things only. Enter the *pooja* room and do *japa* sitting there.

Saturday, 22 October 1983

A beautiful morning dawned with the rising sun's soft rays filtering through the leaves of the coconut trees and the leaves of the *mailanchi plant* (Alhenna shrub) which grew in front of the temple. This diffused light along with the gentle breeze produced a wonderful soothing effect. The chirping of the birds and above all the reverberating sound of the ocean waves made the whole ashram atmosphere more lovely and graceful.

The Holy Mother was sitting on the front verandah of the old temple with a group of educated young men. Cheerful as ever, the Mother's contenance was lit up with a bright smile.

One young man: *Mother, we simply wanted to see you and therefore we came, yet when I saw you I was inspired to ask something. May I ask?*

Mother: A question? To this crazy one? (Mother laughs and after a pause) Yes, yes, you can, son.

Young man: *Mother, some say that this world is a total chaos and confusion. Some others say that there is a harmony beyond all these seeming diversities. What is your opinion on it?*

Mother: Son, these are two different points of view derived from two different levels. Those who run after the external world will always experience nothing but chaos and confusion. Whereas, those who go deeper, who enquire into its real nature, will certainly find that there is only harmony and oneness and no diversity at all. Children, everything depends on the mind. If the mind is well balanced you can experience peace and tranquillity everywhere in the world but if it is agitated the world will seem agitated. When we are on the earth we can see many things, houses, trees, huge buildings, forests, animals, different kinds of people, etc., but when we are traveling in an airplane, flying very high, there is nothing, everything is one, a whole. Son, now there are many thoughts in the mind accumulated from different experiences of life. When thoughts are more we will not get any peace of mind, wherever we are or whatever we have. When they are less we can find peace even if we are not provided with any comforts or facilities. Those who lessen the thoughts through practice can find peace, irrespective of the place where they are or the time. For them, the so-called world of chaos and confusion becomes an abode of peace and harmony. For others it remains as a hell forever. All spiritual practices are methods to decrease the thoughts and to increase peace and thus slowly man can become God. Not only does one enjoy peace oneself but can give peace to others as well.

The Mother suddenly stopped and turning to one of the boys who was carelessly looking here and there said, *"Son, stop fighting with your parents."* One could easily see the visible shock that the boy had immediately when the Holy Mother uttered these words. His face turned pale. Hanging his head, the boy sat silently for a few moments. The Holy Mother, who was smilingly watching the boy, now burst into laughter and asked, *"Did Mother scare you, son?"*

The young man, who still had an amazed look on his face, asked Mother in a soft voice, "No, but how did Mother come to know that? Even my close friends do not know this. Did anyone tell this to you?" The Mother patted his back and said: *"No, Mother was simply joking, don't worry."* The young man in a firm voice said, "No, Mother it wasn't a joke. What you said is true. I always fight with my parents. I am not at all hesitant to admit right in front of my friends and Mother that almost all the time it is my ego which makes me quarrel with them. The reason is that they will not give me money for my lavish way of living."

The Mother lovingly asked, *"Is that correct son?"* Now he could not control his emotions. His eyes were filled with tears. In a broken voice he said: "No, Mother, I know it, but I was never aware of the fact that an unseen person is always watching me. Now it is clear, Mother. I won't repeat it. I promise in front of you." The other young men were silently watching the whole scene with wonder. Tears rolled down his cheeks. The Mother consoled him saying,

Mother: Son, don't be sad. This remorse itself is the best redress for the mistakes that you have committed. The errors committed when we were ignorant will be forgiven by God. But once you become aware that they are mistakes, from then and there onwards try your best to refrain from doing them. Stop brooding. Forget about the bad actions that you have committed in the past. Once you take refuge in God refraining from the bad actions, then they are like a cancelled cheque.

The young man gazed at the Holy Mother's face and again asked surprisingly, "Still, I am wondering about how Mother came to know all these things." The Mother just smiled, looked at him and upturned the palm of her hands (a gesture which means "who knows?").

At this time a householder devotee came with his family and prostrated to the Holy Mother. This was their first visit to the ashram. Mother asked them to sit on the verandah.

Mother: Children, have you eaten anything?
Devotee: *Yes, we had breakfast.*
Mother: Children, you know *bhajans*, don't you? Please sing some songs.

The devotee, his wife and children looked at each other in amazement. They were wondering how Mother came to know that they sang *bhajans*.

Mother: (Loudly) Oh my son Sree (Sreekumar), bring the harmonium.

Sreekumar came with the harmonium. The devotee and his family sang together:

> *nandalála navanita chora*
> *natavaralála gopála*
> *devaki vasudeva kumára deva deva gopála*
> *móhana murali gána vilóla*
> *móhana venu gopála*

Mother: (In great joy) Sing, sing!

They again sang:

> *he nandalá gopál*
> *shyáma gopál venu gopála*
> *he nandalál...*
> *giridhara gopála rádhe gopála*
> *shyáma gopál venu gopála*

Mother: (In a begging tone) One more, please!

The devotee with his family sang:

> *nanda ánanda krishna sundara gopála*
> *ánanda govinda gopi gopála*
> *he mádhava he keshava*
> *manamóhana krishna jagadíswara*

The Holy Mother was very happy. She enquired about the devotee's children's education and their general welfare. The Mother drew very close to them as if she had known them long ago. The Mother said, *"Children, come on, let us go to the seashore."*

The Mother took them to the seashore. There was a stump set deep on the seaside. Only about one foot of the stump was visible from the ground level. Pointing to the stump, the Holy Mother said, *"Formerly it was sitting here that Mother used to meditate."*

The Holy Mother with the devotees went very close to the ocean waves. A giant wave suddenly rose up and broke on the shore. Like a small child, the Holy Mother laughed and called out *"Shivo, Shivo!"* Looking at the sea, the Mother said, *"Where it is not deep there are waves and agitations. The deep sea is calm."*

The Mother with her index finger wrote in the sand "Mother Sea." When the waves rolled up and washed it away, the Mother, like an innocent child laughed aloud.

It was lunch time when they returned to the ashram. The Mother herself served food to the devotees and fed each one with a ball of rice with her own hand like a real Mother and her children.

After lunch the Holy Mother went to her hut. Some of the devotees conversed with the residents and others began reading spiritual books. Some of them sat in the coconut grove and sang *bhajans.*

It was dusk when the Holy Mother came out for the usual evening *bhajan* at 6:30. The Mother sang:

> *O Mother, even though Thou art near I am*
> *wandering unable to know Thee. Even though*
> *I have eyes, I am searching unable to see Thee.*

> *Art Thou the beautiful moon that blooms forth*
> *in the blue winter night? I am a wave that,*
> *unable to reach the sky, beats its head against*
> *the shore...*

Such is the sobbing of the limited individual selves to attain the Unlimited. Knowingly or unknowingly they search for that Supreme Goal but like the waves they again fall down unable to reach the heights of Self-Realisation. The endless search which began aeons ago still continues until dissolution, only to begin once again.

Sunday, 23 October 1983

When the Mother came out of her hut at 10 o'clock in the morning, she was dressed in pure white, wearing ash on the forehead and ornaments made of *rudraksha* on her ears, hands and neck. The Mother smilingly received her devotees.

Her nose ring shone in the sun's rays which made her benign smile more beautiful. The Mother walked towards the coconut grove and sat in a shady place. All the devotees, having offered their prostrations, sat in front of Mother.

The Holy Mother became absorbed in deep meditation. Some of the devotees also sat in contemplation while others gazed at the Holy Mother's form. Now and then the Mother showed different *mudras* (divine ges-

tures) with her hands and blissfully smiled as if she was beholding something. When the Mother came out of meditation, a
woman from a nearby house approached her and began explaining her woeful story. She talked to the Mother as if to a friend or
neighbour. It was quite obvious that her understanding about
the Mother was poor. As there were many people sitting around,
the woman quit the place without spending much time near the
Mother. When she had gone, the Holy Mother said,

Mother: People go to see doctors when they are afflicted by some disease. Likewise, one should go to
spiritual centres when the mind gets sick. There
you will get mental peace. But usually they won't
feel like going. They simply suffer. God is waiting
to help. But there is nobody to receive the help.

Look, haven't you seen that woman? During
Krishna and *Devi Bhavas* she will come and tell everything to *Bhagavān* and *Devi*. She thinks that
Mother doesn't remember any of those things afterwards. Then again she would come like this and
tell many other things but only things concerning
herself and her small family. What a pity! All are
living in their little world made of their own
dreams. (Mother laughs) However much sorrow
comes, these people won't properly turn Godward.

Devotee: *Why is that so, Mother?*

Mother: What Mother would say is *karma phala*
(fruits of past actions). That is how *vāsanas* control people. They lack *sraddha* (care or heedful-
ness) and won't feel to do the needful thing even if
somebody tells them about it. Those are all results
of their previous birth.

The Mother noticed one *brahmachârin* going to do something else during the hour of meditation. When Mother questioned him, he gave certain lame excuses.

Mother: (To the *brahmachârin*) Children, when we set a disciplined routine, we must follow it regularly without fail. Punctuality in following one's discipline is most necessary. A person who has picked up the habit of drinking tea every day at a fixed time will get a headache if he doesn't drink it for one day at that particular time. This is the nature of habits. Likewise, you children should feel that kind of longing if you fail to perform your practice one day. That will show your intensity and *sraddha* to reach the goal.

The *brahmachârin* returned to the meditation hall. The Mother says that one should not get up even for nature calls during meditation.

Mother: A *sâdhak* should have forbearance and endurance. Nothing should move him. Before meditation, you should tell your mind, "Whatever may happen, I will get up from here only after the predetermined hour of meditation is over."

The crows made a big noise cawing while perching on the trees and flying haphazardly in the sky. It seemed that they had seen some food somewhere and were fighting for it. On the other side of the backwaters the fisherwomen were beating coconut husks. That sound mixed with the cawing of the crows echoed in the atmosphere.

One woman devotee: *Mother, what is our path?*

Mother: You children are householders. You should look after your children, husband and home. But all the time chant the Divine Name. Chant your mantra while doing any work. Both spirituality and worldly life should be carried on simultaneously. Let your world be firmly fixed on spiritual foundations.

Daughter, haven't you seen a person feeding ducks while guiding them through the backwaters? He will be standing in a small canoe. There will not be even enough space in the boat for him to stand properly. If the ducks happen to stray away, he will guide them to the correct direction by making a noise splashing the oar in the water. All the time he will be rowing the boat as well as smoking a cigarette. If water happens to enter into the boat through any hole he will bail it out. He will also talk to someone who is standing on the shore. But even while doing all these things, his mind will be fully concentrated on the balance of the boat. If his attention is distracted even for a moment, he would lose his balance and fall into the water. This is how you have to live in this world. Whatever you are doing, your mind should be fixed on God. This is possible through practice.

It is better to tell your sorrows, whatever they are, to God rather than to your husband. You should pray like this, "O God, please give peace of mind to my husband. Please bless my children." In this way, do everything thinking of God. Usually women think only about their family. They should be a little more broad-minded. Remember that all are God's children. We will remove thorns lying in front of our house. Why do we do so? To avoid pricking the foot. To avoid falling down we remove a banana peel from the house or yard. Likewise, we should remove it if it is lying on the public path or road. Think that all are our children or God's children. Our attitude should be that no one should fall, even a person who, out of his ignorance, angrily jumps forward egoistically thinking "I am everything." Don't think "Are they not somebody else's children? Let them fall, why should I care about it?" Our mental attitude should be, "O God, let even the egoistic person be able to pass by without falling down."

First of all, our neighbours should be good. Is it possible for us to sit quietly in our house if a quarrel takes place in the next house? Could concentration be gained for meditation if some thorns are lying here? You will go on thinking restlessly, "Oh, it is piercing, it is paining." Likewise, if there are bad thoughts in the surroundings, that will adversely affect us. Concentration will be lost. Therefore we should pray like this, "O God, make everyone virtuous. It is because of their *samskâras* (mental tendencies) that they are saying and acting like this. O God, give your light to all, pardoning everyone." Always chant your mantra. Whoever you meet, don't forget to chant the mantra.

Daughter, don't waste time talking about worldly things. Life will be wasted if you cling to worldly things forever. Suppose you live eighty or so years in this world. Why should you spend your entire lifetime only for desiring, enjoying and thinking about worldly pleasures? Can't you think and turn to a higher way of living once you understand the momentary nature of these worldly objects? Otherwise, it is foolishness and one leads nothing more than a pig's life. The family man's mind stays in the world, with worldly thoughts gnawing away at his vitals. Even then, ways to save himself are not wanting.

Woman devotee: *Why do you say like that, Mother?*

Mother: Remembrance of God is a *vettuchembu*.[68] Do you know what is the speciality of *vettuchembu*? Once the seedling decays in other roots, it won't sprout again. Whereas, it is not the case with *vettuchembu*. However much it decays, it is said that if there is even a little bit of green portion somewhere the shoot will come from there. Similar is the case with remembrance of God. Suppose it so happens that remembrance of God has entered into our mind at some time or other. It doesn't matter how much the mind is spoiled or how long it has remained under evil influences. When spiritual awareness dawns, that former thought of God will spring up and sprout. This is the special feature of Godly thoughts. So, we don't have to be afraid now, do we?

Nothing will happen if you simply sit feeling happy about it. If you want spiritual progress, intense *vairagya* (detachment) and *sâdhana* are needed. It is laziness to think that everything will turn out well without any effort. This *tamas* (inertia) is a great obstacle.

From the very beginning we should move with care. Suppose we are sowing some seeds. After they sprout, we spread thorns around that particular area. Why? To protect the seeds from getting de-

---

[68] A vegetable that looks like a yam.

stroyed by hens and human beings. In the beginning it
is dangerous because the thorns might pierce people's
feet, but will the seeds sprout if you think in that way
and not spread the thorns? In the beginning thorns
should be strewn in order to protect and help the seeds
to sprout and grow. Likewise, in the beginning stages
the *sâdhak* should protect himself from evil influences
to help his spiritual progress. For that, *yama* and
niyama (the do's and don'ts of yogic discipline) are
necessary. Whoever comes your way, don't mingle too
much with them. The seed of devotion will not sprout
if you gossip and cling to your worldly manners to
please everyone. All that will be trampled and destroyed by relatives and friends. Don't pay heed to
their hatred. They cannot save us. They can only
harm us. *Bhagavân* (the Lord) alone is the Savior.
Therefore, whatever happens, God should be held on
to tightly.

We will lose the certificate of God if we behave
expecting a good certificate from the relatives.
Those who remember God alone are our real relatives. Only those who help us towards that become
our near and dear ones. Others are destroyers.
When such people come, tell them, "You have your
own path. My path is another one. Please don't feel
angry. I take this as the correct path. I must be like
this now."

When milk is set for curdling it should be kept
still. Only then it will become curd. In the
beginning *sâdhana* in solitude is necessary. After
the seed is sown care should be taken to prevent the
hens from pecking or scratching it. Once it germinates

and grows up, then there is no problem. In the beginning don't mingle too much with everyone. Women householder devotees should particularly be careful about this. Sitting alone you should do *japa, dhyâna* and sing *kirtans* without wasting time talking unnecessarily with the neighbours.

Woman devotee: *Mother, what if they come to quarrel with us saying that we are having enmity with them?*

Mother: Daughter, try to make them understand the matter. They will listen if they care. Otherwise, don't bother with them. We shouldn't have hatred towards anyone. Tell those who are about to develop ill feelings, "Look, it is not because of any bad feelings that I am saying this. It is after how many births that we get this human birth? The aim of human birth is God-Realisation. Forgetting the goal, we have passed our time thinking that this body is eternal. Only now, that awareness has dawned. Why should we commit mistakes again? Why should we talk ill of others and find fault with them? What is the use of it? We can chant the Divine Name during that time, can't we?"

Children, we spoil our life thinking of our near and dear ones like husband, children and relatives. Are the so-called children our children? Where were they before birth? Whose children were they? Whose children are they when they die? We say that the children are ours. If it is so, can we stop them from going when death comes? It is certain that they are not our children. All are His children, the Lord's children. It is He who gives life and takes it. He alone is the real owner of the *jîva* (individual soul). Children, what foolishness to think of them as ours! We say that husband is ours. Is he our husband? If so, we must be able to seize and detain him when death comes, mustn't we? If that is not possible, how can we say that he is "our" husband? How can a thing which is not under our control be ours? Therefore, the husband is not ours. Everything is owned by Him. See and behold only the Essence in others. It is not the cashew fruit but the nut that we need. The fruit will get rotten after two days. But the nut won't decay. It is not the husband's body but the soul that we should see. Not only the bodies but the spirits should be united. Thinking and contemplating thus, let us proceed forward surrendering everything to Him. Thus, you should give good advice to your friends and relatives. Even then, if they become envious, don't pay any attention.

We should direct all our attention to God discarding everything else. For example, when our child is sick, we will run to the hospital to see the doctor and get the medicine. On the way while running, one after another of the people by the roadside will ask you, "Where are you going, where are you going?" You would say, "No time now." There is no time to stop on the road and give the answer because you will miss the bus and won't be able to see the doctor. Likewise, ignoring everything else, we should go towards God. When you sit somewhere doing nothing, try to tell stories of the Lord instead of indulging in gossip and finding fault with others.

The woman devotee was very happy and seemed quite convinced. It was a graceful moment. All the devotees were bathed in the nectarian words of the Holy Mother. It seemed as if none had even taken a breath. Everyone sat mo-

tionless like statues listening to the great truths which the Holy
Mother expounded in simple and lucid terms making them alive
and understandable through examples taken from daily life. The
words went directly into the hearts of the devotees. Only if the
Mother finds that the listeners are inquisitive does she give such
long talks. Such occasions are rare. Sometimes in front of people
who are not interested in spiritual matters and people who ask
questions just for the sake of questioning, the Mother would not
even open her mouth. To put it in the Mother's own words,

Mother: However much I tried I couldn't utter even a
word to them. I just got up and came back. Without an
inner feeling springing forth from within, Mother cannot show love or talk artificially. Everything depends
on the children's character. Mother doesn't have any
particular feeling towards anyone. But unknowingly
Mother will feel a closeness to innocent-hearted
people.

But the case is different when people who are eager to
know ask questions even if they are atheists or rational-
ists.

The woman devotee: *We heard that Mother couldn't
sleep last night due to some reason.*
Mother: (Joyfully laughing) Yes, yes, that son's
call. Oh, what an innocent call it was! Eventually
that son slept thinking and thinking of Mother.
From wherever children call, Mother will hear it.

The devotees didn't understand anything about the
son which Mother mentioned, who he was and why he
called so loudly to disturb Mother's sleep. It was quite
obvious from their faces that they were very curious to

know about it. At that time Balu, who was sitting near Mother, solved the puzzle.

Balu: *It is true that Mother couldn't sleep last night. She was so restless and all of a sudden she said in a loud voice, "Son, don't do it, Mother is here for you." It was only at five in the morning that she slept peacefully but only for an hour. We were also a bit worried about Mother's mood. It remained a mystery to us as well until (pointing to a young man who was sitting in the back shedding buckets of tears) he came here today at seven in the morning. I told you that Mother slept for an hour. All of a sudden, she got up at six, came out of her hut at six-thirty and sat outside in the sand as if waiting for someone to come. When it was five minutes to seven this young man hastily came to the ashram. It was obvious that he neither slept nor changed his clothes. Seeing Mother sitting in front of the hut, he went running to her and fell at her feet bursting into tears. The Holy Mother, with overflowing motherly affection, held him and slowly lifted him up. She wiped his tears with her own cloth and lovingly said, "Son, Mother knew that you were coming. I was waiting for you. Mother came to you last night." Hearing this, the young man again burst into tears. The Mother consoled him and talked to him for an hour and returned to her hut.*

Even though the Holy Mother got up and went away, all the devotees were very curious to know about the rest of the happenings, and so to satisfy them, Babu himself said,

Babu: *I was working as an engineer and had visited Mother a couple of times. I had strong faith in her. I received my engineering degree three months ago and fortu-*

nately got employed without much delay. I had a love affair with a young girl who was a medical student. Both of us promised to marry each other soon after the girl's college courses were over and after I had got employed, even if our parents protested. But though my love towards her was pure and sincere, the girl's attitude was not so. Two days before her marriage to someone else took place, I had a total nervous breakdown. Since the last two days I was wandering here and there as one gone mad. Last night I cried and cried, calling out to Mother behind the closed doors of my room and finally decided to commit suicide. I took the thirty sleeping pills which I purchased the previous day when the mental agitation started and was about to swallow them. Then all of a sudden I saw the Holy Mother entering into the room with outstretched arms. The door was still closed, yet I was amazed to see the Mother entering the room in flesh and blood. As she came in, the Mother called lovingly, "My son, don't do it! Mother is here for you." She approached me and took the pills from my hand, opened the window and threw them outside. Then she said, "Don't act like a fool. You are Mother's son. Come to Vallickavu." Saying so, she disappeared. I couldn't even utter a word. I stood tongue-tied. Was it a dream or reality? I looked at the open window. It was closed before. Still not convinced, I went out and searched for the pills outside the window and was wonderstruck to find them lying there scattered around. I had no more doubt. This happened at 4:30 a.m. Immediately I started for Vallickavu.

Babu paused for awhile and looked at the devotees. All of them were sitting motionless like wooden statues. With a joyful smile on his face, Babu said, *"Now, I hope that whole matter is clear."*

It was *Bhâva Darshan* day. At 4:30 in the evening the devotional singing started. The divine mood began at seven. There were hundreds of people. *Darshan* went on until four in the morning. The Holy Mother went to her hut only at 5 o'clock after all the devotees left.

Monday, 24 October 1983

The Mother was sitting under a coconut tree in the coconut grove situated in the front yard of the ashram at about 10:30 in the morning. Though the sun's rays became more and more intense, the shade of the coconut trees and other trees was there to give protection from the heat, just as the loving guidance and help of a *Sadguru* is the protection from the scorching heat of worldliness.

Three youths who were interested in spiritual and religious matters came to see the Holy Mother and were sitting in front of her. On the southern side of the ashram, across the backwaters the people who were beating coconut husks were quarreling with each other. It created a lot of noise in the ashram premises too. Slowly it died down. Then only the sound of the husks being beaten alone resounded.

THE HINDU FAITH AND 'I', THE SUPREME PRINCIPLE

A young man: *Mother, why is Hinduism so liberal and lacking in organisation?*
Mother: Son, the preceptors of old presented the *Sanâtana Dharma* (eternal religion), not as a narrow religion constrained to a particular caste, creed or sect but rather as open to anyone and everyone. All are welcome to this path. This is everyone's. Just like a compassionate and loving mother, it

discards none. This faith declares that anyone, whatever be his or her mental constitution or path, can attain God through constant practice.

Religion should be able to satisfy everyone equally
without any distinction. Take, for example a mother
who has ten children with ten different characters. One
may be a high thinking spiritual person, another one a
scientist. There might be an artist or sensationalist
among them, while another will be doing cultivation
and physical labour. There can also be a rogue or a rob-
ber among the ten children. But the mother will consider all equally. While serving food she won't serve
more for the spiritualist or scientist and less for the artist or the rogue. She will be able to satisfy everyone
equally while serving, talking or in showing love to
them. Sometimes it might even seem that she loves the
rogue more and gives him little concessions. Children,
likewise is true religion. Whatever may be the mental
constitution or level of thinking of a person, true religion must be able to satisfy him fully. This is what Hinduism does. It provides a means to all. There is the path
of *bhakti* (devotion) for the emotionally predominant
person and the path of *jñāna* (knowledge) for the intellectually predominant one. If someone is hard working in nature and is interested in doing physical labour,
the path of action (*karma*) is there for him. But there
are some people who think that their religion alone is
the best and proclaim that Liberation is possible only
through that.

Young man: *Is that correct, Mother?*

Mother: No, it is not. *Kollam* and *Quilon*[69] are one and

---

[69] A town 35 kilometers to the south of the Mother's ashram.

the same, are they not? The ultimate goal of all is one, God. But He is known by different names, that is all. Is it correct if somebody says that you can go to Delhi only through one particular road? There are many roads which will lead us to Delhi, isn't this so? We must be ready to accept this fact instead of fighting each other like dogs in the name of religion.

Young man: *What if they claim that only their path is the direct way to God and all the others are indirect?*

Mother: Nobody has the right to claim so. It is utter foolishness and ignorance if somebody says that. Mother would say that such people are totally ignorant about the purpose of religion. Such statements show the inability of the so-called followers to understand the teachings and life of their masters.

We (the exponents of *Sanâtana Dharma*) have not declared that one path alone is suitable to attain the goal. All will reach the same place whether sitting on a bicycle or in a boat or on an autorickshaw. Whatever vehicle we use in travelling, the destination of arrival is *Quilon*.

Children, no great soul will say "Only through me you will be saved." Has Sri Ramakrishna said, "Follow me alone, otherwise there is no hope?" Has Ramana Maharshi said so? Did any of the great saints and sages of the past declare like that? No. A real knower of the Self will not say so. What they say is to move forward according to your chosen path, having firm faith in it. That is what is said by the founders of all the religions.

But after a religious leader dies, the followers interpret his teaching in a different way. Doctrines like
"Have faith only in our religion" or "Only through our
path" are spread by the followers who have no *visâlata*
(broad-mindedness). Do you know what a *Mahâtma*
means when he says, "Believe in me?" The "I" they talk
about is not the small "I" which concerns the individual. It is that "I" which is the Supreme Principle. As far
as a great soul is concerned, "In me" means "In God."
Taking this and interpreting it as caste or religion, the
followers think in a narrow-minded way. Sri Krishna
told Arjuna, "Have faith in Me," that "I" which is the
Supreme Principle. But now, some Hindus say that
you will get Liberation only if you believe in Krishna;
some others say that Shiva alone is the Liberator. This
is not correct. What we (the *Sanâtana Dharma*) say is,
whether it is Krishna or Christ or Nabi, they all help us
to attain the Supreme. Whether you come through the
southern side or northern side or from the east, you can
reach the ashram. Those who say "Only our religion is
true" are mistaken. Real *Mahâtmas* will never be
bound by an institution. They will go forward keeping
the Supreme Truth alone as the ideal. Therefore, the
great masters of Hinduism, who were all Realised
Souls, have not insisted on any narrow rules. They have
not formed an organisation. That is why, even after
many aeons, the Hindu faith still exists with its roots
deeply entrenched. It is unshakable. No force can destroy it. The infinite power of Hinduism is derived
from the *sankalpa shakti* (strong resolve) of the great
saints and seers. Children, there is no harm in having
many religions and faiths but it is harmful to think that

they are different and that one faith is higher and another lower. Do not see the differences, see the unity in them and the great ideals which they teach. What all religions show is how to develop compassion, love, faith, forbearance, endurance and renunciation. That is what is important. Religion means expansiveness, the ability to accommodate anything and everything. Religion is the merging of mind where all differences disappear.

The second youth: *It is said that* Sanâtana Dharma *is the source of all other religions and that other religions sprung from it. Is this true, Mother?*

Mother: Yes, it is true. In the beginning there was only one religion. It was from that religion that all other religions sprang up according to the need of the different eras. In reality, there are no differences between the religions. There is only unity. Previously, in India, there was only one political party, the Indian National Congress. It is only recently that the other parties came into existence. Likewise, at one time there was only the *Sanâtana Dharma*.

A youth: *The temple authorities in our place play movie songs instead of devotional songs through the loud speakers.*

Mother: Children, you should ask the members of the temple committee, "What is this temple for, what is the purpose of it?"

Young man: *Mother, if we do so, we will be left with no one to support us.*

Mother: Son, don't think like that. You should tell them the matter without getting angry, "Dear elders, you are our fathers. We are young. We would like to ask so we can understand certain things from you. Is it right to do this in a temple? Is this place and its atmosphere meant to develop devotion and love in the hearts of people or is it meant to increase the worldly tendencies in them? As administrators of the temple, are you not responsible for keeping the temple atmosphere pure and holy? Or else what is the difference between a movie theatre and a temple?" Tell them to play devotional songs. If you say it lovingly they will come to the right path. What a pity! Worldly songs are heard from temples. They won't even play "*Harinama kirtana*" (devotional songs) early in the morning.

Young man: *Even if they go to see a vulgar film, out of pride they would say, "I am going to see such and such a film." But if it is to go to an ashram or other holy place, they would simply say, "I am going up to here only." They are ashamed to say that this is where they are going.*

Mother: (Laughingly) They will go secretly. Otherwise, others will tease them. Even if you have to hear their scoldings, tell them frankly that you are going to the ashram. Let them scold. Our sin will be reduced. We are taking on sin when it is told in secret. We must have the courage to tell the truth. Good character is the most important thing in life. That is the foundation on which you have to build your life. Character building is what we get from ashrams and *gurukulas*. Ashamed to visit such places, we consider cheap, worldly things as something great and valuable which, in truth, utterly spoil our life and take away our peace of mind, leaving us in the midst of darkness. They will only increase our negativity. On the other hand, ashrams and spiritual people will lead you to light and bestow peace and bring tranquillity into your life. All this reveals their lack of spiritual culture. You should frankly say, "I am going to the temple or ashram. We have no peace of mind. We are going to the place from where we get it. You cannot give us mental peace. We know that you yourself don't have peace. Then what does it matter if you tease?"

THE SOCIETY WHICH DESTROYS ITSELF

Young man: *Mother, they would say that they see movies to get peace of mind.*
Mother: After seeing such movies, the next step is imitating what they have seen. Many people learn to steal from watching movies. Nowadays what fistfighting the children are doing. They practice after returning from the movie theatre.

Some days back a boy, having fought with another boy, fell down unconscious over there (pointing to the next house). When asked, they said that they were trying the karate which they had seen in one movie. (All laugh)

Another thing is reading cheap novels. After reading such novels, they perform bad actions in an amateur attempt to imitate, and many evil and malicious thoughts pass through their minds which later end in harmful behaviour. Because of this, even the atmosphere becomes polluted.

In the olden days there were less people. Therefore,

the atmosphere was purer. In those days if there was one house here the next house would be far away. In the area where there was only one house previously now there are a thousand houses. Not only that, in the olden days there were plenty of medicinal trees everywhere. No diseases would be contracted if one breathed the air that had blown carressing those trees and leaves. The trees grown in those days were the peepal tree (banyan), the country fig tree and the neem or margosa tree. They were all *ayurvedic* herbal trees. Now, all of them have been cut down and removed. People have started growing fruit-bearing trees, plants and vegetables which are good for eating, but by using artificial means and fertilisers which will do harm to the body. Using these artificial and so-called modern means, they multiply the size and yield of the roots, vegetables and other plants by two or three times of what they would normally be. This is what the people are eating which will definitely be harmful physically, mentally and intellectually. The children born to them will also be affected. Nothing is natural nowadays. Even human beings are after unnatural things. They cannot act or speak naturally. Everything is unnatural. Therefore, they have lost their splendour and glory. The atmosphere has become completely impure. The population and houses have increased. The air has become polluted due to the poisonous gas produced from the factories and industries. Even the health of human beings is quickly deteriorating. The only way to regain the lost natural state of both Nature and human beings is through spirituality.

SATYA NASTI PARO DHARMA
There is no dharma superior to truth

Mother: In those days there was only truth. All families lived up to a truthful life. People of those days lived truthfully even if their lives were in danger. Even though one were a servant, he would not give up truth even if somebody offered millions to him. If you catch hold onto truth, everything else will come back to you. Without truth, *Lakshmi* (the Goddess of prosperity), *Bhairavi* (an aspect of Mother Durga) and even *jñâna* (knowledge) cannot exist. Truth is everything. Truth is God.

In the olden days, everyone practiced truth. The wife lived for the husband and the husband for the wife. They had the fruit of truth and self-sacrifice. They had an all-surrendering attitude, courage, love, righteousness and justice. Without truth, there is nothing, no *dharma* or *Lakshmi*. Even if one's life was in danger he would only tell the truth. (Laughingly) Nowadays what lies people are telling even in court, touching (taking an oath on) the *Ramayana, Srimad Bhagavad Gita* or *Bhâgavata!* In those days there was *bhaya bhakti* (devotion endowed with reverence and fear) to *the Ramayana* and other holy texts. But now, after taking an oath on the *Ramayana* saying, "This is truth, what I am going to say is truth," the first word they utter will be a lie! (All laugh) Today the *Ramayana* is only a stack of paper.

The youths and the devotees present greatly enjoyed the Holy Mother's talk. It was quite clear that they were really amazed to hear these highly enlightening words from a seemingly simple village girl who did not even have any formal education.

Young man: *I have told some of my friends about Mother. But they were not convinced.*

Mother: Son, when it is time, it will ripen. Don't squeeze and make it ripen too early. There are people of different natures. You shouldn't try to argue with them. Each one's experience is their *pramâna* (valid means of knowledge). Even we might not believe it if somebody else tells us their experience. When we tell about our experience to others, let them accept it or not. Otherwise, don't insist. Don't waste time on all this, children. And then, if someone comes to criticise you, say, "On the basis of our faith we go there. You have nothing to do with this matter. Would it be for nothing that we go to the ashram, spending money from our houses? Consider the fact that there may be something valuable there. We are going to the place where we will get mental peace. What about you? You give the money that you have at hand to liquor shops and tea shops. That is your habit. You don't have time and money for beneficial things. Because of that, you suffer."

Young man: *Do you send the resident* brahmachârins *to give speeches?*

Mother: It is no big deal to give a speech after studying books. You should speak having gained the experience. That which comes through experience is valid. Sometimes Mother will send one or two for giving a speech. Mother had sent one son to study the scriptures. But others had not studied the scriptures at that time. Even then, they have conducted speeches in many places. They have shown others that one could conduct speeches nicely even without learning the scriptures. It is possible as the result of their *sâdhana* and experience.

Young man: *We don't have irrevocable bonds of relations like the people of other religions, do we?*

Mother: They have many problems and entanglements concerning their existence as a religion. Therefore they are forced to stand together. The *rishis* (the seers) thought not to bind the Hindu religion. Where is the end to catch hold of and tie? Whom do you think can seize hold of the vast sky and tie it? Therefore, they could not bind it. It lies open. Still, the fact remains that there is no unity. Yet because there are no bonds it still exists without decaying. Organised religion also has its drawbacks. Look at the decline of the Buddhist faith.

Look at the people of some sects of Hinduism. They say that Liberation is possible only through their God. That is an extremely narrow attitude. They are giving speeches standing in market places and street corners as if God is for sale. They will beat you if you say that there is another God other than theirs. This is an uncivilised nature. But real Hindus will accept everything. What is there to reject? Everything is God only, is it not? It is said, "I am *Gayatri* among mantras, Himalaya among mountains, peepul tree among trees," isn't it?

Two elderly people arrived and sat among the group of devotees after prostrating to the Holy Mother.

Mother: Children, where do you come from?
First man: *From Trivandrum (capital city of Kerala).*
Mother: Children, have you eaten anything?
First man: *Yes, we have eaten earlier.*
Mother: Here lunch is at 12:30. All children can take food from the ashram. Will you be going soon?
Second Man: *We came to see and speak with Mother.*
Mother: Yes, it should be for *satsang* that we should go to spiritual people and spiritual centres. It is good to spend some time in this way. *Satsang* is the best thing for spiritual advancement.

The newcomers were spiritually inclined. It seemed that they were *sâdhaks*. Mother also felt some kind of closeness with them. When they were about to ask something, the Mother said,*"Children, have your lunch and then come. Mother will talk to you later."* The Holy Mother went to her hut after taking them to the dining hall.

In the afternoon the Mother called the newcomers to her hut. Getting up from the cot, Mother also sat on the floor on a mat with them.

First man: *Mother, are all* satsangs *equally good?*
Mother: Son, whichever kind it is, all *satsangs* will have at least a little benefit. The confluence of people who think of God is good, is it not? All will be thinking of the same thing. The homogeneous thought wave will lessen unnecessary thoughts, and peace will be enjoyed. But the meeting should not be for arguing and disputing, which will only increase arrogance and ego. It should be for meditation, singing devotional songs,

contemplating and discussing scriptural statements. It is most beneficial if you get a chance to see *Jivanmuktas* (Liberated Souls) or *Avatârs* (Incarnations of God). Their mere presence itself will benefit us.

NIRVIKALPA SAMADHI AND AN AVATAR

Second Man: *Can one come back after experiencing* nirvikalpa samâdhi?

Mother: Children, if they are people who have descended from above, they will return after experiencing *nirvikalpa samâdhi* but won't return if they are people who ascended through *sâdhana*. The latter would just go (leave their body). Having thought about a particular thing before entering into *samâdhi*, one can return to the same thought which he had before entering into that state. This is possible. But this is possible only if one does it intentionally. Only those who know how can do it. Otherwise, it will just be like a kite going up in the air with a broken thread. Incarnations can come back. In fact, an Incarnation doesn't have different states like *nirvikalpa samâdhi*, the state above and the state below, etc. They are always *That* only, *Purnam* (whole). They have only certain limitations which they themselves have accepted for the *avatâra karma*.[70]

Both the newcomers were very happy. The one who seemed to be the eldest said, "Mother, we are very much

---

[70]The activities that should be launched during that particular Incarnation.

blessed to be in your presence. We are ignorant children who are still very much involved in worldly affairs. Mother, please bless us to come to you now and then so that we can unload our burdens and regain our peace and tranquillity."

The Holy Mother smilingly replied,

Mother: We ourselves have taken the burden and now we ourselves have to give it back. Mother doesn't want anything from her children except the burden of their sorrows and sufferings.

The elderly people saluted the Holy Mother and took leave of her. It was 6:15 and soon the *bhajans* began.

Friday, 28 October 1983

The day passed. The sun slowly moved to the western horizon ready to dive deep into the Arabian Sea. It was five in the evening. Some of the *brahmachârins* were meditating in the meditation hall, others under the trees and a few went to the seashore. The ashram atmosphere was calm and quiet. All of a sudden the Holy Mother, who was usually very cheerful, was afflicted by breathing trouble (asthma). No particular symptoms were seen before this started. This created a great amount of confusion in the ashram. As each moment passed the disease became worse. All were very much distressed seeing the Holy Mother struggling to breathe properly. The *brahmachârins* ran here and there in the hope of getting some medicine. Though they tried different medicines, no effect was seen. Some of the householder devotees and *brahmachârins* shed tears looking at the Mother. Some began chanting Divine Names and mantras for healing the Mother's sickness. The Holy Mother in great pain rolled on the ground. Several hours went on like this. At 10 o'clock at night the Mother drifted into a seemingly sleepy mood.

Saturday, 29 October 1983

This sudden attack of asthma remained a mystery until the next morning. It was only 7 o'clock in the morning when a lady came to the ashram from Quilon, urgently stating she wanted to see Mother. She sat outside Mother's hut, waiting for her to come out. That day Mother came out before the usual time. All the residents were anxious to know whether the asthma attack of the previous night was lessened. But since the Mother was very enthusiastic and cheerful as usual, it was quite apparent that the disease had gone. Not only that, there was no trace of the attack either on her face or in her movements. Everyone was very happy and amazed at the same time.

The woman devotee suddenly came forward and having saluted the Mother, stood with joined palms in front of her.

Mother: Why so early daughter? Is not your sickness cured?

Hearing these words, the woman stared at the Mother's face in wonder and as if in a dream she uttered,

Devotee: *Mother, you saved me yesterday. So it was true. Now it is clear. The whole day I suffered a terrible attack of asthma. In the afternoon it became worse. Unable to bear the pain and difficulty it created in my respiratory system, I cried aloud calling Mother. In a few minutes the illness was cured. The asthmatic trouble completely disappeared. Everyone was struck with wonder. The children in the house said that it was Vallickavu Amma who removed the illness. Then they started singing the Divine Name with great devotion. I also thought, "Who else could remove this horrible disease except Mother." Now I heard it from your own mouth. I came running to see you and to offer my salutations. O Mother, I have nothing else to offer.*

The woman burst into tears. The Holy Mother lovingly patted her on the back and comforted her.

Later the Mother related, *"Mother could not help taking her illness when she heard that daughter's heartbreaking cry."*

YOGASCHITTA VRITTI NIRODAH

The ashram clock rang ten. The *brahmacharins* came out of the meditation hall after their morning meditation. One young *brahmachârin,* who joined the ashram a week earlier, approached the Holy Mother who was sitting under a coconut tree in front of the temple lost in meditation. The *brahmachârin* stood at a short distance away from Mother looking at her. A few more minutes passed when the Mother opened her eyes uttering *"Shiva, Shiva."* She smiled at the boy who then came closer to the Mother and saluted her.

Before meeting Mother, this *brahmachârin* was a *nirgunopâsaka* (worshipper of the Formless) although he worked as a priest in a temple of the Divine Mother Kâli near his home. He later started meditating on the formless Self as instructed by a scholar. Before switching his meditation to the formless Self he had meditated upon the fierce aspect of the Divine Mother Kâli. For a long time he used that form of Mother Kâli as his Beloved Deity. He never used that form of meditation after he started the new technique. On his first visit to the ashram, he had an informal talk with the Mother, expressing to her his decision to join the ashram. Before he could mention anything about his practices, the Mother took a small picture of Mother Kâli from the wall made of coconut leaves and handing it to him, said, *"You are not mature enough to meditate on the Formless. Therefore, meditate on this form of the Mother. Without love, nothing can be gained. Your mind has become very hard. Sprinkle the water of love and make it soft."* The astounded boy was tongue-tied. He alternately looked at the small picture given by the Mother and at the

Holy Mother's face. Do you know why? Because it was exactly the same pose of Mother Kâli on which he used to meditate. Even the size of the photograph was the same. The boy, still unable to control his wonder said, "Mother, I used to..." The Holy Mother then interrupted and said, "*Yes son, Mother knows it; you used to meditate on this form of the Divine Mother and that is why Mother gave it to you. Attain the Nirguna (attributeless) through Saguna (God with attributes)."*

Now the boy sat near Mother and said, "Mother, I would like to know something about yoga."

Mother: Son, yoga is not something that should be told in words. It is an experience. It is the yoking of *jîvâtma* (the individual self) and *Paramâtma* (the Supreme Self). The bliss of that unity is inexpressible just as you cannot explain sweetness after eating honey. Many talk about it but have not experienced it. Though there are many paths, there are mainly only four - *bhakti yoga, karma yoga, jñâna yoga* and *râja yoga*. The purpose of all *yogas* is control of the mind which means thoughts. Whatever may be the path, attainment of the goal is possible only if the *vâsanas* are attenuated.

Do you know for what these different *yogas* are? Different paths are needed according to each one's nature. The doctor treats the patient according to the patient's bodily constitution. Some people are allergic to injections. Liquid medicine will be given to them. There are some others who would vomit if liquid medicine is taken. They will be given pills. But there are some for whom even allopathic treatment is not suitable. They will be told to take *ayurvedic* medicines. The doctor knows what the patient needs. The aim is to cure the disease, whereas the treatment can be done only according to the body's stamina and other conditions. Likewise, when the disciple comes to the Guru, the Guru knows which path is suitable for him. For some it would be *rāja yoga*, for others it is *bhakti yoga*. Each person will be given the appropriate teaching according to his mental state. He will be guided on that path which suits him. For an emotionally predominant person, the Guru might advise *bhakti yoga* instructing him to direct all his thoughts towards God. For an intellectual person the Guru may suggest the path of knowledge and be asked to discriminate and understand the ephemeral nature of the world. The path of *rāja yoga* will be given to someone who is interested in observing and analyzing the functioning of the mind. He will be asked to closely observe the mind and its tricky ways, to trace from where the thoughts originate and how to control them. A dynamic person who is hard working in nature would be asked to follow the path of *karma yoga,* dedicating all his work at the feet of the Supreme Lord, renouncing the fruit of all actions. Thus, the path of *yoga* differs according to the nature and taste of the disciple. But there is one thing; it cannot be said which path is better than another because each one is great and unique in its own way. Some people may be weak by nature, others might be hard-hearted. The Guru knows how to guide all these different types of people.

Each one has qualities inherited from past births. Suitable treatment is needed. If we think it over carefully, *bhakti, rāja* and *jñāna yogas* which say, "I am neither the mind nor the intellect," are all a kind of *bhakti*. *Bhakti* comes even when you say "I am *Brahman*." It is not possible to perform *sâdhana* without devotion unto the eternal and pure *Brahman*, saying, "I am That." *Karma marga* (path of action) is also good. What is needed is to act, seeing everything as God and renouncing the fruit. Selflessness is the goal of spirituality. All *sâdhanas* are for achieving only that. However much *sâdhana* you do and whichever be the path, no spiritual progress will be gained if there is selfishness in the mind. It cannot be said that one path is better than the other. The path will be prescribed according to *âdhikâri bheda* (the qualification of the student). Different paths are suitable for different people. There is no one path which is suitable for all. In fact, the apparent differences in each of the paths do not really exist. Each path merges in the other.

The path expounded by Patanjali Maharshi is known as *râja yoga*. There is importance given to *pranayâma* in this one. *Kundalini yoga* also comes under this. The vital force which sleeps in the *mulâdhâra* (bottom of the spine) is awakened through *pranayâma*. The principle of both *râja yoga* and *kundalini yoga* is the subjugation of the mind. The purpose of all spiritual practices is nothing but that.

SAMATVAM YOGA UCHYATE

The Mother stopped talking and started singing,

Come, O Mother,
Who art the Enchantress of the mind.

Give me, O Ambika, Thy Vision.
Let Thy Form shine
In the lotus of my heart.

When will dawn that blessed day
When my heart will become full
Of devotion to Thee?
Satiated with the repetition of Thy Name,
When will blissful tears flow
From my eyes?

The Holy Mother went into *samâdhi*. She shed tears of bliss. Regaining her external awareness, the Mother said,

Mother: Son, the taste of devotion is something unique. The purpose of *bhakti yoga* which declares "I am nothing, everything is You" is meant for mental purification. The path of *jñâna yoga* which considers "I am the Self, everything is Me" is also intended to attain purity of mind. The aim of *karma yoga* in which one does selfless action seeing God in everything is also for mental purity. Through the attainment of concentration of mind, *râja yoga* also aims at this. All *yogas* aim at *samatva bhâva* (attitude of equality). What is known as *yoga* is *samatva*. There is no God beyond that, whatever may be the path. That state should be attained.

(To one householder devotee) The different paths are for people endowed with different natures. Look at this son. He used to do meditation on *suddha bodha* (Pure Awareness). But understanding his nature and mental constitution, Mother asked him to meditate upon the form of Kâli.

This would also soften his mind which became very hard due to lack of love and devotion.

One who knows how to make paper flowers beholds flowers in a sheet of paper whenever he sees a sheet of paper. That memory comes because he learned how to make flowers. How could this vision spring forth in a person who has not learned that art? Therefore, we should first learn. That means mental purity should be gained. For obtaining that, it is said that *bhakti* is necessary. Only those who have attained mental purity could say, "*suddha bodha.*"

We are not mature enough for that. The ego has not been removed. Such being our condition, there is no use in walking around speaking about *suddha bodha.* In the beginning, there must be *bhakti* alone. Otherwise, talk of *suddha bodha* will only go to inflate our ego.

Turning again to the *brahmachárin,* the Holy Mother said, "*Bhakti alone will help to eliminate the ego. At present that is what is needed. Nothing else is needed now. Try to call God shedding tears. Don't run after different yogas.*" The Mother sang:

> Except through devotion,
> There is no other way to get
> The Lord's Vision and to know Him..

Mother: Werner says that he likes *átma dhyána* (self-inquiry). He does *sádhana* on that. Therefore, Mother tells Werner, "*Atma dhyána* is the best." He is able to do it. Mother asked him to sit and meditate and he is doing accordingly.

It is good to do *sádhana* but self-observation also should be done to see whether you have attained concentration and the strength to love everyone equally, act selflessly and manifest other spiritual qualities.

THE EXPANSIVE 'I'

Mother: Even here there are so many distinctive natures. For each one Mother shows a different path. Mother loves all those who follow different paths but Mother likes the path of devotion and gives importance to that. That is how Mother grew up. There is the expansive "I" and the narrow "I". The expansive "I" is the Pure Principle (*suddha tattvam*). It doesn't have any connection with *Maya* (illusion or Nature). The narrow "I" is the mind or *jīva* (individual soul). The mind and Creation are the result of desire. It is not correct to say all that is seen is that narrow "I." In the expansive meaning, Mother is in everything that is seen. There is no Mother who is different from this Universe.

We were talking about Yoga. All that is explained by Mother can be known through experience if one moves forward firmly holding to any one of these paths. Nothing will happen by simply hearing about it.

One Devotee: *Mother, what should be done to melt the heart with God's love?*

Mother: You should call God in solitude and pray, shedding tears. The mind of one who has a wound on his body will be always on that. He will always be thinking of ways to cure it. Likewise, we are afflicted with the disease of *samsāra* (transmigration). We should have the desire to treat and cure it. Then the prayers will become sincere and love will fill the heart.

It was 1 o'clock. Having told everyone to go and have their lunch, the Holy Mother entered the temple.

Monday, 31 October 1983

Mother did not sleep or rest properly after the previous night's *Bhâva Darshan*. Some of the devotees were still waiting to see the Mother and offer their salutations before they leaving. Perhaps because of their intense desire the Mother came out of her hut at eight in the morning. When they left, the Mother sat on the southwestern corner of the temple verandah, keeping her feet on the footstep. The chanting of *the Lalitasahasranama* emerged from the temple. All the *brahmachârins* were in meditation.

A group of people from the extreme northern part of Kerala arrived to see the Holy Mother. There were some scholars in the group. The Holy Mother happily said, *"Come, children, come and sit here."*

They all stepped onto the verandah and sat, having offered their salutations and the fruit which they brought. The Holy Mother distributed oranges as *prasâd* to everyone. After some time one of the *pandits*, who was a bit egoistic in appearance and movements, started asking certain questions to the Mother.

Scholar: *What is* moksha *(Liberation)? Is it attenuation of* vâsanas *or elimination of mind?*

Mother: Son, both attenuation of *vâsanas* and *mano nâsa* (elimination of mind) are one and the same. That itself is *moksha*.

Scholar: What is the way to it?

Mother: Different people have different paths. For you it is enough if you get *bhakti*. If a balloon is inflated too much it will burst. Beauty is in humility, not in being egoistic thinking that one knows everything. This can be attained only by sowing the seeds of *bhakti*. *Bhakti* when fully ripened and developed becomes the huge shady tree of *jñāna*. All are waiting to get that *bhakti*. We will have succeeded if *bhakti* is attained. Hollow utterances of being a *jñāni* or scholar are of no use. The picture of a cow drawn on a sheet of paper won't eat grass. Those who have experience won't say that *bhakti* and *jñāna* are two. When love for God comes, that is *bhakti*.

There was a sudden change in the scholar. He was really humbled. He clearly understood that the Mother's talk was aimed at him. His next question was with full humility and reverance.

Scholar: *Mother, what is needed to get love?*
Mother: Faith should come. *Vairagya* (detachment) also is needed.
Scholar: *Mother, is it possible to attain* bhakti *through faith?*
Mother: Yes, definitely it is. Faith and love are not two. They are interdependent. Without faith we cannot love someone and vice versa. If we have complete faith and love for someone, the mere thought about that person itself will give us a special joy. Do we get any joy if we have no faith in him and consider him as a thief? The lover opens his heart to his beloved because he has faith in her. That faith is the foundation of love. Love springs from faith.
One devotee: *Mother, does love arise through* japa?

Mother: Through *japa*, mental purity is gained. While chanting, we are replacing other thoughts with that particular mantra. Just as saline water loses it's salty taste by constantly adding fresh water to it, through constant repetition of a mantra, the number of thoughts can be reduced. In due course, all the thoughts can be eliminated except one, that is God. Love will spring through *japa* if one has complete faith and intent to reach the goal.

Devotee: *What change will chanting of the Divine Name bring in us?*

Mother: Son, when Divine Names are chanted sincerely and with devotion, peace of mind and tranquillity can be gained. As Mother said before, it will lessen the number of thoughts. When the thoughts are less, you will get more peace of mind. Tension and mental agitation are caused by the numerous thought waves which in turn bring forth all other kinds of negative tendencies like lust, anger, jealousy and greed. Divine Names, when chanted with one-pointedness, will enable us to accept both good and bad experiences of life as God's Will and blessing. This is not possible if your prayers are only to fulfill desires. That will only help to increase your sorrows and disappointments in life. Peace of mind is the most important thing without which one cannot enjoy even worldly comforts. Son, when we have the desire to be healed of a disease, we will move carefully. If medicines are taken, there occurs a change in our state of health, doesn't there? Likewise, when we chant with concentration thinking, "I want to be healthy and wish to be healed," there occurs a change in our character. In the same manner, all our ways will change when the mind is on God. If you read the biographies of devotees and *Mahâtmas* you will understand the difference between them and other people. Look at the lives of Chaitanya Mahaprabhu and Sri Ramakrishna. You will understand what change *"Nâma"* (chanting the Divine Name) can bring in us.

Scholar: *Mother, is adherence to the physician's (Guru's) prescription regarding diet, habits etc., necessary while taking the medicine of* Nâma *to remove the disease caused by worldly existence* (bhava roga)?

Mother: That is absolutely necessary. In the beginning it is indispensable. It is not so much needed after gaining concentration of mind. A mode of life is very important. The character of a deer which eats grass and a tiger which eats meat are different, aren't they? Those who do meditation should not talk about worldly things during the period of *sâdhana*. In the beginning, complete silence is needed. Silence, sattvic food, abstinence from worldly talk, satsang, regularity and discipline in doing *sâdhana*, all these will come under the rules and regulations which a serious *sâdhak* should observe.

You should become introspective. Speak only when it is necessary. Only an introspective person can look within. Ability to endure will arise when desire to cure the illness is there. In the hospital at Vallickavu, Mother had seen people going and lining up in a queue. However much time they would have to wait they would still wait. It is because of their desire to get rid of their disease that they come and stand there for long hours having walked all the way from their house in the sun and undergone many difficulties. What a patience they have! Their only concentrated thought is to see the doctor and get medicine. How would you see the doctor if you think that you do not have a disease and therefore cannot stand waiting? How will you cure the disease? One who thinks that he has no disease will not have the patience and won't wait for such a long time either. When patience comes, the mentality to sacrifice also comes. Mere chanting of *Nâma* is not enough. It should be done with concentration. Otherwise it is like pouring water on the surface of a rock. *Japa* is beneficial only if there is concentration. Both sitting ten hours with eyes closed and chanting Divine Names with concentration for one hour are equal. In pyrotechnics (fireworks) there is a kind of rocket which goes upward with great speed and a hissing noise and then bursts when it reaches a certain height. Likewise is *bhakti*. Liberation can be attained in a moment. That call, that one call with love, forgetting one's mind, intellect and body, that will take one to the goal.

Just then a devotee named Ayyappan from Mavelikara[71] came and prostrated to the Holy Mother. Having conversed with him for some time, the Mother sat with eyes closed for a few minutes. Everyone waited gazing at the Holy Mother's form until she came down from the ecstatic mood. Some more moments passed, and with a smile on her countenance, the Mother opened her eyes.

[71]A town about 25 kilometers north of Mother's ashram.

After a few more moments of silence, one devotee asked, "Mother, what is real devotion?"

Mother: The devotion of Hanuman[72] is an example. *Bhakti* is surrendering or sacrificing oneself to Divine Love.

Devotee: *What about the devotion of the Gopis?*

Mother: Son, the devotion of the Gopis is also superior. But, it was a little bit mixed with *vásanas* in the beginning. Knowledge had not yet arisen. In the beginning it won't. Otherwise, why did they get angry when Akrura[73] came? There was still the attitude of duality. What was the reason for *Bhagaván's* (Sri Krishna's) departure from Ampadi (His birth place)? The Gopis had not attained complete mental purity. Mother is talking about the beginning. Later they attained a state where they could see Krishna inside, outside and everywhere. The seed has to be sown in the shade first. It can be transplanted when it has grown to a certain height, but until then, shade is necessary. Likewise, the seeds of the Gopis' love were sown and grew to a certain level under the shade of the huge tree called Krishna. Then, all of a sudden, He left them to enable them to see Him within and become more expansive, i.e., to teach them self-dependence. In the beginning, the selfishness which the Gopis had in their love towards Krishna helped them a lot to increase their devotion.

[72]The great monkey devotee of Sri Rama. He is revered as an Incarnation of Lord Shiva who wanted to enjoy the bliss of service to Sri Rama and therefore, took the humble form of a monkey.
[73]A devotee of Sri Krishna who came to give a message to the Gopis from the Lord telling them to see Him within and as identical with their Real Self.

A young man who worked as a leader in the social and spiritual field was present among the devotees. He was keenly listening to the Mother's words.

Young leader: *Mother, it is seen that many are approaching spiritual subjects with a negative attitude. Why is this so?*

Mother: Son, such things will happen if it is served to anyone and everyone. What Mother says is that Hari Sri (the first letters of the Malayalam alphabet) should be taught only to one who has a surrendering attitude. Only when the child approaches the teacher stretching out his fingers saying, "I don't know anything, please teach me" will the teacher make the child write the letters in the sand while catching hold of his fingers. How could a teacher teach a child who doesn't stretch out his fingers? If you approach those who don't have humility, trying to make them understand about spirituality, they will deny it. Anyhow, you are doing good work in propagating *dharma*. It is God alone who entrusted this work to you. But the only thing is that you have to do it selflessly.

Young leader: *But Mother, there is a problem when we talk about selflessness. Suppose some aggressors forcefully pluck coconuts from the coconut trees of the ashram and take them away. Now, what would Mother do? Would you simply allow them to take the coconuts or would you call the police? It is selfishness if you call the police, is it not?*

Mother: There is one thing. Everything is one Self. But a dog should be seen as a dog and treated accordingly. Holding a stick against it as if to strike doesn't fall under selfishness. There is no fault in driving away an ignorant dog when it comes to harm us. Mother does not say that this is selfish. There is nothing against selfless action in obstructing a person who does things out of ignorance. Not only that. If he is not prevented, he will become a public nuisance and will create many problems in the society. What is important is that when you punish him, it should be done with a pure intention, that is, to correct him for his future good. It should not be done out of dislike or revenge. One shouldn't act desirous of selfish ends. It is beneficial for the world if you help to punish an aggressor who forcefully climbs on somebody's coconut tree. There the stress is not on selfishness but on *dharma*.

A *Mahâtma*, if he really wishes, can create another world. But he won't do anything against the pre-established laws of Nature. It was they *(Mahâtmas)* who formulated the rules and regulations of life and if they wish they can break them, but they will not do so. Just as the supreme authority of a nation would not do anything which is against the constitution, in a like manner, great souls do everything only according to the rules and regulations set by the ancients.

Above all, as far as great souls are concerned, they look upon everyone and everything equally. They won't waste their power to achieve trivial worldly things. For them, nothing is insignificant. That is, each and everything has its own place, neither more nor less. They know that even a needle has its own use.

TO THE SADHAKS

The Holy Mother then noticed two *sâdhaks* sitting on the bare ground.

Mother: In the beginning, *sâdhaks* should be careful about many things. They should use sandals while walking. The earth has got gravitational power. Try sleeping on the black sand on the seashore. You will become so fatigued that you can't even get up. The gravitational power of the earth is capable of absorbing our energy. Now we are standing enslaved by that attractive power. We are trying to overcome that. Therefore, wherever the *sâdhak* may sit, also spread something on the ground. In the initial stages a serious *sâdhak* should wear clothes so as to cover his whole body. Do not give negative vibrations any chance to affect your body. It is said that a *sâdhak* should cover his body so that if others happen to look at him, they will not see his full form. All these are necessary during the *sâdhana* period. Besides that, a *sâdhak* also should not gaze at anyone. Don't speak too much. A lot of vital energy will be lost through speech. In this way, only if there is much external alertness can the *sâdhak* in the beginning stages withstand and overcome the obstacles. All these observances may seem to be a kind of weakness to a non-dualist but such people can only speak about non-duality. Those who reached the goal are people who have observed the disciplines in this manner.

There are also people who have attained the goal without all these disciplines but they had a tremendous spiritual disposition inherited from their past birth. We who long to go from the level of the *jīvātma* (individual self) to the state of *Paramātma* (Supreme Self) need all the discipline. It doesn't matter for a *Jīvanmukta* (a Liberated Soul) if he lies in the sand or water. But one can do all those things only after attaining a particular stage. After attaining the state of *Jīvanmukti*, the power won't go out without their will because their mind is fully under their control. Even if they may look at a person or an object with their eyes, they won't fix their mind there. Only if the mind is fixed will the power flow out. It is beneficial for us if they look with that resolve. Until that state is attained, a *sādhak* should move very carefully.

Young man: *Mother, then are not the charges lodged against Sankaracharya correct, saying that he has* tindal *and* todil?[74]

Mother: It is definite that it will do harm to the *sādhak* if he mingles with those who don't have spiritual culture. If we live with a leper, doesn't that disease affect us also? Likewise, in the beginning stages it is very advisable for the *sādhak* not to associate with others. Even if it is said that all are human beings, are all human beings the same? Some are thieves, some are innocent, some others are embodiments of compassion, yet there are some who have leprosy or tuberculosis. While others are perfectly healthy. It is harmful if mingled together without any control. Therefore, Mother cannot find

---

[74]The Sankaracharya, the ecclesiastic head of a large section of Hindu society, observes an old custom of India existing among the priestly caste forbidding the people who belong to the other castes to touch or come close to them for fear of pollution by touch and proximity.

any fault if Sankaracharya doesn't touch anyone.
Maybe it is to set an example for *sâdhaks*. All those rules
are necessary for a *sâdhak* before the attainment of
Jîvanmukti. In a math (monastery) discipline and a
regular routine are indispensable. A path is needed for
human beings. The birds don't need it. An *Avatâr* or a
Jîvanmukta doesn't need a path. We can proceed only
through *yama* and *niyama* (observance of rules and
regulations prescribed by the scriptures and the great
masters).

BEYOND DISCIPLINE

Mother: Some people would say that a hand fan is
not necessary if there is an electric fan. A fan is not
needed on the seashore. Likewise, if there is
satsang, rules and regulations of worship are not
necessary. But it should be real *satsang*. Who does
satsang like that? Real *satsang* is the yoking of
jîvâtma and *Paramâtma*; at least it should be a sincere and dedicated effort to attain that unity. If
that kind of effort is there, then nothing else is
needed. We are all seeds from fruits which are
caused to ripen unnaturally. It is a bit difficult to
sprout. Whereas, there are some others falling
down from the beaks of birds on to the top of rocks.
They will germinate lying there. The saliva which
comes out from the bird's mouth is its fertiliser. It
needs neither sand nor water nor a protective fence to
grow. It doesn't need someone to look after it either. It
will grow lying there. It came enriched with fertilisers
necessary for its growth. Such people are *Jîvanmuktas*.

They will be able to lead a life without any attachment to anything. They are people who came with fully developed spiritual qualities inherited from the previous birth (*purva samskâra*). They won't become weak-minded under any circumstance. They will only act understanding the subtlety of a thing. They do not act in accordance with the external appearances of things. They do not need sâdhana, but ordinary people do. Otherwise it is not possible to attain the goal.

As she was talking, the Mother entered into *bhâva samâdhi* (ecstatic trance). .After some time, chanting *"Shiva...Shiva...Shiva,"* she became her normal self. The Mother continued,

Mother: Wherever *Jîvanmuktas* go, people will go after them. They don't have to look nor do they have to search for disciples. People will go on following them. People will be attracted to them even without their knowledge, just like rubbish caught in a whirlwind. That is the power of a person who does *sâdhana*. Either their breath or the wind that blows over their body is enough to benefit the world.

Ordinary people should gain concentration through spiritual practices, observing the prescribed rules and regulations. Otherwise, they will collapse. Whether it is a stone or paper, the artist beholds the object which he can make out of it. Likewise, a Self-Realised soul beholds the Essence in all objects. He neither sees the differences that we see nor think that anything is without significance. Others may see a stone or paper only as a useless thing. They don't see the object which can be made as an artist would. Therefore, move forward observing things subtly.

Young man: *Certain spiritual persons are being abused by some people for wearing silk clothes. Is there any significance of such things as silk clothes?*

Mother: Son, there are good effects in wearing silk clothes as well as in wearing certain animal skins. They will protect us from several evil external powers. *Rudraksha* has medicinal power. It is good to wear it on the body. Especially beneficial is wearing it on the neck touching the cavity of the throat. Likewise, applying ash from a burnt corpse is also good. It has the power to prevent germs. Ash from the burial ground *(chutala bhasmam)* will also prevent polluted air from entering the body. Different things will be needed during each stage of spiritual practice.

The Holy Mother got up and went to the hut. Some devotees left, having taken leave of her. Others came to stay overnight in the ashram. The western horizon slowly became pink in colour. The sun dived deep into the ocean to have his evening bath. Dusk had fallen. The ashram atmosphere was saturated with peace and tranquillity. The *brahmachárins* began singing *bhajans*. The Holy Mother also came and sat for the *bhajan*. There was no light except the light from the oil lamps kept inside the temple. The Mother sang in an intoxicated mood,

> O Goddess, Great Goddess, bless me.
> O Leader of all, my salutation to Thee.

Since how many days have we been crying like this, O
Treasure of Compassion, O Embodiment of Truth.
Please shower Thy Grace on us, O Krishna, Lover of
Thy devotees.

For what reason have we been pushed Into this
hell and are being tortured, O Krishna, who
nourished the Pandavas, O Holy One?

The Mother sang like an innocent child calling out
"Amma...Amma!" now and then. The *bhajan* lasted for
two hours. After the *arathi* (vespers) the Holy Mother
sat in the sand by the side of the temple. Everyone offered
their prostrations to her. Some went to meditate and
others sat near her.

NITYANITYAM
The Eternal and non-eternal

An aspirant: *Mother, what is meant by* "nityânitya
vastu vivekam" *(discrimination between the eternal and the non-eternal)?*
Mother: Shiva...Shiva...what do we know? Your
Mother is crazy. She is uttering something or
other. Accept what you feel is right.

If a traveller happens to stand in a bus stop, a
person may look and smile at him. He will talk to
him. At that time another person will come near.
Thus, some people will gather together. Quickly
all of them will become friends. As they are talking the
bus comes. Everyone gets into it. Having travelled for
sometime, when the first traveller turns back and
looks, none of the friends who had gottten into the bus
from the bus stop with him are there on the seats. "Alas,

are they all gone? I thought that all of them would be with me until the end." The poor fellow thinks that all those people who travelled with him would be his friends forever. He is disappointed when each one of them alights and goes their own way when the bus reaches each person's destination. He would not have been dejected if he had understood this earlier. In a like manner, whether it is your father or mother or wife, they will leave you when it is their time. Disappointment will be the result if you live fixing your mind on all these ephemeral objects.

Therefore, children, don't be deluded by these dreams which you see externally. They are all things and people who have to go when the time comes. If you are attached, then what remains is only sorrow, is it not? Therefore, despair will not arise if you live understanding this beforehand without getting tempted by external affairs Instead, remember God with an attitude of surrender to Him. God alone is the Eternal Truth. It should be understood that the world is not eternal. This is discriminating between the eternal and the non-eternal.

Everything will be all right if you move along this path. Suppose a person has a job in a bank. Many people will come to see him in the bank. They will speak sweetly to him. A clever person will understand that those people are coming not because of their love towards him but to fulfill their desire. Understanding this, he will do his duty properly without being deluded by their sweet words and manners. He won't waste time talking. He will even be ready to lodge a case against them if they don't repay the amount that they had taken as a loan. Many people will come to see you when you have a position of power. But what will happen when the position is gone? Then admirers will not be there. One should take refuge in the eternal God after thinking about all this with discrimination.

A person handles millions of rupees in the office or in the bank but he knows that it is not his wealth. He has no attachment to it nor does he desire it. Likewise, the headache is over if we understand that none of these things in this world are related to us. One will not have any more problems if the awareness that the wife and children are not one's own dawns in one. What we have as our own is God alone. Perform your actions in the world thinking "It is my duty." Don't sit idle. You should work. In the beginning a regular routine is needed. If you take tea today, tomorrow a headache will come if you don't drink it. That is because of the habit. Therefore, good habits should be developed through a regular routine.

In the beginning external rules and external attentiveness are necessary. One must move with discrimination. That is beneficial. Otherwise, you might simply sit and say, "I am also *Brahman*" (the Absolute). You can see *Brahman* jumping up and down with pain if a thorn happens to pierce the foot. (All laugh) There is no use in babbling without attaining that state of experience.

All these years we worked thinking that the world was eternal. Now, having understood the truth, we should set aside some time for the Self. Out of twenty four hours, we should try to know the Self for at least one hour. Spiritual practices should be performed. That should be done regularly. Time lost cannot be regained. If millions are lost we can make it up by doing more business but if even a second is lost it can never be regained. You should live understanding this.

Sâdhak: *Mother, you have said that we are in the* vyâvahara *(empirical plane) and that we should move with subtlety. What does this mean?*

Mother: Empirical means meaningless things and actions. *Mithya* does not mean perishing but rather everchanging. The world is transforming from one state to another. Each and every object is changing. First whole lentils, then the broken ones and finally *parippu vada*[75] But the basic thing is not getting destroyed. It only transforms into something else.

When we say *Brahman*, everything is included. But discrimination is needed because we are standing in *vyâvahara*. In the beginning only if we think, "This is day, this is night, this is good, that is bad, etc.," can we progress.

All that is related to *Maya* will come under *vyâvahara*. That which is *mithya*, that which is not the Truth, is changing. Move endowed with subtlety. *Nitya* is God, *anitya* are worldly affairs.

Sâdhak: *Mother, is it very necessary that one should do* mantra japa *using a rosary?*

Mother: Children, kids learn to count using pearl

---

[75] A kind of crispy food made from ground grams or pulses with spices and fried in oil.

beads. Using this method they can quickly learn to count. Likewise, in the beginning a *japa mâla* (rosary) is good to fix the mind firmly on one point. Later, you can continue even without a rosary. It will become a habit. The *japa* will go on automatically even without our knowledge. One person used to write dipping the pen in the ink bottle. For ten days the ink bottle was kept on the right side. On the eleventh day he shifted it to the left side. Even if he knows that the ink bottle is on the left side his hand will automatically move to the right side. Therefore, *japa* should become a habit. Then it will go on while walking, sitting or sleeping. *Japa*, prayer and meditation are good for concentration. Once compound letters are learnt then there is no need to learn the letters by writing them down. But in the beginning all these are indispensible. Otherwise, it is not possible to learn, my child. Upon first showing the picture of an elephant or a horse to the child, the father or mother would say, "This is an elephant, this is a horse." The child will think that the elephant and horse are in the picture. Later, the child will understand that the elephant or the horse is not the picture but something entirely different. Showing the picture when the father told him, "This is an elephant or this is a horse," the child did not have even one iota of doubt in his words. He may even be frightened if the father says, "Look, the elephant is going to pierce you with his tusk." Just like the child, you must first have innocent and blind faith in the Guru's words. That faith will serve as a vehicle in which you can easily travel towards the goal.

Son, whatever the Guru does is only for the spiritual progress of the disciple. It is absolutely impossible for him to act otherwise. Mother is referring to a *Sadguru*, not just anyone who simply declares himself to be a Guru. A true spiritual master sometimes may even behave strangely. He may get angry at the disciple without any particular reason and might scold him severely, blaming him for errors which he hasn't committed. But those seemingly strange behaviors are not because the Guru is angry with the student. That is the Guru's method of teaching self-surrender, patience and acceptance. For example, sometimes the Guru might ask the disciple to make a beautiful idol of Krishna or Devi. The disciple, forsaking food and sleep and applying all his artistic talents, would make one in twenty days or a month. Eventually, he will bring it to the Guru. The Guru may not even look at it or sometimes he may even smash it into pieces after snatching it from the disciple. During such occasions a perfect student would remain totally calm accepting it as the Guru's will and for his spiritual good without responding negatively at all. Each reaction which arises from us causes a delay in attaining the goal. Whereas acceptance will cause the Grace to flow without any break. Son, the Guru has no selfish interests at all. He or she lives in *tyâga* (renunciation); his or her whole being is *tyâga*. The Guru burns his or her own body which he or she has taken by self-will, in the flame of *tyâga* for the uplifting of the disciples and for the good of the world. From that blazing flame of *tyâga* each one of us can kindle a wick so that we can also become a street light in the dark path through which the entire human race walks.

Sâdhak: (Bowing down to the Mother) *Mother, this has cleared many of my doubts.*

He sat with joined palms and bowed head for awhile in front of the Mother and then asked, "Mother, Ramana Maharshi propagated the path of jñâna, didn't he?"

Mother: He has said everything. When instructing foreigners, who are predominantly intellectual, in accordance with their nature, he asked them to enquire "Who am I and where did I come from." But he also said that one should attain concentration by performing the proper *sâdhana* to attain this goal. First, the Guru might act according to what the *sâdhak* likes. Then gradually rules and regulations concerning *sâdhana* and regularity in spiritual practice will be insisted upon. *Sâdhana* is necessary if the attainment of the goal is wanted. Ramana Maharshi said that one needs devotion also. Imagining each stone on Arunachala Hill as Shiva, he cried calling, "My Father, My Father!" He perceived Arunachala as Lord Shiva Himself.

Then he also had done *sâdhana* sitting in the Patalalinga Cave. He practiced silence too. There is a picture of Ramana Maharshi cutting vegetables. In one or two books he talks about worldly affairs as well, but nobody would notice all these things. The followers always want to limit the unlimited Guru. That is a pity. They *(Sadgurus)* are expansive; whereas, the followers, wearing the spectacles of narrowness, try to impose their own narrow point of view on them which is like trying to put the vast ocean in a small bottle. Sincerely think for a while. Are we trying to accept the teachings of the Great Masters or to bring them under our little world of chaos and confusion to make others also confused? It is not enough to pay attention to only one part of the sayings of great souls.

Without some resolve *(sankalpa)*, how is it possible to concentrate on the Self? For that, Ramana Maharshi has introduced the method of going around the hill chanting the Divine Name. A raft is needed to cross the river. It is not necessary after crossing the river. *Sâgunârâdhana* (worship of an idol of a God or Goddess) is there at Ramana's ashram. But some are doing nothing saying "I am Brahman." Having drawn the picture of a house, they want to live in it. Simply keeping Ramana's picture, they do nothing, no meditation or other spiritual practices. Instead of this, why don't they chant the Divine Name so that they can become a true follower of Ramana Maharshi or any other *Mahâtma?* How much he meditated! The *Mahâtmas* will still retain *bhakti* even after attaining the state of *Jîvanmukti.* Do you know why? To stay in this world. They won't give up *bhakti.* They accept it of their own will. The greatness of *bhakti* is something unique. They enjoy *bhakti,* having created it by self-will. You may ask, what is there for them to enjoy; is there "I," "you," etc.? But they will retain *bhakti* to stay in the world.

One devotee: *Mother, what is needed to attain concentration?*

Mother: Son, there are no short cuts. Constant practice is needed. It is difficult to get one-pointedness. In the beginning, it is a great thing if by chance we get even one or two minutes of concentration when we do *sâdhana* for one hour. *Sâdhana* should be done continuously and sincerely without stopping until one-pointedness is gained. Once the seeds are sown, then you should water them every day until the seedlings grow and reach a certain level. In between, if you stop watering, they will wither away, especially if it is dry land. One day they will become strong enough to withstand the heat. Then you can stop watering. Likewise, we have sown the seeds of spirituality in us. But the inside is very dry due to being in the scorching heat of worldliness for a very long time. It might take some time for the sprouts of spirituality to come out. Sprinkle the waters of *sâdhana* regularly without any fail and wait patiently. But if you stop the *sâdhana* owing to lack of concentration and patience, then no result will be gained. *Japa* is necessary.

One young man: *What benefit does the world get if one sits and meditates with eyes closed?*
Mother: Nature is benefitted by the concentration of a *sâdhak*.
Young man: *How?*
Mother: Son, such concentration will purify the atmosphere. At some time in the future, modern material science will discover it. Not only that, we should not forget the services done by the *Mahâtmas* who were *dhyânis* (meditators). They derived power from meditation.

Son, in order to magnetize an iron rod, a powerful magnet should be rubbed on it in one direction alone. When it is rubbed for some time the iron will become another magnet. The molecules in the iron rod which were previously lying in disorder, were systematized by the rubbing process. But it needed another powerful magnet to do this. Mother thinks that this is what happens in meditation also. By fixing the mind firmly on one thought, i.e., a selected mantra, Divine Name or Form, the thoughts are rearranged and directed towards one object. Thus, power is generated when thoughts constantly flow in one direction, i.e., towards God.

This power is always radiating from a *Mahâtma* which certainly creates spiritual energy in us when we sit in his presence. He can transmit that power to us through a mere touch, look or thought. But like the iron rod, we must allow ourselves to be magnetized, without raising any objection or words of protest.

Children, look at a river which flows into many branches. The force of the current will be very little. But if a dam is constructed closing all the small channels, the water current will increase tremendously and we can generate electricity from it. Likewise, if the mind which is flowing outwards as thoughts and desires is directed to one point, infinite energy can be created which will definitely radiate from all around you, revitalising anything and everything. But the quantity will differ depending upon each one's subtlety of mind.

Son, television stations always telecast programmess, but if you want to see them you must turn on the television which is in your house and tune it. In the same way, tuning of the mind to the *Mahâtma's* world is necessary. If that is done, then you can experience the flow of spiritual energy from them to you, that which was, in fact, always there. For that, spiritual practice is a must.

The Mother paused for a while and distributed the sugar candy brought by a devotee as *prasâd* to all. A few grains fell and scattered on the floor. One by one the ants came and gathered there. Pointing to the ants, the Mother said,

Mother: Children, look here. First there was only one ant on the sugar candy grain, then many. One is enough for others to follow. If even one *vâsana* remains, other *vâsanas* also will follow. All *vâsanas* must be destroyed without leaving even one.

Mother noticed one *brahmachârin* passing by at a distance. She called, *"Come here, son."* The perplexed *brahmachârin* came near her.

Mother: Son, tomorrow you should go and have your hair cut.

The *brahmachârin* nodded his head in approval and left the place silently.

A householder came with his family in the evening. They were devotees of the Holy Mother for quite a long time. They had a lot of problems. The wife had no obedience to her husband. Their family life was not very peaceful.

Mother: This daughter has devotion to Mother but (smilingly) what kind of *bhakti* is it?! What *bhakti*, what *japa* and what *dhyâna* is it having thrown the husband into the midst of sorrow? Who needs the devotion of a wife who gives trouble to her husband? That is why the people of old gave more importance to mental unity than physical beauty concerning marriage. If the wife is a pious woman endowed with patience, forbearance, devotion and endurance, she can transform the character of the husband even if he is a rogue.

Just then a father came with his little daughter. The Holy Mother called the little girl and made her sit near her. The father of the girl said, "Mother, please advise her not to cry, adamantly saying that she wants to see Mother after having returned home from the ashram."
Hearing this, the Holy Mother hugged the little girl and laughed with great happiness.

One devotee: *How fortunate it is to cry for God. That is how all of us have understood it.*

All laugh happily.

One young man: *Does Mother ever suggest* prânayâma?
Mother: During the present age, *prânayâma* is very difficult to practice. *Kumbhakam* (retention of the breath) will arise with love for God alone. What is *prânayâma* for then? With hatha yoga and *prânayâma*, insanity will be the result if a perfected master is not there to guide the aspirant.

Monday, 14 November 1983

The time was about nine-thirty in the morning. The Holy Mother was sitting in her small hut on the cot facing towards the north. Four young men came to the ashram to see the Mother. Coming to know from a resident that the Mother was sitting in her room, the young men peeped into her room from outside. The Mother saw them and said, *"Come in, children."*

All four of them entered the hut and sat on the carpet spread on the floor. The Mother got up from the cot and sat down. The young men, one by one, looked at her quite surprised. They were all educated and had read a few spiritual books which had kindled an interest to know more about spirituality. Recently they heard about Mother and were curious to see her in person and possibly ask certain questions. It was quite clear that the Mother's simplicity, humility and her loving call, *"Children"* influenced them to some extent.

Mother: (Smilingly) Children, from where are you?
One among them: *We are from Paravoor. It is near Quilon (pointing to one young man sitting near him). This is my friend and the other two are his acquaintances. Together we came to see Mother.*
Mother: (Laughingly) Shiva, Shiva, Shiva, to see Mother? Mother is crazy. Because the children call her "Mother" she acts in some way or other, doing some crazy things. Children, have you eaten anything?
Young man: *Yes.*
Another young man: *We came having heard about you. We have visited many ashrams.*
Mother: How far have you studied?
Young man: *I have passed B.Sc. and he has a B.A.*

By this time the Mother entered into a trance. A few moments went by in silence. The roaring Arabian Sea could be seen from the Mother's hut. The beating of the coconut husks by the fisherwomen could also be heard from across the backwaters. The Mother slowly opened her eyes chanting *"Shiva, Shiva, Shiva,"* whirling her uplifted hand which showed a divine gesture *(mudra)*.

One young man: *We would like to know certain spiritual things.*

Mother: (Laughingly) Shiva, Shiva, Shiva! What do we know about spirituality! He (God) knows everything. Children, you may ask. Mother may blurt out some crazy things. Accept it if you feel that it is correct. Mother would tell her children, "There is a crazy Kâli here. You will know her nature only when you get closer." Shiva, Shiva! (Mother laughs)

The young men were really surprised. After a pause, the young man continued, "It is rich people more than the poor who are visiting the ashrams, is it not so?"

Mother: Is there such a thing that only the poor should go to visit *Bhagavân* and the rich shouldn't? The rich have their own problems, don't they? Children, more wealth means more problems. In spirituality there are no distinctions like small and big, rich and poor. For God, all are His children; none will be discarded. The rich who come into contact with ashrams and spiritual people will do a lot of good things. Doesn't it take money to do charitible things? Can the poor give it? No, they have no capacity to do so. Ashrams and spiritual people inspire the rich people to do *sat karmas* (virtuous actions). It is the poor who are getting the benefit of that, aren't they? This is not so bad.

Spirituality is the right of both the poor and the rich. If remembrance of God is done with concentration and if you make one step towards God, God will make a hundred steps towards you. Are you ready for that? Son, are we getting concentration even for a minute? Without striving for that, we simply find fault with others. First try to correct our own drawbacks. You know, son, if one rich man becomes interested in spirituality many who are poor will be saved because of the *dharma buddhi* (charitable mind) that he gets from the spiritual person or ashram which inspires him.

Young man: *What must be done in order to gain concentration?*

Mother: Son, to gain concentration we must be intent on reaching the goal. Suppose one person is learning to ride a bicycle. Even if he falls down several times he would again climb onto it. Why? Because he has the intent to learn. At that time, falling down or getting injured is not a problem. Concentration will arise if the intent to reach the goal comes. It is not possible unless you strive hard. Attainment of the fruit is possible only through concentration.

WORLDLY LOVE

At this time, a few householder devotees entered the hut and sat down after prostrating to the Mother.

Mother: Take the case of worldly love. Does anybody love selflessly? Is it either for the woman or for the children that one gets married? Is it not for one's own pleasure only? Is it not to satisfy one's own desire that one loves one's wife and the father loves his children? Now, let us take the case with the child. We love the child because he or she was born from our blood and semen. Other than that, do we love him or her selflessly? If so, why are the children of other people not loved? Therefore, we love our child only because the child was born with our blood and semen. Even then, we are loving ourselves only. Let that be for the present. Suppose that the house catches fire. The child is inside the house and you are outside. We would only cry, calling out, "Please, somebody save my child!" We won't save the child by jumping into the fire because we know that death is certain if we jump into the fire. So, then whom are we loving and who loves us? We love ourselves only. This is the nature of worldly love. Is this not so? Allured by this love, we wander away from God, thinking, "He loves me; she loves me." We become friendly with others only for our own pleasure. Selflessness won't arise as long as the awareness "This body is I" exists.

So, that is what people are doing. They become enticed, thinking the people who they had seen in the bus stop were relatives. The so-called relatives will go to their own places. That Supreme Self, the Eternal Principle, that alone is the real friend. Understanding this truth early, we must always contemplate on it in whatever path we walk while doing our work.

DON'T GIVE UP THE
INTENT TO REACH THE GOAL

Mother: Many obstacles will arise. However many kicks we get, we won't get angry while being in the queue to buy tickets for the cinema. Why? Because our aim is to see the movie, isn't it? When we are really desirous of seeing the movie, these kicks and sufferings are not a sacrifice. Likewise, suppose we are getting in a bus. There are many people trying to get in. They are pushing and pulling. One comes and hits us. We would also hit him back. It is not out of anger. Somehow he or she just wants to get into the bus too, in time to reach the office or home. That is the reason. If it was another occasion we might have quarreled and even might have lodged a case. Therefore, when one is intent on the goal, all differences are forgotten. While travelling, two strangers or even enemies might sit on the same seat.

In the same manner, we will sit patiently waiting till evening in the court verandah. Why? Only to win the case. That is it. However rich one may be, he will sit waiting in the front yard of the court. He is not hesitant to endure any amount of suffering. Don't we understand that nothing is difficult if *lakshya bodha* (intent to reach one's goal) is there? He does not complaint that the wife is sick, the medicine is not yet purchased or that the food is not cooked. He doesn't feel that it is a sacrifice when he lies down in the courtyard from morning until evening because he wants to win the case. That is the goal.

Those are not sufferings. But when you come to the spiritual field, even a little suffering will be felt as big. The reason is the lack of *lakshya bodha*. So when we suffer for spirituality's sake, we should think over all this. We undergo sufferings for silly things. Not only that, don't we proceed, enduring all the obstacles that arise during our effort to fulfill our desires? Likewise, impediments will arise in the spiritual path as well. We should move forward enduring everything.

Having lived so many years thinking that we are the body, we will not get concentration simply by saying that we are the Self. We are lucky if we can get even one minute of one-pointedness. Son, in the beginning you will feel it to be a bit difficult. Even the ocean can be emptied, but the mind cannot be brought under one's control. It is very difficult. One can move forward overcoming everything if *lakshya bodha* is there. No obstacle will be a problem if we remember the Beatific Vision that awaits us. Nothing is a problem when we think of that. We should try to control the mind through *tyâga* (renunciation).

Another thing is that we must have faith. Faith is what is important. But Mother doesn't say that you must believe in God. It is enough to believe in one's own Self. Our Real Nature should be known. *Atman* is eternal. The world is not eternal. You should become convinced about this. One should move forward believing in one's own Self.

MANIFESTATION OF SIDDHIS

Young man: *What is Mother's opinion about the display of* siddhis *(psychic powers)?*

Mother: What the *rishis* (sages) have written is that it is not correct if *sâdhaks* display *siddhis*. But in today's world *siddhis* might become necessary. In the olden days, the type of education which existed was *gurukula vidyâbhyâsa*.[76]Even at a young age obedience to the parents and the Guru would be taught. After that, the purpose of life and what we took birth for will be understood. In the olden days, it was not taught to get married and procreate five or ten children. One virtuous child was enough, and even only after doing *tapas* for a long time at that. They procreated a child with the semen of their *tapas shakti* (power of *tapas*). That child would be a brilliant and intelligent one. The parents would go for *vanaprastha*[77] life having raised him and made him fit after giving him a proper education. That was the system in olden times. Whether it was a king or a servant, *sannyâsa* (total renunciation) was the goal of their life. But what about today? "I want to become a minister in the government, I want to become a doctor. I want to grab all the wealth! And then I want a scooter, a car, a house, etc." This is today's way of thinking. Trapping the mind in this restlessness and tension, we attempt to kill and rob everyone. We are ready to get our share of wealth even by killing our own parents. Today we don't give any value to our parents. We live in the midst of such desires and false sense of values.

In those days, each step was made keeping spirituality as the goal. Today, we do not do that. Even

---

[76]Staying in the Guru's residence, serving the Guru and spending one's time in studies and contemplation for a number of years until all the scriptures were mastered.

[77]The third stage of life, renouncing the hearth and home and going to the forest for doing penance.

children studying in nursery school are shouting political slogans. Many children during *Bhâva Darshan* come to Mother and say, "Mother, I want to kill a person, Mother should help me." This is what tiny little children say! There is enmity in the name of political parties. The children of today think that their party should thrive even by murder. In those days this was not so. The attitude was "Love your neighbour as yourself" as Jesus said. Today it is just the opposite. Display of *siddhis* should be evaluated in this background.

As the young men keenly listened, the Holy Mother continued,

Mother: *Siddhis* might not have been necessary in the old days when the people had spiritual culture. Then there was selflessness and *tyâga*. Today, all is selfishness only. People are desirous of seeing *siddhis*. If they don't, they won't believe in God.

Son, during this age people will go only after desires. If the desires are fulfilled, they will believe. Thus, slowly they can be brought to the path of devotion. Nowadays, nobody would go anywhere if it is not to fulfill their desires. If there is sickness they will go to see a doctor, otherwise not. Whereas some who do not have any disease will also go to see doctors. Do you know what for? To get advice as to how to prevent disease. They see the doctor to know where and when to do purification, how to live, what food stuffs are good, etc. They are people who have good insight into affairs. Likewise, there are people who would approach great souls with the thought, "I must know what spiritual life is." Still, they may have desires to fulfill but they will consider those as secondary. But such people can be counted on one hand. The majority crave to fulfill their desires. Manifestation of *siddhis* is necessary to lead them to goodness.

In the world of today, all are afflicted with the disease of worldliness. They go after desires only. Their fear is whether the wife would err, the husband would err, the children would err, whether they will be able to become wealthy or become grandparents, etc. They do not want spirituality other than for providing the solution for such problems. Most of the people are of this kind. Certain things will be needed to attract such people. This is like *katha prasangam.*[78] The story will actually be only half an hour long but it will take hours to tell it. This is because in order to attract the audience it should be embellished with humorous or appealing touches. Only then will the people be attracted. No one will listen if the story is narrated in a nutshell. Some *Mahātmas*, according to the desire of the devotees or people who visit them, manifest *siddhis.* The intention of that is to attract the people towards God. They will be attracted to God and the Divine Power when they see the display of *siddhis,* is that not so?

One young householder devotee: *Mother, this conversation about* siddhis *reminds me of one incident which occured in my life only two weeks before.*

With a child's curiosity the Mother asked, *"What is that, son?"*

---

[78]A public narration of a story with musical accompaniments.

Devotee: *Mother, though like an innocent child you pretend as if you do not know anything, this son is fully convinced that without your knowledge nothing would happen.*

Mother: Mother knows only one thing, that she doesn't know anything.

Devotee: *Mother, I know you are trying to fool me. Anyhow, I like to be fooled by you.*

Another devotee: *We are anxiously waiting to hear the incident which you were about to tell.*

Devotee: *Two weeks ago my wife had a dream in which the Mother appeared in front of her and said in a very clear voice, "Watch Resmi." That is the name of our only girl child. She is only two years old. My wife immediately got up but the child was comfortably sleeping near us. She woke me up and told me about the dream. I said, "Go back to sleep; it might have been a mere dream, don't worry." Both of us didn't give much importance to the dream. But my wife Sarada had the same dream again during the following two days in which Mother appeared in front of her and said the same sentence, "Watch Resmi," but more loudly. On the third night as my wife got up she screamed. The sound woke me up. When I turned on the light I saw my wife sitting, trembling and sweating, on the bed. Resmi also woke up and started crying. My wife took her and held her tightly to her bosom. Like one gone mad, she went on saying, "Mother, what is going to happen to my child Resmi; what is going to happen to my Resmi? Protect her." Although the dream seemed insignificant to me on the other two nights, I couldn't remain at peace when the same dream was repeated on the third* *night, especially when my wife narrated the way it happened. I myself was very confused but even then I tried to console my wife, saying "Don't worry, Mother is there to protect us." We could not sleep that night.*

The next morning Sarada and myself went with Resmi to the family shrine room and offered our morning prayers to the Mother, seeking her protection especially for the two year old child. Since I had no more leave of absence and owing to the heavy work load at the office because of the closing period of the yearly accounts, I could neither come to the Mother nor could I take leave for a day. Therefore, dedicating everything at the Mother's feet and instructing Sarada to have a careful eye on Resmi, I went to the office with a totally upset mind.

When I returned from the office that evening, I was shocked and at the same time wonderstruck hearing Sarada's narration about the unbelievable incident which happened that day before noon. At a quarter past ten my wife went to the kitchen to cook lunch. Resmi was fast asleep. Afraid of the warning which was in the dream, Sarada didn't lay Resmi on the cot to avoid the possible danger of her falling down from it. Instead, she lay her down on a mattress spread on the floor. It was eleven-thirty. Sarada was immersed in cooking and other household chores. All of a sudden, as she was about to chop the vegetables, somebody pushed her strongly from behind and simultaneously was heard the Mother's voice as if scolding her, "I warned you to watch your child. Go, hurry up to the pond." Sarada rushed to the pond situated on the southern side of the house which was only a few yards away from the room where Resmi was sleeping. Sarada screamed aloud, perceiving the horrifying sight that she saw there. Resmi was about to step into the waters of the deep pond. Sarada, like one gone mad, cried aloud and rushing towards the child, grabbed her posthaste. Hearing her loud cry, all the neighbours came running to the house. All felt relieved seeing that the child was saved from the great danger which would have occured.

It was only then that Sarada thought about how Resmi happened to get there. Noticing Resmi's plastic playball floating on the surface of the water, the whole incident flashed through her mind. Before falling asleep, Resmi was playing with the ball. Upon waking, she might have again played with the ball which probably rolled out of the room to the yard through the open door. Thus each time the ball slipped away and rolled, the child followed it and eventually reached the pond.

The devotee stopped. He was silently shedding tears. After a few seconds he asked, "Mother, what you said is true. Who can help themselves from feeling attracted to you, my God, when they directly come into contact with such experiences?"

Half of the time, while the story was being narrated, the Mother was deeply immersed in *samâdhi*. The Mother smilingly replied, *"Son, this happened only because of your innocent devotion and faith, not because of this crazy Kâli."*

The Mother continued talking about *siddhis*. She said,

Mother: It is a *sâdhak* who must not show *siddhis*. If he gets deluded by *siddhis* they will cause a downfall for him. Whereas, as far as an *Avatâr* is concerned, displaying *siddhis* is not a problem. The wonderful power which we call as *siddhi* is God's innate nature. Power will not be wasted if a Godly person shows *siddhis*. Did not Rama and Krishna manifest *siddhis*? How is God affected by the rule that a *sâdhak* shouldn't manifest *siddhis*? You come desiring an imitation. That is not the real thing. The real gem is there within you. Nobody is searching for that. Therefore, after having shown the *siddhis* first, they teach them the essential principles.

Young man: *Sri Ramakrishna didn't encourage* siddhis *at all, did he?*

Mother: Children, don't compare one *Mahâtma* with another. Don't ask, "If he has done that, why is this one not doing likewise?" There are no two people alike. Is Sri Rama like Sri Krishna? No. Parasurama is not like Sri Rama.[79] Hanuman is not like Parasurama. Sri Ramakrishna is not like Hanuman. The incarnation of Narasimha is not like Vamana.[80] There are differences between Incarnations. Even though the goal of all the Incarnations is one, the way in which they act is different. Don't compare one with another. Is it possible to tell one person's features while looking at another's?

Sri Ramakrishna said that *siddhis* should not be shown. There are two reasons for it. First, it was to *sâdhaks* that he said not to get deluded by *siddhis* as they would fall spiritually and this is true. Secondly, he was setting an example to show how a true *bhaktha* (devotee) should live. In order to set an ideal example of a true devotee, he did not show any miracles.

---

[79]Parasurama and Sri Rama were both Avatars of Lord Vishnu and both lived at the same time.

[80]Narasimha and Vamana were also both living at the same time and were both Lord Vishnu's Avatars.

Usually *Mahâtmas* won't show any *siddhis*. If ever they show them it would be a spontaneous manifestation in a befitting circumstance. They manifest *siddhis* not for the spectators but naturally according to circumstance.

Children, don't go after *siddhis*. They will turn black in a moment. The Incarnations come in order to destroy desires, not to create them. Therefore, it is good if nobody shows or gets deluded by *siddhis*. Otherwise, one may fall. Usually spiritual people will desire to attain siddhis. Because of that, they will be ruined. Those who approach them also will be ruined without gaining any spiritual uplift. When a person displays *siddhis* before us, we will also develop a desire to learn them. Having learned *siddhis*, we pave the way for our own destruction. Children, try to shed at least two drops of tears calling God. Ah, *Bhakti*! It's taste is something unique.

INCARNATION
AVATAR

Another young man: *Mother, is an* Avatâr *a person whose mind has become perfectly good?*
Mother: Son, it is not that one is an *Avatâr* because his mind has become good. *Avatârs* will have full awareness from birth itself. Others will not have it. Not only that, because the *Avatârs* are in total identity with Nature, their mind is not what we usually call as mind. All minds are theirs. In other words, an *Avatâr* is Himself the Universal Mind. *Avatârs* will be far be-

yond all kinds of *dvandas* (pairs of opposites) including purity and impurity. Therefore, *Avatârs* cannot be called, "One whose mind has become good." When God descends in a human form, He or She is an *Avatâr*. Therefore we cannot limit Incarnations saying, "*Avatârs* will appear in such and such a period of time at such and such a place." If God is omniscient, omnipotent and all-pervading, He can easily assume any form at any time, at any place irrespective of caste, creed and sect. That depends on the urgency or need of the era.

Young man: *Mother, will the infinite God come in a human form?*

Mother: All forms have a limit. God, the Supreme Principle, is beyond that limit. An Incarnation (the infinite God in a limited form) in *Brahman* (the infinite Reality) is like an iceberg in the ocean. All the water in the reservoir will come through the tap but the tap is not the reservoir. There are limitations for whatever has a name or form. But through this small body, God can act as He likes. That is the greatness of the form of an Incarnation. This is the reason that it is said that God and an Incarnation are one. There is no need to assume a body and descend in order for God to act. Even then, *Avatârs* are beneficial for human beings to bring them closer to God.

Young man: *Is there any meaning in calling a person who is alive as* Bhagavân?

Mother: Child, that depends on our faith. Is not our father dear and great as far as his son is concerned?

The young man's friend: *Does it mean that we don't have to believe if there is no faith?*

Mother: Not so, son. A mosquito will get only blood from an udder which is full of milk. Someone else squeezes milk out of it. Faith alone is important. Two different things can come from the same udder. The thief, when he sees a post in the night, will think that it is a policeman; the girl will think that it is her beloved; one who is fearful in the night will think that it is a ghost. Is there any change for the post? The post is the post only. It reflects differently according to each one's nature. In which way did the Gopis see Krishna? In which way did Kamsa (an enemy of Sri Krishna) see Him, and what was Arjuna's attitude?

Therefore, our faith is the cause for what we perceive. The principle is that if we believe that God is in a blade of grass, we will get power even from that. Did not God appear from a pillar as the Man-Lion? If so, can't God's Power manifest in human beings too?

INCARNATION AND AN ORDINARY SOUL

Extract from a talk which occurred on 27th December, 1981.

Devotee: *Mother, what is the difference between an ordinary* jîva *(individual soul) and an Incarnation?*
Mother: There are differences. A date palm tree that is giving sweet fruit to everyone can be considered as an Incarnation. It can satisfy those who come hungry. Others can pluck its fruit and eat. Likewise, an Incarnation is able to give peace, tranquillity and spiritual power to both those who take ref-

uge in him and others as well. There is no meaning if a seed of the date palm says lying down, "Listen, I am the date palm." The seed has to be grown with attention and care, being given water and manure properly. If grown properly, a date palm will spring forth from the seed. There is no sense if the fruit of that tree, when it attains perfection, pompously says, "I came from this date palm; therefore, I am a tree." There exists a difference between the two until the fruit becomes the palm tree. It can become a date palm. As said before, it would need to be grown with proper care, with a fence to protect it from stray animals and with water and manure. Even then, it might wither away due to the heat of the sun or it might be eaten by some cows or other animals. Likewise is the difference between a *jīva* and an Incarnation. There are 500 watt bulbs, 100 watt bulbs and night lights, but all shine with the same electricity which comes from the same power station. Even then, the light will be different. We are all just sparks, not even night lights. We have not become perfect. An *Avatār* is perfect.

15 December 1988

MOTHER'S TALK TO WESTERN DEVOTEES

Mother: Children, you have come to the ashram because you had a pure resolve to fulfill certain things. Mother is not trying to put forth rules and regulations or to impede your freedom but there are some things that she must tell you so that your stay here will be fruitful.

In every corner of India you can see people in colleges. Those students who failed in their examinations when studying in colleges will go to tutorial colleges. Most of these tutorials do not give proper discipline or coaching to the students. But there are some tutorial colleges where students will get good training and they will come out successful. Because those tutorial colleges have trained their students properly, the students have good discipline. So, in the beginning stages, discipline is very important, without which we cannot attain the goal. When the goal is attained, you can surrender this discipline at the Feet of the Lord. Discipline is a must.

Some of you might feel that having to follow the rules and regulations here (in the ashram) is like being in a prison, but it is not so. Mother does not want to restrict your freedom. But, if a child is given to much freedom, it may jump into water or fire due to lack of proper discrimination. Likewise, if to much freedom is given now, that will culminate in tomorrow's jail. If rules and regulations are followed now, then you can be fully free tomorrow. It is for tomorrow's freedom that Mother is giving these rules and regulations today.

First of all, you must have love and respect for your mantra, the mantra that was given to you by your Master. Always repeat this mantra wherever you are, whatever work you are doing irrespective of time and place. Without talking unnecessarily, chant your mantra, have love for your mantra. These mantras will help you to purify the mind and are vehicles to take you to the Supreme. If you can repeat your mantra silently within, that is best. If you are unable to do that, then you can just repeat it softly moving your lips.

Some may feel that even though one is repeating a mantra, the thoughts that continue to rise from within will dissipate one's energy. This is not so. For example, take the water in a dam. When the wind blows, there will be ripples on the surface, but even then, water will not be lost. Likewise, even if there are thought waves within, the energy will not get dissipated if a mantra is repeated mentally. It is talking about worldly things and indulging in worldly activities that dissipates our energy.

If you simply do your spiritual practices once a day, such as, after your bath or after your breakfast or lunch, it will not help you reach the goal. Constant practice is needed. However much we do, it will not help us to reach the goal without constant practice. Even if you take hundreds of births and do a lot of penance, this kind of intermittent spiritual practice will not help you reach the goal. Whatever work you do, irrespective of place and time, you should be able to chant the mantra or reflect on the Vedic dictums or on the spiritual things that you have learned. Only then will you be able to attain the goal.

Children, do not think that all these prayers and chanting of a mantra and other external practices are only for weak minds. The more you chant and the more you pray, the more the mind will become clear and pure. For example, take a washing machine. When we put dirty clothes in, the more they get rinsed, the more they will become clean. Likewise, the more you chant your mantra, the more the mind will become clear and pure. Mother is just reminding you about certain things. You have your own freedom and you can choose whatever you like.

It is easy to realise God if you see God in each and every action you perform. Take the Gopis of Brindavan for example. Their business was selling milk, ghee and butter. On each and every bottle and container they would write the different names of Krishna. On the bottles of spices they would write "Madhava," and on some other bottle they would put "Keshava." When they went out selling, instead of calling out "Butter! Ghee! Milk!" they used to call out, "Krishna! Hari! Mukunda! Madhava!" They could easily see unity in diversity. It is easy to attain God if you see God in each and every action you perform.

It does not matter which path you follow. It may be *jñāna*, *karma* or *bhakti*. It does not matter if you are one who meditates on the formless Self or one who meditates on God with form. What is needed first is to cleanse the mind. Without that, however much practice you do, it will not enable you to attain Perfection. Before we sow seeds, the weeds must be removed. Only then will we get a good harvest. Likewise, negative tendencies, likes and dislikes must first be uprooted. Prayer and chanting of the Divine Name will enable us to attain that goal easily. Whether it is worshipping the Formless or God with form, what we need is a pure resolve, then we can worship it. Even to worship the formless God we need a pure resolve.

The Realization of God is not possible in a moment. It will not arrive one fine morning. It needs a lifelong practice. In the *Srimad Bhâgavatam* there is a story about a character named Ajamila. He did all kinds of evil deeds while he was alive. Eventually, when he was breathing his last, he wanted to see his younger son named Narayana. He called out "Narayana!" but instead of his younger son, the messengers of Lord Narayana (Vishnu) Himself appeared before him and forbade the messengers of the Lord of Death from taking him. After reading this story, a businessman thought that it must be easy to attain God. Simply you call God's Name at the end of your life and God will appear and take you to heaven. With this in mind, he named his three sons Krishna, Rama and Govinda. During his life he did all kinds of evil acts. He had a shop and committed many atrocities like cheating and lying. Finally when he was bedridden and was breathing his last, he called his three sons, Krishna, Rama and Govinda. When all his sons came near him, the thought that came to his mind was, "Didn't you open the shop today?" (Isn't there anyone in the shop?). This was the thought that sprang up in his mind because all his life he was thinking about the shop and how to make a profit. So, the thought that you follow all of your life is the one that will spring up at the end of your life. Definitely that will be the thought that comes to you first. So do not think that God-Realisation is possible in a day or two. It requires a lifelong practice.

Why should Mother say all these crazy things to you? All of you have read a lot and heard a lot. Mother is telling you in order to remind you of these things, that is all. What you want is experience and Mother is asking you to do whatever is necessary to gain that experience.

If we simply read and learn things, then there is no difference between us and a tape recorder. Whatever is recorded will be repeated. What we want is to apply all these scriptural statements to our lives and live them.

At the bus stop, you can see a board giving the timetable of the buses going to different destinations. If you simply stand there reading all the details, you can not catch the bus and reach your destination. If you want to reach your destination, you must catch the bus and get inside. Suppose there is a billboard saying that there is a jewellery shop in the next town. If you simply ask the billboard, you will not get the jewellery. You must go to that shop and purchase it.

Mother knows that you know all these things. Now what is needed is practice. The ego should be uprooted. The practice is for eliminating the ego. We always think that we are greater or better than other people. This feeling follows us wherever we go. Even if we apologise to someone, later we may think, "Oh, I shouldn't have said that. I am greater than him, so why should I apologise?" These egoistic thoughts will always pull us down. Only in the presence of a Perfect Master can we remove these egoistic thoughts and actions. This is why we go to ashrams and live in the presence of great Masters. Only they can remove the ego in us. There is a huge tree dormant in the seed, but only if the seed is buried in the ground will the tree sprout. If the seed egoistically thinks, "Why should I bow down to this dirty earth?" then its real nature cannot manifest. Likewise, only if we cultivate and develop humility is it possible to realise the Supreme Truth, our real nature.

In the beginning stages, a Perfect Master is a must. Otherwise, it is impossible to remove the subtle tendencies (*vāsanas*) of the mind. For example, a child is more inclined to play than to study. If he does study, it will be out of fear of his parents or teachers. But after his high school studies, he will have the desire to become an engineer or a doctor. Then he will concentrate on his studies and abandon all other play because now the awareness of a goal has arisen in him. He will automatically concentrate on his studies. Once discrimination arises, then the Guru within you will be invoked. Then you do not have to depend entirely on an external Guru, because you will get instructions from within. But until then, a Perfect Master is needed to guide you.

A parrot raised in a church or temple will have one type of culture. It will always be chanting God's Name. But a parrot raised in the liquor shop will always use vulgar words, won't it? When you go to an ashram or when you are in the presence of a Great Soul, there will be radiant spiritual power in the atmosphere surrounding them. We will be able to become one with that if our mind is properly tuned. Being in the world in the midst of all material pleasures is like sitting at the seashore. Due to the salty breeze, our body will also become coated with salt. But being in the presence of a Perfect Master is like going to an incense stick factory. After leaving there, your body will smell of that fragrance. Similarly, slowly and gradually our mind will become purified due to the presence of a Great Soul.

When you are in the ashram atmosphere, it is good if you move with utmost alertness. Selfless service and repeating your mantra is enough for attaining the goal. If these are lacking, however much penance you do, you will not be able to attain the goal. If you do spiritual practices without performing selfless actions, it will be like building a house without any doors, or a house which doesn't have a path to enter. Be courageous. Do not be idle.

Now we do not have the requisite mental harmony. Because of that, Nature's harmony also is lost. Even now one can clearly see the after-effects of this disharmony. Either there is not enough rain or there is too much. If we become harmonious within, then Nature also will be benefitted and there will be harmony without.

Children, Mother is not saying that you should give up your present way of life or pleasures. But in whichever way you choose to live, you should discriminate between that which is eternal and that which will pass away. Slowly and steadily cultivate and develop detachment. If you do that, then you can enjoy peace of mind and spiritual bliss wherever you may be and whatever the circumstances may be in which you live.

GLOSSARY

Achâra: Traditional customs and observances.

Adhâra: Substratum.

Advaita vedanta: Philosophy of Non-duality.

Agnâna: Ignorance.

Akâram: Form.

Anandam: Bliss.

Antarika prakriti: Inner nature, as opposed to external Nature.

Anâchâras: Contrary to custom.

Arati: Waving burning camphor before the Deity as the conclusion of worship.

Archana: Worship through repetition of Names of God.

Asana: A seat; a posture in Hatha Yoga.

Asana siddhi: Perfection in sitting unmoving in one posture for more than 3 hours.

Asura: A demon.

Asura svabhâva: Demonic nature.

Asuric: Demonic.

Atma bhâva: The spiritual attitude; to be established in the Self.

Atma dhyâna: Meditation on the Self.

Atma gnâna: Self-knowledge.

Atma vichâra: Self-enquiry.

Atmachaitanya: Spiritual power; the illuminating soul.

Atman: The Self.

Atmâvin dukham: Sorrow of the soul.

Avadhûta: A Realised Soul who has transcended all the rules and regulations of the Scriptures, tradition and society.

Avatâr: Incarnation of God.

Bâla bhâva: Attitude of a child.

Bhagavati: The Divine Mother.

Bhagavân: The Lord.

Bhajan: Devotional singing.

Bhakti: Devotion.

Bhakti marga: The path of devotion.

Bharat: India.

Bhaya bhakti: Devotion with fear and reverence.

Bheda buddhi: Differentiating intellect.

Bhoga: Enjoyment.

Bhukti-mukti-pradâyini: Giver of worldly enjoyment and Liberation.

Bhâgavatam: Scripture about the life and deeds of Lord Vishnu's Incarnations.

Bhâva darshan: The Holy Mother giving an audience in the mood of the Divine Mother or Krishna.

Bhâvas: Moods, feelings or attitudes.

Bijâksharas: Seed letters preceding mantras.

Brahma pâda: The Absolute State; the highest position.

Brahmacharin: A celibate student studying the scriptures and undergoing spiritual guidance and discipline under a Guru.

Brahmagnâna: Knowledge of the Absolute.

Brahman: The Absolute.

Brahmanubhuti: Experience of the Absolute.

Brahmânanda: Bliss of the Absolute.

Brahmachârya: Celibacy and sense control.

Chitta: Intellect; mind.

Dakshina: Reverential offering in cash or kind.

Darshan: Audience or vision of the Deity or holy person.

Dâsa bhâvana: Attitude of being a servant.

Dâsatvam: Servitude.

Dâsoham: "I am a servant."

Deha bhâva: The feeling that oneself is a body.

Devata: A god or deity.

Devi bhâva: Divine mood as Devi, the Goddess.

Dharma: Righteousness.

Dhyâna: Meditation.

Dhyâna rûpam: Form on which one is meditating.

Dosha: Evil or defect.

Dvaraka: City where Sri Krishna lived.

Ekâgrata: One-pointedness.

Gauranga: Sri Krishna Chaitanya, considered as an Incarnation of Sri Radha-Krishna, who lived in Bengal about 400 years ago.

Gopas: Cowherds of Brindavan.

Gopis: Wives of the cowherds of Brindavan; divine lovers of Sri Krishna.

Grahasta: One living in a house, i.e., a married person.

Grahastâshrami: A spiritual-minded grahasta.
Gudakesa: A synonym for Arjuna; one who has conquered sleep.
Guru: Spiritual master.
Guru bhâva: Attitude of a Guru.
Guru mahima: Greatness of the Guru.
Gurukula: Residential school of a Guru.
Hrîm: A seed letter associated with the Goddess.
Iswara amsa: A partial manifestation of God.
Iswara bhâvana: The attitude that oneself is identical with the Lord.
Jagat: The world.
Japa: Repetition of a mantra.
Jîva: The individual soul; life force.
Jîvanmukta: One who has achieved Liberation even while tenanting the body.
Jîvâtma: Individual soul.
Jnâna: Spiritual wisdom or knowledge.
Jnâna marga: The path of knowledge.
Jnâni: A Knower of Truth.
Jnânâgni: The Fire of Knowledge.
Kaliyuga: The present Dark Age of materialism.
Karma: Action.
Karma phala: The fruit of action.
Kauravas: The enemies of the Pandavas during the Mahabharata War, representing unrighteousness.
Kirtana: Devotional singing.
Koladi: A country folk dance.
Krishna bhâva: The divine mood as Krishna.
Krôdha: Anger.
Kumbhaka: Retention of breath during pranayama.
Kundalini dhyâna: Meditation on the kundalini.
Kurukshetra: The battlefield on which the Mahabharata War was fought.
Kâma vikâra: Lustful feelings.
Kâma: Lust or desire.
Lakshana: Symptoms or signs.
Laksharchana: Worship by repeating the Divine Names 100,000 times.
Lakshya: Aim or goal.

Lakshya bôdha: A mind intent on reaching the goal.

Lalitasahasranâma: The 1000 Names of the Goddess Sri Lalita.

Laya: Merger or absorption.

Leela: Play.

Mahamântra: Great mantra.

Manonâsa: Destruction of the mind; permanent subsidence of the mind.

Mithya: Unreal.

Moksha: Release from the cycle of rebirth.

Navarâtri: Festival of 9 Nights dedicated to the worship of the Divine Mother.

Nirguna: Without qualities.

Nirgunopâsaka: One who meditates on the qualityless Absolute.

Nirvâna shatkam: A composition of Sri Sankara consisting of 6 stanzas on Nirvana or Final Emancipation.

Nishkriya: Actionless.

Nishta: Established; regularity in practice.

Nitya: Eternal.

Nityânitya vastu vivekam: Discrimination between the eternal and the transitory.

Nâma: The Divine Name.

Omkâra: The divine sound OM.

Padmâsana: Lotus posture.

Paramahamsa: A God-realised Soul.

Parâ bhakti: Supreme devotion.

Peetham: Seat or throne.

Pramâna: Knowledge; means of knowledge; proof.

Prasâd: Consecrated offering to God or a saint.

Prema bhakti: Loving devotion.

Prema swarûpa: Of the nature of love.

Prâna: Life force.

Pûja: Ritualistic worship.

Purâna: Ancient scriptures written by Vedavyasa.

Purnagñâni: Fully realised soul.

Purnakumbha: Lit., full pot; a pot of consecrated water offered to a holy person on their arrival at a temple, house, etc.

Purva samskâra: Previously acquired tendencies.

Pûrnam: Full or perfect.

Rajas: The principle of activity; one of the three gunas or qualities of Nature.

Rasa: Taste; juice; elixir.

Râdha bhâva: Attitude of being Sri Râdha, Beloved of Sri Krishna; supreme devotion.

Râja yoga: The Royal yoga; the eight-fold yoga of Liberation.

Saguna: With attributes.

Sahaja samâdhi: The Natural State of being established in the Supreme Reality.

Sahasradala padma: The 1000 petalled lotus chakra on the top of the head wherein resides the Supreme Lord, the Goal of all Yogas.

Sahôdhara buddhi: Treating all as one's brothers and sisters.

Sama chittata: Equipoised mind.

Samatva bhâvana: Attitude of equality.

Samatva buddhi: Mind endowed with the equal vision of beholding all as One.

Samatvam yoga uchyate: "Equipoise is yoga."

Samâdhi: The equipoised state of Oneness with God.

Sankalpa sakti: Power of resolve or creative imagination.

Sanâtana dharma: The Eternal Religion of the Vedas.

Sarvatra samada: Equal vision everywhere.

Sâstra: Scripture; science.

Sat karma: Good or virtuous action.

Sattva: Principle of clarity; one of the three qualities of Nature.

Satya nasti paro dharma: "Truth is the supreme righteousness."

Seva: Service.

Shânti: Peace.

Shivoham: "I am Shiva."

Siddhi: Psychic power; perfection.

Sishya: Disciple.

Suddha bodha: Pure awareness.

Suddha sattva: Pure sattva (see "Sattva" above).

Suddha tattvam: The pure Principle.

Suprabhâtam: Good morning; verses requesting the Deity to wake up in the early morning hours.

Svadharma: One's own duty.

Svayambhu linga: A self-manifest linga or symbol of Lord Shiva.

Sâgunârâdhana: Worship of God as having attributes.

Tamas: The principle of inertia; one of the three qualities of Nature.

Tamasic: Pertaining to tamas (see above).

Tapas sakti: The power generated by austerities.

Tindal and todil: An old custom of avoiding impure substances and people for fear of pollution.

Tiruvâtira kali: A village dance.

Trigunas: The three gunas or qualities of Nature, sattva (tranquil), rajas (active), and tamas (inert).

Trikârtika: A star or constellation.

Turiya: The fourth state of Bliss beyond the waking, dream and deep sleep states.

Vairagya: Detachment.

Vanaprastha: The third stage of life in which one leaves all worldly activity and devotes oneself to austerities.

Vedas: The revealed scriptures of Hinduism.

Vettuchembu: A kind of tuber root.

Vidya devi: The Goddess of Knowledge.

Visâla buddhi: Broadmindedness.

Visâlata: Expansiveness.

Viveka: Discrimination.

Vyavahâra: Empirical.

Yama and Niyama: The do's and don't of the path of Raja Yoga.

Yogaschitta vritti nirodah: "Yoga is the control of mental modifications."